A SONG FOR SPRINGFIELD

Words and Music:
Fred. S. Hyde

Edited and Arranged:
Gilbert T. Vickers

1. Now raise a song for Springfield, Let hearts and voic- es blend To

2. May vic - to - ry, de - scend-ing, E'er keep her ban- ners bright, And
3. Earthwide, may hap- py child-hood Lift high his wond'ring eyes, Strong

cel - e -brate her prais- es. Whose fame shall have no end; While

dye with new ef - ful - gence Our rare ma -roon and white; Bring
youth bring back the vis - ion Of earth-ly par - a - dise; To

fel - low- ship makes ho - ly, While ea - ger hope e'- lates, And

fair-ness with thee wing- ing, And en - er - gy to dare, To-
fol- low truth to wis - dom, Nor faint thro' fal-t'ring fears, Be

vis -ioned youth come throng-ing her spa - cious gates.

geth - er shall ye guard- ian Her field so fair.
this thy task, O Springfield, Thro' all the years.

Springfield College:
In Spirit, Mind, and Body

Notes and Scenes
from Our First 125 Years

1885-2010

By Richard C. Garvey and Ronald S. Ziemba

Preface to the First Edition (1984)

This is a Springfield College family album, the latest proof that this century-old College is different.

Like other families, this one has had its dinner table arguments and sibling rivalries, and has even tried to deny the familial relationship which suggests paternalism/maternalism.

Indeed, the Springfield College Collegium decided in 1970 that the College is a community, not a family. As soon as the Collegium student members graduated, their successors went right back referring to the Springfield College family, and it is for that family that this album is intended and dedicated.

For those who think of Springfield College as a community, a history book will come, some day.

This album is out of balance. Family albums always are. Uncle Harry gets more space than Uncle Samuel just because Uncle Harry was more interesting, not more worthy.

The prudent trustee who argued that the first building should be designed for reuse as a soap factory is in the album. The quiet trustee who donated and worked to build receives less attention.

Similarly, the president who prudently collected undated resignations from all faculty members makes the album for that more than for all the other contributions he made.

The donor who dug deeper perhaps because his daughter had married the president of the College gets more attention than the benefactor who loyally but quietly wrote checks.

Included here are some things that must be kept in the family, such as the decision of the founders that students would pay no tuition. (We must not mislead new applicants.) We include all the dreams here, including the ones that didn't quite make it.

The album's compiler makes no claim to scholarship or even objectivity. He admits to familial affection for his subject.

The compiler received help from all the usual places and people—libraries and librarians, college employees (present and retired), alumni and alumnae, trustees and corporators—and material from books, newspapers, diaries, and memories. Julius Appleton, a trustee for more than half the college's history, shared the perspective of a man who recalls Leslie Judd as an undergraduate from Australia.

Of greatest help was Charles Weckwerth, who was associated with the College as a student, alumnus, professor, and administrator for more than half of its first century. Because of his devoted and detailed assistance, many errors of commission and omission have been avoided. Those that remain are the sole responsibility of the compiler.

Richard C. Garvey

Preface to the Second Edition (2010)

Welcome to the Springfield College *quasquicentennial!* You are holding a new edition of the book first published in 1984 on the 100th anniversary of Springfield College's founding.

This book includes, on pages 1-139, the text written by Dick Garvey and the accompanying photographs for the 1984 edition—updated and revised to take into account the passage of 25 years.

This book also includes, beginning on page 140, four new chapters, written by the undersigned, on the presidencies of Frank Falcone (1985-91), Bill Bromery (1992-98), and Dick Flynn (1999-present).

Just as the chapters on President Locklin (1965-85) were longer than most of the others in the first edition, Flynn warrants the "incumbent's bonus" this time. It's also fair to say, as it was in Locklin's case, that the sheer number of significant accomplishments during the Flynn years demands the extra coverage.

In addition, a number of listings of importance and an Index have been added to this new edition.

The book's title has been changed from "The Springfield College Family Album." The reason is simple: When you say "Springfield College" what other words seem to follow naturally? "In spirit, mind, and body," of course. In that context, it only makes sense to use our traditional triad in the title, especially in these days of web searches, which Dick Garvey never had to concern himself with in 1984, we're sure. We rather liked the "Family Album" title, but we believe more people will go to Google with "Spirit, mind, and body."

Garvey suggests that the first edition is no comprehensive or balanced "history book." That goes for the second edition, too. It seeks to continue along the road taken by Garvey—tell the stories like the newspaper reporter he was, put in some good photographs to make the stories come alive, and try to be fair to all concerned.

So this book is not the work of academics or traditional historians. It's the product of two reporters who happen to like story-telling, but don't know much about footnotes.

Another thing the two authors have in common, across the 25-year gulf: An unabashed affection for the subject. One came to his affection from his job as editor of the city's newspaper and his position as a trustee of the College; the other from growing up in nearby Chicopee, newspaper training, 30-plus years of writing for corporations, and the past decade as marketing and communications director and writer for Springfield College.

Ronald S. Ziemba

Contents

The original building for the School for Christian Workers. Before this building's completion, the school's first classes were conducted in nearby Hope Church. This building eventually became the home of the Armory Hill YMCA, but before then the YMCA rented space from the school.

Henry S. Lee, a bank president and a driving force behind the founding of Springfield College, which was then known as the School for Christian Workers. Lee served as part-time president of the school from 1891 to 1893.

Chapter 1

In the Beginning . . .

Henry S. Lee, out for a walk in Springfield, Massachusetts, with two friends on a Sunday afternoon in the winter of 1865, turned the conversation to one of his favorite subjects— Sunday school.

His companions were ready to join in. They, too, were active laymen in South Congregational Church, one of four churches joining that day in a union service to discuss Sunday schools.

The walkers met children sliding on newly iced streets (the temperature had dropped sharply after a Saturday rain), and it can be safely assumed that it was Lee, not the children, who brought up the subject of Sunday school.

They had not been to Sunday school because there was not one in their neighborhood. Lee convinced thirteen of the children that they would prefer Sunday school to sledding. The weather might seem to favor the latter, for the editor of *The Sunday Republican* thus described the day: "The air was delightfully bracing, and people who remained housed up all day, afraid to venture out to church, don't know what they lost."

Out of this delightfully bracing day, the persuasive Lee led his sledders' parade to the nearby home of Eli Davis, a former slave, who was a homeowner only because Lee, head of the city's oldest and largest savings bank, had arranged a mortgage. Davis opened his home for Lee's Sunday school.

The school outgrew three homes and a converted barn. Within five years, a chapel was built. But when Sunday school membership reached 220, Superintendent Lee had to deny admission to those who attended Sunday school elsewhere. (His school's weekly concerts did nothing to dampen the childrens' interest.)

The chapel soon became a parish and, when the founding pastor left, it needed a pastor as young and vigorous as itself. It chose David Allen Reed. When Reed was received into the ministry the next year, Hope Church's membership had increased to 260, but its Sunday school had 550 enrollees. Rev. Reed was faced daily with the need for well prepared laymen to help administer such expanding parishes and Sunday schools.

By the time Lee called people together at the parsonage to discuss ideas for meeting such needs, the Hope Church Sunday school had grown to 864 students, necessitating the naming of five assistant superintendents. The parish had also opened satellite Sunday schools for another 150 students. One of the pastor's brothers, Rev. Orville Reed, was helping with these mission chapels, but the need for properly educated laymen was becoming more and more evident.

During a meeting in the home of Rev. David Allen Reed in 1884, the decision was made to found the School for Christian Workers, precursor of Springfield College. The young minister was elected president and led the institution from 1885 to 1891.

THE FOUNDER FINDS A HOME

On the Tuesday of Thanksgiving week in 1884, men who had indicated an interest in the idea of a School for Christian Workers met at the home of Rev. David Allen Reed on State Street in Springfield.

Rev. Samuel G. Buckingham, pastor of one of Springfield's largest churches, presided. By the time the meeting was over, the participants had agreed to establish a legal corporation, elected officers for a year, picked the faculty, arranged for temporary quarters, agreed to erect a new building on land already acquired, and announced the opening date for classes. It hardly needed to be mentioned in the newspaper accounts the next day that most of those attending had the project explained to them earlier.

Rev. David Allen Reed was chosen president, and Rev. Samuel L. Merrell, secretary, to receive student applications. The initial announcement ended, "Anyone desirous of aiding the work by contributions will please send the money to Henry S. Lee, treasurer of the Springfield Institution for Savings." Lee had found one of his niches, and the School for Christian Workers, which was to become Springfield College, had been born.

E. C. Rogers, treasurer of Riverside Paper Co., of which Julius H. Appleton was president, was a trustee, along with another Holyoke paper manufacturer, Charles H. Southworth, treasurer of Hampshire Paper Co. The board included one professional educator, Simeon F. Chester, principal of Springfield's Elm Street School.

Published with the announcement was a list of leading professional, business, and industrial leaders of Springfield and Holyoke who would serve as corporators. Some of them would become loyal benefactors of the new school.

How could a young minister, pastor of a relatively new parish, himself in town only a few years, galvanize so many of the community's leading citizens to undertake this work? Credit has to be given to Rev. Reed's missionary zeal and to his ability to inspire people to work as hard as he did. Also, however, he had been making Springfield connections for years.

When David's brother, Rev. Edward Allen Reed, was accepted for ordination as the eighth pastor of First Congregational Church of Springfield, Rev. Buckingham was moderator of the examining council that had representatives from twenty-seven churches.

The Sunday Republican account of the event reported: "The examination was unanimously pronounced satisfactory, and the council took a recess for dinner at the Massasoit House, which was generously offered to all the council, and was also found to be highly satisfactory." Host at the dinner was the ever-generous Marvin Chapin, owner of the Massasoit House, Springfield's finest hotel and dining room. This may have been the first meeting of the new pastor's twenty-year-old brother, David Allen Reed, and the host's daughter, Gratia Rebecca Chapin, but it certainly was not their last.

On August 20, 1878, in the Chapins' new home on Springfield's fashionable Mattoon Street, they were married, and Rev. Edward Reed was the officiating clergyman. "A quiet wedding removes another from the circle of Springfield's best young people," was the comment of *The Republican*, which also noted that Rev. Dwight L. Moody and Rev. Ira B. Sankey were among the wedding guests. Rev. Edward Reed had led Moody revivals that overflowed his church into City Hall, and David Allen Reed had been assisting the Moody and Sankey revivals in New Haven and elsewhere.

Rev. Dwight L. Moody, a prominent evangelist, was assisted by Rev. David Allen Reed in religious revivals throughout the Northeast.

One indication of the school's close ties with the YMCA was the election of Robert Ross McBurney as vice president. As "the father of the New York City YMCA," McBurney was one of the nation's most prominent and influential YMCA leaders.

When Rev. Edward Reed was released from the First Church pastorate only a month before the wedding, some of his congregation believed he had overtaxed himself at the revivals, and they offered him a substantial salary increase and six-month annual vacations in each of the following two years if he would reconsider.

Amherst College President Lucius Hawley Seelye, who had studied at Auburn Seminary and in Germany, was moderator of the council which, in 1878, after highly praising Rev. Edward Reed, released him to the pastorate of a German Reformed Church in New York City.

Immediately after the wedding, David Allen Reed and his bride left for Germany to continue his studies. He had graduated from Hamilton College in 1877 and had begun theology studies at Auburn Seminary. In Germany, he studied at the University of Leipzig for the first year, and the University of Bonn the second. It was while in Germany that he translated *Protestant Foreign Missions* by Theodore Christlieb into English, and that 264-page translation was published by the Boston Congregation Publishing Society in 1880, making his name familiar to many who had never met him.

The Reeds returned to the United States, and David finished his studies at Auburn Seminary in 1881. The Hope Church pastorate, where Reed's older brother had been pastor, and where Reed himself had been married, then became vacant. There had also been an earlier wedding that connected the Reeds to Springfield. In 1866, the Reeds' cousin, Helena Sarah Allen, from the Reeds' home village of Lansingburg, New York, had married Julius Appleton of Springfield.

So Reed came to a city where he married, where his brother had been pastor, and where his cousin was married to a leading citizen. Even at his arrival, he was no stranger, and in only four years he was ready for even more labors of leadership.

Reed was able to attract not only local, but nationally known figures. His friend, Rev. Dwight Moody, became a trustee and agreed to be a guest lecturer at the new school.

The School for Christian Workers was founded by a group consisting primarily of leading citizens of Springfield, including a number of clergy. The school's founders were quite familiar with the work of the Young Men's Christian Association (YMCA), though the school was not officially tied to the YMCA. This tie could be seen in the only out-of-town officer among the founders; the vice president, Robert Ross McBurney, was the founder of the New York City YMCA. This tie was destined to continue, and to strengthen.

New York trustees included another YMCA leader, Richard S. Morse, as well as Reed's brother, Rev. Edward Reed, and Rev. George F. Pentecost (then midway through the ten-year labor which produced his ten-volume *Bible Studies*), who agreed to be a guest lecturer.

"SAD FALLING-OUT AMONG OUR CLERGYMEN"

The new school was making news, most of it good. Under the headline, "A Very Important Enterprise," *The Springfield Union* printed a lengthy report on the new school, and told where young men could apply for admission and where supporters could send donations.

The Sunday Republican, reporting on the school's first prospectus, mentioned the letters from Rev. Dwight Moody, Rev. George F. Pentecost, and others. The news story stated that, "One spicy letter warns the school not to fail, as too many seminaries and colleges have, in accepting scholars whose only qualifications are piety and poverty." *The Republican* did not identify the author (Rev. A.F. Schauffler of Olivet Church, New York City), but obviously agreed with him, for the article concluded: "Applications for admission are still coming, but good judgment is demanded of the managers in discriminating between the cases to secure only such good men as they want."

A different kind of letter appeared in *The Republican* three days later. It was in response to a notice sent by Rev. David Allen Reed and others to Springfield pastors offering tickets at one dollar for a series of lectures to be given by Professor M.B. Riddle of Hartford Seminary, Rev. Moody, Rev. Pentecost, and others. The letter had noted that the cost per lecture would be only three cents. The responding letter was from Rev. John Cuckson, minister of the Church of the Unity, who noted that the School for Christian Workers was "strictly evangelical" and "Unitarians would be denied its advantages and privileges, if they felt the need of them. It is too much like the Young Men's Christian Association to command our sympathy or support," the Unitarian minister concluded.

Rev. Reed may have believed that a soft answer would turn away wrath, but Rev. Thomas W. Bishop, pastor of one of Springfield's Methodist churches and one of the signers of the notice, thought otherwise. Explaining that he was writing only because Rev. Reed was in New York, the minister responded with a letter which *The Republican* accurately headlined, "A Sharp Response to Mr. Cuckson."

Bishop wrote, "Had the writer of that letter lived here long enough to become acquainted with Springfield before rushing into print ... in this mad fashion, it is to be hoped that he would have known better...." Understandably, Cuckson responded, and what *The Republican* called, "this sad falling-out among our clergymen" continued for a week.

School opened on the very day the first Cuckson letter appeared, and, according to the newspaper accounts, Rev. Reed was not in New York but in Springfield, meeting with the school's first five students. At the initial session were the righteously indignant Rev. Bishop and two other Springfield ministers, Revs. Samuel L. Merrill and Theron H. Hawkes.

The first decision of the faculty was to suspend classes for a week because the ministers were too busy with Week of Prayer services to undertake teaching duties. Thus did Springfield College begin.

YMCA Strengthens the Family

The Commonwealth of Massachusetts incorporated the School for Christian Workers on January 28, 1885, but the school didn't wait for that technicality.

The administration and faculty had started classes in the Old Chapel of Hope Church and also purchased the land immediately to the west for a new building. The property was purchased from the McKnight brothers, John and William. (Their last name is still associated with the city neighborhood they developed.) Until the papers of incorporation arrived, the land was held in the name of Charles H. Barrows, a trustee of the school and an officer of the Armory Hill YMCA, who would later become the school's president.

Jacob Titus Bowne, the first head of the school's YMCA department, came to the school from the post of secretary of the YMCA International Committee.

In April, the school acquired from the McKnights' associate, Theodore Haynes, land adjacent to the first purchase. This gave the school the complete tract from the chapel to the street that the firm of Haynes & McKnight had laid out and named for General William Tecumseh Sherman. The architectural firm of Francis R. Richmond and B. Hammett Seabury was chosen to design the building, and E.W. Shattuck Co. to erect it.

It was then that Trustee Noyes Fisk of Springfield gained a measure of immortality when he recommended that the new structure be convertible to a soap factory in case the new enterprise failed. His family's candle-making business had progressed into soap manufacture, but it was not until a decade later that he put his ideas, money, and energy into a new product—the *Fisk* tire.

Rev. Reed was determined that his dream would never be transformed into a soap manufactory. Stating that it was only an assumption that he could not do the work in the church and in the school at the same time, Reed nonetheless asked a parish committee to name his brother, Orville Reed, as associate pastor. By a vote of 29-11, the committee accepted that arrangement with no salary increase, allowing the brothers to divide the salary as they wished, requiring the new associate pastor to devote his whole attention to the parish, and David Allen Reed to be free to devote such time as might seem best to him to the School for Christian Workers.

At about the same time, the school's appeal to the YMCA International Committee to recommend the best man to head the YMCA department at the school brought Jacob Titus Bowne to Springfield. Five years earlier, when Bowne was general secretary of the Newburgh, New York, YMCA, he formed there a "training station" to prepare men for YMCA secretary posts. In 1883, he was named one of the secretaries of the International Committee, and it was from that assignment that he came to Springfield.

Along with Bowne came a written endorsement from, in Rev. Reed's words, "four of the most successful Christian association workers in the world," Henry M. Morse, Russell Sturgis, Richard C. Morse, and Robert R. McBurney.

"We heartily commend this department of the School for Christian Workers to the sympathy and help of all who are interested in the Young Men's Christian Association," they wrote. What they recommended to others, they embraced themselves. They led the Boston donors to the new building, and all four became trustees of the school. When McBurney died after a lifetime of service to the YMCA, he left one-fourth of his estate to the school.

When the fall term opened September 9, 1885, there were eighteen students "and a prospect of plenty more to follow as soon as accommodations can be provided," according to a contemporary account. The students meeting in the Old Chapel of Hope Church could see the walls of their new building nearing completion. Bowne was there, and quickly showed his concern for one of the students. This newspaper advertisement appeared: "Wanted—A place on Armory Hill for a worthy student with unexceptional references, who is willing to care for a lawn, sidewalks and furnace, and do other chores, say three hours or so a day, in return for his board and lodging. J.T.B., 32 Clarendon St." Tuition was free, but meals could cost as much as $3 a week.

When the students returned from Christmas recess, they found their building partly occupied—by shopkeepers who had rented the first-floor stores. (The school had asked the contractor to complete the stores first, because two tenants were ready to pay $1,200 a year for the space.) For more than a century, the story has been told of the early faculty member who said he had to raise his voice to be heard over the thuds from the butcher's block in that first building. The never-before-identified butcher was Landomir E. Pease, a good neighbor by day and by night (his home was at 17 Sherman Street), who paid his rent, and so, at least, merits mention in this history.

In February, the Armory Hill YMCA moved into its quarters in the new building, so their former home in the old chapel could be converted into a dining room and other school facilities. Bowne moved into his study, and into his library—"the most complete collection of YMCA literature in the world," which was displayed in bookcases and files before the secretaries of the New England YMCAs arrived for a special tour in March. (Much of Bowne's library is housed today in the Springfield College Archives.) According to *The Springfield Republican* account, the new building "called out bursts of praise" from the secretaries.

The celebration of the school's 1st anniversary was in two parts. The first was held at the city's First Congregational Church on May 31, 1886. Its program showed that the school had succeeded in attracting strong support within the YMCA. The speakers included Edwin D. Ingersoll, whose salary as secretary of the Railroad YMCAs was paid by Cornelius Vanderbilt, Jr. and other railroad officials.

One speaker raised a prophetic but futile call; Montreal YMCA Secretary David A. Budge wanted to make certain that the young Canadians coming to Springfield would not be turned into United States citizens.

The Sunday school department had one part of the ceremony. Rev. E.P. Armstrong of the faculty led the students in song, the beginning of a school tradition. The celebration concluded the next day with the dedication of the new building, with an address by Rev. Michael Burnham, pastor of the church that had hosted the previous day's ceremonies. Speaking for the faculty was Rev. William Herbert Perry Faunce, pastor of Springfield's First Baptist Church, whose greatest service to the school was to come to Springfield when he was pastor of Fifth Avenue Baptist Church in New York City ("the Rockefeller Church") before beginning his thirty-year tenure as president of Brown University. At their meeting, corporators and trustees heard the good news that more than half the total cost of the building, land, and equipment had been received, and that student rooms were being made available as soon as donors could be found to pay for furnishings.

When the secretaries had toured the building in March, only one model room was furnished. But now, the corporators and trustees saw sixteen finished rooms, each with a plaque on the door to identify the donor of the furnishings.

There was no rest for Reed. The next day, he was on his way to Harrisburg, Pennsylvania, where the conferring YMCA secretaries responded generously to his appeal for funds.

DISTINGUISHED FACULTY SETS THE TONE

By the time school opened for the fall term in 1887, all debts had been paid, and the school achieved financial stability.

Some of the gifts reflected the growing interest of YMCA supporters (Cornelius Vanderbilt gave $1,000) and the geographical spread of that interest (donations had come from twenty-four states and four Canadian provinces.)

Neighbors began a tradition of generosity to the school, with the largest gift of all, $10,000, coming from Rev. Reed's father-in-law, Marvin Chapin. Other major gifts came from Julius H. Appleton, whose wife was related to Rev. Reed, and Appleton's close friend from boyhood, Henry Lee.

Other faithful supporters included Horace Smith of Smith & Wesson and William H. Haile, who had served the city as mayor and would later serve Massachusetts as lieutenant governor.

These men met in other board rooms. All were trustees of Lee's bank, or directors of Springfield Fire and Marine Insurance Co., founded by Marvin Chapin; Haile was both. One local donor was John H. Southworth of Southworth Paper Co., who served with Chapin on the board of one of Springfield's national banks. Southworth's son was a trustee of the school.

To some a difficult man to work with, Luther Halsey Gulick nonetheless was an undisputedly gifted teacher and innovator. At the age of twenty-three, he was named to direct the school's physical department.

The dramatic appeal of the school's physical education program is illustrated in this 1887 photograph of a summer session class. The instructors were Gulick (center row, fourth from left), and Robert J. Roberts (center row, fifth from left).

THE BIRTH OF PHYSICAL EDUCATION

Wishing to learn more about the German gymnasium system of education, Harvard sent George Bancroft there after his graduation in 1817.

When Bancroft returned, he found Harvard unready to test the German gymnasium system, so in 1823 he started Round Hill School for Boys in Northampton, Massachusetts, the first American educational institution to offer such a program, and hired Charles Beck of Germany to teach gymnastics.

Considering that it cost more to send a boy to Round Hill than to send a man to Harvard, it is remarkable that the school lasted ten years. Bancroft left the place even earlier to become a prominent American historian, the founder of the U.S. Naval Academy at Annapolis, presidential cabinet member, and ambassador, and to do other useful things.

8

Harvard finally took the step and hired Beck's fellow exile, Charles Follen, as "instructor in German and superintendent of the gymnasium" just in time for Rev. William A. Stearns to see this discipline and develop a lifelong interest in it.

In his address on being installed as president of Amherst College in 1854, Rev. Stearns said, "physical education is not the leading business of college life, though were I able, like Alfred or Charlemagne, to plan an educational system anew, I would seriously consider the expediency of introducing regular drills in gymnastic or calisthenics exercises."

Rev. Stearns was delighted to find the spirit of Round Hill still alive in nearby Northampton in the person of Benjamin Barrett, who had gone to Harvard with Bancroft. With Barrett as major donor, Rev. Stearns built Barrett Gymnasium on the campus of Amherst College. There, Edward Hitchcock, the first full-time teacher of physical education to achieve the rank of full professor on an American college faculty, endeared himself and his discipline to Amherst students for half a century. Fortunately for Springfield College, those students included the Pratt brothers—Charles, Frederic, George, Herbert, John, and Harold.

The year that brought financial stability to the school also brought two men important to its history: Luther Halsey Gulick and Robert J. Roberts.

A trail that would lead to Springfield began when the Boston YMCA, the nation's oldest YMCA, unexpectedly came into possession of an equipped gymnasium. (There was still considerable opposition within the YMCA to physical education, even though the first American YMCA gymnasium, developed at New York City in 1869 by Robert R. McBurney, had won some supporters.) They reluctantly hired as "janitor and gymnasium superintendent" an unemployed wood-turner, Robert J. Roberts.

It was Roberts who coined the word "body building" for his system and made it popular. Reed and Bowne agreed in 1887 that Roberts was the man for the new school.

During Roberts' brief tenure, Lewis Warren Allen, who had come to the school during its second year, received the first diploma in physical education. Allen began his long career with the YMCA in Springfield and for many years was director of physical education at Hartford (Connecticut) High School. It was seventy-eight years after his graduation and twenty-two years after his death that his residual estate, more than $200,000, came to Springfield College. To this day, this fund memorializes Allen, Roberts' first graduate.

Roberts had met Gulick when the latter came from Oberlin in 1885 to spend the winter at the new school for physical training founded by Dudley Allen Sargent at Harvard. Gulick had been born in Hawaii of missionary parents, and uncertain health during his boyhood seems to have turned his own missionary fervor to physical education.

Gulick was hired in 1887, along with Roberts. Roberts was to have special charge of the floor work and Gulick took charge of the studies, correspondence, and office work. Two years later Gulick was named director of the physical department.

(When the school was empowered to grant honorary degrees, in 1906, it awarded its first master's of physical education to Gulick.)

Over some opposition from the YMCA department faculty, the school's administration added a physical education program. They hired Robert J. Roberts, the Boston YMCA's "gymnasium superintendent," as a gymnasium instructor.

Before the turn of the century, the school was able to acquire additional land at its new campus overlooking Lake Massasoit. In purchasing property from William R. Purple, the trustees granted Purple the right to enter the land to remove his "Slaughterhouse." Unfortunately, he never exercised that right. It wasn't until decades later that the eyesore was torn down and the bricks buried beneath the parking lot to the rear of Marsh Memorial Library.

A New Campus ... a New Game

Hindsight credits the administration with foresight in locating the athletic fields near Lake Massasoit, and reserving land there for the entire campus.

Actually, the trustees tried in vain to find land near the original building for playing fields. The first athletic field, "within five minutes' walk of the building," according to early documents, was opposite the Springfield Armory's Government Square, west of the new school. It was there that Amos Alonzo Stagg G'91 prepared the football team that defeated Amherst College at Hampden Park in Springfield.

The trustees were certainly not thinking about buying land when they gave a committee "power to rent suitable grounds" on November 5, 1890.

The committee discovered that two prominent, intermarried Springfield families wanted to settle an estate by selling a large tract of land on Alden Street. The acreage had been owned by the nationally famous editor and publisher, Samuel Bowles, and his sister's husband, Henry Alexander, bank president and onetime mayor of Springfield. The family relationship had been somewhat strained since the mayor ran for Congress, and his brother-in-law's newspaper, *The Sunday Republican*, endorsed Alexander's opponent, who won.

The land was left with two sets of heirs owning two undivided half interests in the Alden Street property, unfortunately cut in its western portion by a fifty-foot-wide strip of land sold fifteen years earlier to accommodate the New London Railroad. The strip still runs west of what is today Locklin Hall, but no train traffic is evident.

Soon thereafter, the trustees were able to purchase the adjoining land of William R. Purple, a wholesale meat dealer, who reserved to himself "the building known as the 'Slaughterhouse' and sheds connecting, and the brickwork under same," and preserved the right to enter the land to remove this property.

Unfortunately, Purple did not exercise that right. The deteriorating building became an offense to the eye, and the brickwork continued to cause trouble until broken and buried under the Marsh Memorial Library parking lot generations later.

The Purple acreage was nonetheless a bargain at $2,000, and it added another 450 feet to the school's waterfront.

As enthusiasm for this lakefront site waxed among YMCA secretaries, it waned for the earlier plan to build a companion building to the east of the old chapel, retaining the tower as the center of the complete structure.

Although this trend ran counter to Reed's dream of a Christian university, he increased rather than decreased his enthusiasm for the school.

On December 23, 1889, Rev. Reed resigned his ministry so he could give full time to the school. The following year, the name YMCA Training School was separately incorporated (following a 17-6 vote of the trustees). Reed retained the presidency of both schools until June 10, 1891, when he resigned as president of the Training School but remained as a trustee. Also in 1891, the school name changed once again, to the International YMCA Training School.

Reed remained in the presidency long enough to have the formation of the alumni association fall within his tenure. Only a few weeks before Reed's resignation took effect, the alumni association was formed at the International YMCA Convention in Kansas City, with Frank N. Pratt '87, as president. After Reed's resignation, students of both the International YMCA Training School and the School for Christian Workers attended classes on both campuses until the separation became total in 1894. At that point, the School for Christian Workers became the Bible Normal College, which later moved to Hartford as the School of Pedagogy of Hartford Seminary. The International YMCA Training School continued on in Springfield and ultimately became known as Springfield College.

Another school within Reed's projected Christian university was the New England Industrial and Technological School, of which Reed was president, and Milton Bradley, the game manufacturer, vice president.

Reed had started the school to teach building and machine skills to men going into the Latin American and African missions. After he helped to bring the French Protestant College (now known as American International College) from Lowell, Massachusetts, to Springfield, Reed introduced a typesetting course into the industrial school curriculum so that the college's French evangelical tracts could be published more inexpensively. This was yet another step toward the admission of students not necessarily mission-bound.

To allow students to finance their education, Reed set up a work-study program with the Elektron Co., which manufactured electric motors in an adjoining building in what was then called Winchester Square (today, Mason Square).

When J. Frank Duryea came to that company for help in solving ignition problems for a gasoline engine he was building, Reed learned of this young man's efforts to build a "horseless carriage."

Typically, Reed later said only that he had made space available for Duryea to build his first automobiles. Actually, Reed was a founder, stockholder, and first treasurer of the Duryea Motor Wagon Co., the country's first automobile manufacturer, located in Reed's industrial school building. This school program was absorbed later into the city's public school system, and the new Technical High School was built to accommodate it.

Reed maintained his interest in all the schools with which he had been connected. For years, he provided flowers from his beautiful gardens which Springfield College students would place on the graves of Henry Lee and alumni who had died in Springfield. Only two years before his death in 1932 he donated the materials for the erection of the Pueblo of the Seven Fires on Springfield College's east campus.

The institutions that Reed founded or helped to perpetuate remain as good neighbors, but have never gravitated toward merger into his original Christian university ideal.

Hartford Seminary Foundation and Springfield College maintained a cooperative arrangement for many years. It was most active in the 1950s, when President Glenn Olds was also a trustee of the foundation.

James Naismith G'91, a graduate of McGill University in Montreal who continued his studies at Springfield College, enjoyed a variety of sports. But he earned immortality in 1891 by devising an indoor game that could be played between the football and baseball seasons. He invented basketball.

At that same time, Springfield College and American International College (successor to the French Protestant College) launched a joint eight-month capital campaign, properly called "unique in the history of the two institutions." Although it failed to reach its $850,000 goal, another joint campaign was launched five years later for a smaller goal, which also fell short.

To other schools and colleges, Reed was a solicitous uncle or a devoted family friend; only to Springfield College was he the father.

THE BIRTH OF BASKETBALL

Reed's "earnest prayer that God will guide you in the selection of a suitable and consecrated man for this important post" was not quickly answered. Henry Lee agreed to assume the post of president of the school temporarily and remained for two years. It was to be an eventful tenure.

For one thing, Instructor James Naismith G'91, seeking a way to keep students active between football and baseball seasons, invented "basket ball."

In the winter of 1891, Naismith devised thirteen rules, found two peach baskets, and introduced "basket ball" to his physical education class as an indoor game for the cold New England winters. In the first public game, the students defeated the faculty, 5-1.

Amos Alonzo Stagg, G'91, who had entered the school with Naismith and joined the faculty with him, scored the only "basket ball goal" for the faculty, according to a contemporary account. After that first public game, the name came to be spelled as one word, and the scores also seem to have increased.

Stagg, it turns out, was one of Springfield College's greatest sons, and truly a man for all seasons. He was one of the greatest college athletes *ever*. He was the College's first football coach, in 1891, and later became the dean of college football coaches, having coached continuously for fifty-seven years. He pioneered such innovations as the huddle, the man in motion, the end-around, and the Statue of Liberty play, among others. Though he also coached baseball, basketball, and track and field, football was his first love, and it is as an innovator, player, coach, and teacher of football that he will be remembered.

Back then, President Lee and his associates may not have realized what it meant for the school to be the birthplace of basketball. But they certainly knew that these two outstanding young educators, Naismith and Stagg, were the very ones who were almost denied admission to the school because they were not planning to join a YMCA staff. It was a good lesson in humility for those administrators and trustees, and remains so for those who have followed them.

If Lee had been a lesser man, he might have resented the appointment of Rev. Hanford Burr to the faculty. Rev. Burr was the founding pastor of Park Congregational Church, founded as a mission by Lee's Hope Church and raised to independent status by an ecclesiastical council over Hope's strenuous opposition. Also, there was the fact that Rev. Burr was a free agent, in that his salary was being paid by Mrs. Eleanor S. Woods until the school recognized his value.

The gymnasium where basketball was born in 1891.

Mrs. Woods was the daughter of the late Charles Merriam, the "C." of the G. and C. Merriam Co. of Springfield, successors to Noah Webster as publisher of the *Webster's Dictionary*.

Under the circumstances, Lee might have thought of young Rev. Burr as salt in a wound. He didn't; others did.

When Mrs. Woods fulfilled the terms she had agreed upon to pay Burr's salary, Lee quietly assumed that responsibility, whereas others would have preferred that Rev. Burr depart.

After teaching at Springfield College for several years, Naismith acquired a medical degree at Gross Medical College in Colorado, worked briefly at a YMCA in Denver, then joined the University of Kansas faculty. Despite his years at Kansas, he consistently expressed the hope that a Basketball Hall of Fame would be erected at Springfield College, "the birthplace" of the game.

A Yale graduate, Amos Alonzo Stagg G'91 joined the faculty and coaching staff while completing his graduate studies at Springfield College. His extraordinary career as a football coach at a variety of institutions made him the dean of college football coaches.

Some may simply have been jealous of the young man's popularity with students and with distinguished and highly placed older people. Rev. Burr's minister father privately tutored him for Amherst, where he was admitted to Phi Beta Kappa, and then for Hartford Seminary. His first assignment after ordination was in Lowell, where he worked among millworkers, and his lifelong concern for the poor and powerless was sometimes expressed in rich and potent language, which some found disconcerting.

Those who love the mother tongue often are loved by her in return, which makes them eminently quotable. So, let Rev. Burr describe life under the faculty triumvirate in those days: "I served three masters. Oliver Morse supervised my theology with obvious disapproval. Bowne deplored my lack of a 'Y' background. Gulick wanted me to change my courses from month to month to suit his whims."

During the years in which there was no full-time president, the operation of the school was left in the hands of these three men, and the hands did not always pull in the same direction.

For all the complaints that Gulick was a difficult man to work for or with, he attracted some of the school's finest graduates to the faculty, among them Stagg, Naismith, James Huff McCurdy, who would become Gulick's successor, and Frank N. Seerley, who was to become dean.

Bowne—recognized even then as the father of professional education in the YMCA—had the respect of the alumni, who were holding more and more responsible positions within the YMCA.

Morse set two goals for himself and faithfully fulfilled them: Keep Bible instruction fundamentalist, and keep the school solvent.

Rev. Burr made the phrases, the triumvirate made the rules, and Lee made the decision that the trustees needed these committees: *Executive*, to make policy directions quickly; *Instruction*, to oversee curriculum development; *Endowment*, to assure the future; *Construction*, to build the new lakeside campus; and *Presidency*, to find a full-time president as soon as possible.

In the meantime, the trustees were ready to act on important matters. At the spring meeting in 1893, they agreed that it was "undesirable to permit a cow to be kept on the grounds indefinitely and that the faculty act in the matter." They also decided that it was prudent to buy $50 worth of plumbing tools for the janitor-watchman-groundskeeper so he could keep the water and the new gas system in repair.

The trustees proved their prudence in other ways. Instead of retaining an architect to design the new dormitory, they added the task to a faculty member, David F. Graham. Also, they voted to install an ordinary telephone in the gymnasium, rather than the more expensive metallic circuit.

During his tenure, Lee and the school lost a friend with the death of Horace Smith in his eighty-fifth year, but Smith had found a way to show his friendship forever. He left $5,000 to the school, its first bequest. He also established a fund, naming Lee and his bank successors as trustees, to help young people from nearby with the costs of education.

At the first commencement over which Lee presided, the printed program contained the school's new emblem, the inverted triangle devised by Gulick to symbolize the unity of man in spirit, mind, and body.

The trustees had adopted this emblem only three months earlier, but not for the last time, the students were far ahead of the trustees. They had been using Gulick's symbol for more than two years, and the Class of 1891 wore triangle-decorated jerseys when having their class photograph taken, sending a strong hint to the trustees.

At that, the school was more responsive than the YMCA, which debated another five years before accepting Gulick's symbolic triangle as its official emblem. (In contrast, the adoption of an interestingly modified Gulick triangle by the Camp Fire Girls of America was without delay or debate. That organization was founded by Gulick and his wife, Charlotte Vetter Gulick.)

When Lee declined to remain as president, Charles M. Barrows, a local attorney and another pioneer of the Armory Hill YMCA and of the school, agreed to accept the part-time presidency. A graduate of Harvard College and Harvard Law School, Barrows had served as assistant attorney general of Massachusetts before opening a law office in Springfield. The Barrows family was well known in Springfield because his father had worked for the school system for fifty-three years, including forty-four as principal of the school, later renamed Barrows Grammar School.

Barrows was a gifted writer from his days as editor of the *Harvard Advocate* to his autumn years, when he wrote books on local history. He was chosen to deliver the historical address on the city's 275th anniversary. He never forgot the College he helped to found and served as president. After the death of the last family member named in his will, one-sixth of his estate came to Springfield College.

After completing his studies, Stagg received an International YMCA Training School diploma in 1891. He was appointed to the faculty and was the only faculty member to score in the first public basketball game, against the students.

Ever the innovator, Gulick designed the school's first emblem, a triangle, which has remained the foundation for all school seals, representing the school's Humanics philosophy of spirit, mind, and body. The symbol was so popular that students were wearing it two years before the trustees adopted it as the official symbol. Later, the YMCA would also incorporate the triangle into its logo.

Succeeding Lee as a part-time president was Charles M. Barrows, a Springfield attorney, who also was one of the original founders of the school. He served from 1893 to 1896.

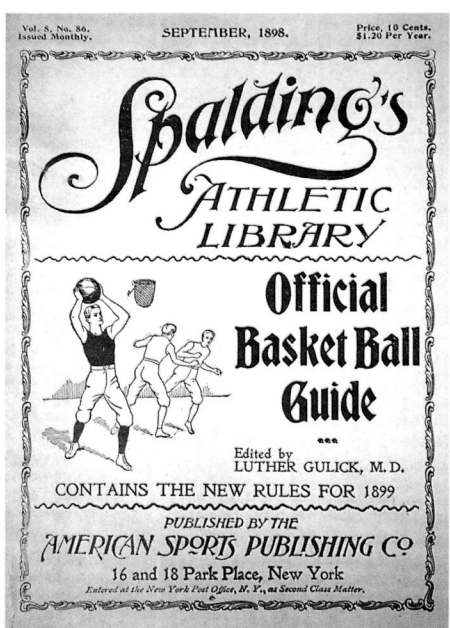

Official "Basket Ball" guide for 1898

If Lee could claim (not that he would) that basketball came during his presidency, Barrows could claim (not that he did) volleyball. The sport was actually invented by William George Morgan '94, in 1895 while he served as physical director of the YMCA in Holyoke, a few miles north of Springfield. When Gulick heard of Morgan's new game, "mintonette," he invited him to the campus for an exhibition contest. Alfred Halstead, a professor at the College, watched the game and suggested the name "volley ball."

MONEY, BRICKS, AND MORTAR

With a hymn and a prayer, the cornerstone for a gymnasium, the first building on the new campus, was laid on May 12, 1894.

The hymn was sung by the school's glee club, with Gulick conducting, and the prayer was by the now-departed David Allen Reed. The cornerstone was put in place by John McFethries, president of a Springfield land development company, who had been recruited by his friend and associate, Henry Lee, to head the campus planning committee. (McFethries told the audience that his Scottish burr lent the necessary "international" character to the proceedings at the International YMCA Training School. If he had not been so economical in speech, he might have added that he had married a British subject in an American chapel in Russia.)

President Barrows called on Rev. Burr to say the final prayer, which was certainly needed by the speaker at the ceremonies, Oliver Morse, who had the job of raising the money for the gymnasium building and for the dormitory soon to follow.

Lee could be both practical and visionary. A month later, speaking at the 50th anniversary of the founding of the YMCA, he told the attendees about the buildings they would see when they returned to the campus in 1944 on the 100th anniversary of the YMCA founding. On a more timely and mundane note, he said that the school had received $500 from the Class of 1894 to furnish the reception room in the new dormitory, and it would be named Jubilee Hall to honor the YMCA's golden jubilee.

Lee was back the next year with a gift of $1,000 to be applied to the Alumni Association dormitory fund, if the graduates were willing to add to their pledges either $1 a year for ten years or fifty cents for twenty years. Lee scored again in his campaign for recurring income when the alumni voted for the $1 option.

Ironically, it was in that newly finished Jubilee Hall early the next year that the trustees' executive and instruction committees met together for eight hours to discuss the critical financial condition of the school. President Barrows reported that the school needed an emergency fund of $50,000 in order to stay open. He told them that, two weeks earlier, he had collected from each faculty member an undated letter of resignation to prepare the way for money-saving reorganization. (Didn't anyone see the irony of meeting in Jubilee Hall to receive these messages?)

Fred Washington Atkinson, Harvard President Charles W. Eliot's protégé, then principal of Springfield Central High School and later president for twenty-one years of Brooklyn Polytechnic Institute, and W.R. Newhall, headmaster of Wilbraham Academy, offered to work with the department heads to consider reorganization.

Pivotal to the school's early academic plans was the construction of a gymnasium. Built in 1894, it was the first building to be erected on the new campus overlooking Lake Massasoit.

Morse was not present at the meeting; he was still away on an even more important mission. Five days later, he was back on campus with pledges of $34,500, many of them conditioned on raising the entire $50,000 by August 1, 1896.

The decision to have Atkinson and Newhall review all the academic offerings now seemed less important, but proved to be providential.

The good financial news turned the trustees' attention to the selection of a new full-time president, and they invited one of their prospects, Laurence Locke Doggett, to attend the 1896 commencement.

In 1895, the second building on the new campus rose on a hillside overlooking Lake Massasoit. Never named in anyone's honor, the structure—now known simply as the Administration Building—originally housed classrooms, dormitory rooms, and offices.

Doggett saw the new buildings on the tract that had not favorably impressed him on his first visit, but he still had misgivings about the academic programs, which he feared were superficial. However, he found that two of the trustees, Atkinson and Newhall, were both knowledgeable about the academic programs and enthusiastic about them. Like Doggett, Atkinson had also done graduate work in Germany, but Doggett's later identification of Atkinson as a fellow alumnus of Leipzig may have been a reflection of his enthusiasm. Atkinson received his doctorate in 1893 from the University of Jena in central Germany.

The commencement speaker was Rev. William Herbert Perry Faunce, who had spoken for the faculty at the dedication of the Winchester Square (now Mason Square) building, and had since left Springfield for the pastorate of New York's Fifth Avenue Baptist Church. He, too, helped prepare Doggett for the call that was to come a few weeks later.

Viewed from the lake, the Administration Building sits atop what became known as "Rally Hill." During World War II, when there was little to cheer about, the military used the College as a training site. Because of structural problems, the government removed the building's top three floors. Today, the Administration Building has only two floors.

ICE HOCKEY

Ice Hockey Team

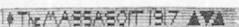

The Massasoit 1917

ALUMNI

Mission Study

Prohibition Society

Training School Lights

Chapter 2

Doggett:
The Legendary President

T he man the trustees chose to be the school's first full-time president was Laurence Locke Doggett, thirty-two years old, an Iowa native who had been educated at Oberlin, the Union Theological Seminary, the University of Berlin, and the University of Leipzig.

Only a few months earlier, Doggett had become state secretary of the YMCA of Ohio, and the trustees commissioned Oliver C. Morse, who had been general secretary of the Cleveland YMCA when Doggett joined the YMCA at Oberlin, to carry their proposal to him.

At Marion, Ohio, where Doggett was attempting to organize a YMCA with the assistance of Warren G. Harding's father-in-law, Morse delivered the school's offer.

There were many reasons for Doggett to decline. He had tried to start at Oberlin a training school for YMCA secretaries, and shared the view that Springfield College was a "straining school" rather than a "training school." He believed that the Springfield College program, without the benefit of a university milieu, was superficial.

Doggett's visit to the campus in September 1894 had generated other misgivings. He found the new campus "a disheveled sandy spot" on a section known as "Whiskyville" because of "Betty Hogan's bootleg house." (The 1894 listing of Springfield's thirty-two legal saloons does not include any establishment near the campus nor any license issued to Ms. Hogan, so Doggett's judgment that it was a bootleg house appears correct.)

Doggett had succeeded his admired mentor, Samuel D. Gordon, as secretary of the Ohio YMCA, and reports of the Ohio YMCA leadership and of Doggett show how pleased they were with each other and with the progress being made.

Why then did he accept the presidency? It certainly wasn't for the money, because he was paid $3,000 and returned $500 to the College the first year, making his net income the same as he had received in Ohio.

Along with his memories of sandy "Whiskyville," he had more pleasant recollections. He greatly appreciated Jacob T. Bowne's generosity in loaning him a trunk full of priceless records of the early YMCA with which the young scholar won professorial approval of his plan to write a doctoral dissertation on the beginnings of the YMCA.

He also remembered the students. As he recalled years later in his autobiography: "The students impressed me as being not so much a body of students as a body of active men who were engaged in pushing a project in which they were deeply interested. There

Laurence Locke Doggett, president for forty years, from 1896 to 1936, at first expressed reluctance at assuming the position. During his first visit to the campus, Doggett described it as a "disheveled sandy lot...." What changed his mind about the place was the fervor of its students.

was a fervor and enthusiasm and pioneer quality about the life of the school that attracted me greatly."

Doggett spoke at an evening gathering and recalled a half-century later that the students opened the session, as they did all their classes, with prayer. As College president and chairman of the Board of Trustees, he continued the practice of opening all board meetings with prayer.

Springfield College had another attraction that was difficult to assess. Doggett's family had lived in Massachusetts for eight generations, until his parents moved to Iowa a couple of years before his birth. His wife, the former Carolyn Durgin, was also a New Englander, daughter of Rev. and Mrs. Dewitt Clinton Durgin of Rhode Island. The Doggetts' first child was due in August, and Doggett knew that his wife would enjoy being near her parents when August came.

Doggett's biographer, Lawrence K. Hall, offered the best explanation for the decision: "If God's guidance abides in one's will to make oneself ready and well-prepared for the work at hand, then God led Doggett to Springfield."

Pictured here are the faculty members who established the International YMCA Training School as a world-recognized center for educating young men and women for service to mankind. In no small measure, this was accomplished due to Doggett's support of academic freedom. His support of William G. Ballantine, a faculty member, cost the College both in contributions and in enrollment.

CONTROVERSIAL DECISIONS ALTER HISTORY

During the first two years of his administration, Doggett made two decisions which were to greatly affect the school even longer than the thirty-eight years remaining in his tenure. They were the appointment of Rev. William G. Ballantine to be professor of Bible, and the president's decision to assume the major responsibility to raise funds for the school. The two decisions were not unrelated.

After he resigned as president of Oberlin, Ballantine made a lecture tour of the eastern United States. While making a stop at Mount Holyoke College in nearby South Hadley, he called on Doggett, who had been Ballantine's student and admirer at Oberlin.

As he was discussing his work at Springfield College, Doggett mentioned that he was seeking an instructor in Bible, and seems to have been as surprised as he was delighted when Ballantine expressed an interest in the position. Only $1,500 had been budgeted, but Henry Lee provided another $1,000 from the Horace Smith Fund, and Ballantine joined the faculty.

As seen in 1898, the Administration Building—with its classrooms, dormitory rooms, and offices—was a key part of the base from which Doggett began to build the College in his own image.

The combined classes of 1899 and 1900 majoring in YMCA studies engaged in work for the Army during the Spanish-American War in 1898.

A year later, Oliver Morse, whose heroic work had kept the school out of bankruptcy, sent a letter of resignation to the trustees, expressing his enthusiasm for the school and his confidence in its future, and suggesting that the trustees find a younger man who would command less remuneration to replace him.

When Doggett reminded Morse of their agreement that Morse would be responsible for the fundraising while Doggett raised the school's academic standards and YMCA connections, the real reason for Morse's resignation was discovered. Morse said that he could not raise money for the school so long as Ballantine was teaching Bible, because many in the YMCA were alarmed by his liberal attitude toward Scripture.

Doggett replied that Ballantine would stay, so Morse left.

"With me, it came down to a matter of who was to be the ultimate authority at the school, Mr. Morse or myself," Doggett wrote later.

Doggett and Morse also had their family traditions to separate them. Doggett was proud of his great-grandfather, a liberal clergyman who founded the first Massachusetts academy free of religious ties; and Morse was proud of his grandfather, who had helped to found Andover Seminary and was devastated when it became theologically liberal.

The departure of Morse saddened Doggett, but the departure of sixteen students at the same time edified him. They responded to the call for YMCA camp workers to serve during the Spanish-American War. The Student Association gave $100 for their support and Henry Lee added $1,000. Nine alumni joined the group, so that one-sixth of all YMCA men involved in this work were from the school at Springfield, which itself was not yet fifteen years old.

PERSISTENT PROBLEMS: FINANCES AND THEOLOGY

The year that ended the century ended Gulick's career at Springfield College. McCurdy rose to replace Gulick on the faculty and eventually also to replace him as one of the leading physical educators of the country. The last year of the century also tested the president in handling two problems which would recur during his tenure. The problems which were not so happily and quickly resolved were financial and theological.

Doggett launched a $100,000 endowment fund campaign with great enthusiasm and little planning. He asked the widow of Frederick Billings, the railroad magnate, for a donation. She gave him $10,000 and, half a century later, he could still recall his elation. When her son added $5,000, as did Frederic B. Pratt, Doggett raised the goal to $200,000—a mistake—and solicited pledges conditioned on receiving at least $100,000 —a worse mistake.

As the deadline approached, Doggett had to make a whirlwind tour of the Northeast to beg donors to waive the conditions he had set, and had to resolicit local friends to meet even the $50,000 level. In pain, he had learned some expensive lessons, but he learned them well, as his later fund-raising successes proved.

The theological problem was caused this time not by Ballantine, but by Rev. Burr, writing on "The New Reformation" in the school's periodical, *Association Outlook*. For many of its readers, the old Reformation was sufficient, and those genealogical and/or spiritual descendents of the people who brought Calvinism to the New World saw no need to echo the old accusation that Calvin had been a "Protestant Pope."

When Rev. Burr learned that many had threatened to withdraw financial support from the school unless the professor was fired, he offered his resignation to the president, who replied: "A college without academic freedom would not be worth having. You stick."

Rev. Burr admired that courage, but he had his own brand. When Eleanor S. Woods, who had sponsored his advent to the school, offered to endow a chair for him, he urged her instead to provide something the students urgently needed—a dining and social hall.

Rev. Burr envisioned something more homelike than the top-floor refectory in the Dormitory building. So Mrs. Woods funded the construction of Woods Hall, north of the Dormitory building, and herself presided at Thanksgiving dinner there in 1905, two months after it was opened.

She invited students to come back often to Woods Hall, and even suggested: "Come in by twos, sometimes, being not too bashful to borrow now and then from Smith's and Mount Holyoke's pretty garden of girls, though there is many a fair one in our own Springfield."

She died soon thereafter, leaving the College another $5,000.

TRAGEDY HITS CAMPUS

Mrs. Woods was not forgotten, however. Since the death of Henry S. Lee in 1902, seniors would decorate his grave at commencement time, and now they added her grave to that ceremony, a tradition that was continued for twenty years.

A death that affected students in a different way was that of Henry Seifert, an orphan who had been supported at Mount Hermon School by members of the St. Mark's German Evangelical Church in New York City.

Rev. Hanford M. Burr was an Amherst College graduate who trained for the ministry at Hartford Seminary. Like Ballantine, his theological teachings offended some of the College's benefactors. Doggett fully supported the idea of academic freedom.

Eleanor Woods, a member of the Merriam family, publishers of successive editions of *Webster's Dictionary*, supported Rev. Burr and offered to endow a chair for him.

Seifert's fellow graduates of the Class of 1904 knew he would not be in Springfield for the start of commencement week. He was going to help oversee the St. Mark's Sunday school children on their annual outing to Locust Point, on Long Island, but would be back in time for class day and graduation.

Seifert and the children left on the *General Slocum*, a wooden paddle-wheeler that went up the East River with a band playing gaily. A man on shore noticed a fire aboard the ship and sounded the alarm. A fireboat raced to the scene but the steamer maintained full speed ahead, sending the flames racing back through the ship.

Hundreds of the children were killed by the fire, or by the paddle wheels when they jumped to escape the flames. Among those rescued were the captain and all his crew (except one who, weighted down with money, drowned), but more than 1,000 passengers, most of them school children, were killed. Among the dead was Henry Seifert.

When word of that disaster, one of the worst in American history, reached the campus, a memorial service replaced class day, and Doggett, recalling his days at Leipzig, said that this young man had reflected the finest in the German tradition.

RACISTS NEED NOT APPLY

The 20th commencement in 1906 was to be different. For the first time, the participants would wear academic gowns, for the Commonwealth of Massachusetts had granted to the College the right to confer degrees of bachelor and master of Humanics, and bachelor and master of physical education.

Who would have the honor of receiving the first degree ever granted at Springfield? First of all, it would have to be a person who entered the College as a high school graduate. (The College established a college-preparatory course so that those without high school diplomas could receive one on campus and then qualify for a degree.)

Dinner time in Woods Hall, circa 1910.

In declining an endowed chair, Rev. Burr urged Mrs. Woods to provide a suitable dining hall instead. Woods Hall was completed in 1905 and provided the College with a central dining and social facility. Mrs. Woods presided at Thanksgiving dinner—one of several occasions she hosted for the entire student body.

There were two other qualifications. A candidate would have to complete his College years with an 80 average, and he would have to present a thesis "worthy of praise."

The College also decided that those who qualified for degrees would receive them alphabetically, and that would apply to the division names also. Therefore, those qualified for bachelor of Humanics would precede the bachelor of physical education recipients.

The first degree was awarded to William H.J. Beckett of Baltimore, and one evidence of the campus' color-blindness is that no one considered it of sufficient interest to record that the first degree ever conferred at Springfield was awarded to a black man.

Beckett later served the black YMCA in Baltimore, and black high schools in Washington, D.C. and St. Louis.

It was during the previous year that the school's football team had won Doggett's admiration. After the Yale game, the team had gone to a New Haven restaurant for dinner, but the hotel declined to serve Robert P. Hamlin, who was black. Doggett became aware of this only when he saw Hamlin's teammates parading out of the hotel in protest, followed by the proprietor who arranged to have the entire team served in the banquet hall. (Hamlin became a YMCA state secretary, and later a member of the staff of the YMCA International Committee.)

Some of these early black graduates faced greater difficulties on the job, and Burr even speculated in a letter to one black graduate that the campus, "almost totally color-blind," might ill-prepare black graduates for those later problems.

Only three years after Doggett's arrival, the Rev. William N. DeBerry, a graduate of Oberlin Seminary, came to Springfield as pastor of the city's oldest black church, St. John's Congregational. Soon, students were assisting in youth programs there, and

The Class of 1906 holds a special place in the College's history. Its members were the first to receive baccalaureate degrees as a result of a decree issued by the Commonwealth of Massachusetts. Previously, graduates received diplomas. The first degree was awarded to William H.J. Beckett, a black man from Baltimore. In 1947, Beckett also received the Alumni Association's highest honor, the Tarbell Medallion.

Erected in 1901 through the efforts of students, the Boathouse served for forty years as the College's center for aquatics instruction. It was located at the bottom of Rally Hill.

Frank Beebe, donor of the Boathouse and first contributor to the College's new gymnasium fund, donated a six-room cottage where students could conduct athletic and other programs for young people from St. John's. This was a forerunner of what is now Springfield's Dunbar Community Center.

Doggett was later to write: "The cordial relations that have existed between our white students and students belonging to the Negro and other colored races are among the happiest of my recollections of Springfield College."

However, when the Junior Prom started, Doggett refused to overrule the student committees that failed to invite black students. He was pleased, and perhaps relieved, when the student committees soon made that decision on their own, and black students attended the Junior Prom at Springfield's Symphony Hall. "The roof did not fall, nor the campanile tumble down," Doggett noted.

1904 Campus panorama, showing Hickory Street, a nine-year-old Administration Building, and, in the distance, Woods Hall under construction.

HELP FROM SOME FRIENDS

It was in 1908 that Doggett reported to the trustees that the College was free from debt for the first time since the Lake Massasoit property had been acquired seventeen years earlier.

John D. Rockefeller, Jr., had agreed to pay $2,250 if other gifts were sufficient to pay off the mortgage by July 1, 1908. And on June 30, Doggett received the final $500 needed to meet the deadline.

It could not have come as a surprise to the trustees that Doggett, at the same meeting he announced the end of the debt, recommended another fund drive.

He said that the College needed $200,000 for a new library, another gymnasium, an athletic field, and a power plant. The president noted that tuition was paying only one-third of College costs, and that endowment was needed to help meet the other two-thirds. So the trustees authorized a capital fund campaign of $300,000, of which $100,000 would be for endowment.

The campaign got off to a quick start. William Thayer Brown of New York City, treasurer of A.G. Spalding Co., was named chairman of the athletic field committee, which included Herbert L. Pratt, with Frank N. Seerley and Elmer Berry of the faculty. After the committee received estimates that it would cost $10,000, Pratt offered to pay the entire cost.

Fred T. Ley Co., Springfield contractors, offered to build the field at cost, and the students honored the school's tradition of offering free labor. They worked for three

Herbert Pratt, president of Standard Oil Co. and one of the College's staunchest friends, financed several projects, including Pratt Field, home field for the football team for fifty years, and McCurdy Pool in the gymnasia complex.

A tradition in the College's early years was for students to volunteer as laborers on construction projects. In addition to working on the Administration Building and Boathouse, students dug trenches, laid 1,200 feet of drainage pipe, and loaded fifteen horse-drawn carts to help build Pratt Field.

Edward W. Marsh of Bridgeport, Connecticut, who contributed $38,000 to the 25th Anniversary Capital Campaign, was the principal benefactor for the library that later bore his name.

days to remove trees, dig trenches, lay 1,200 feet of drainage pipe, and make the dirt fly, loading and reloading fifteen horse-drawn carts. The contractor estimated the value of their labor at about $1,000. Nevertheless, with the tennis courts, quarter-mile track, baseball diamond, and football field, and its surrounding concrete wall and iron gates, the cost reached $15,000, and Pratt paid it all.

The gymnasium project also had its friends, who wanted to move fast. One trustee, Herbert A. Wilder of Boston, offered $10,000 if the remaining $40,000 was raised within six months. (Wilder's gifts did not end with his death in 1923. As his estate was settled, the College received $2,500 in 1924, $52,000 in 1961, and $27,000 in 1966, from the Wilder estate.)

When McCurdy had been physical director of the 23rd Street YMCA in New York City, Cleveland H. Dodge had been chairman of its gymnasium committee. McCurdy asked Dodge if he were still interested in gymnasiums, and Dodge matched Wilder's gift and deadline.

Arthur Curtiss James, Amherst College graduate and trustee, was a director of Phelps Dodge Corp., of which Dodge was vice president. James gave $5,000. The goal was reached, and work began as soon as frost was out of the ground in 1910.

It was Jacob T. Bowne's library of YMCA history that had enticed young Doggett to the College, and it was Bowne's gracious generosity that Doggett never forgot. He was determined to move that valuable collection into a fireproof building, and thus free thirteen dormitory rooms for new students.

One of Bowne's earliest students, John W. Cook '89—recipient of an honorary master of Humanics degree in 1907 and the Tarbell Medallion in 1939—initiated the library project. He was then general secretary of the YMCA in Bridgeport, Connecticut, where Edward W. Marsh had already proved his friendship for Cook, the YMCA, and the College. Marsh promised Cook $38,000 if other donors would provide the remaining

Pratt Field was surrounded by an eight-foot-high concrete wall. The wrought-iron gates were stored away when Pratt Field was later replaced by Benedum Field (known today as Stagg Field). They were taken out of storage in 1981 and are now at the entrance to the Child Development Center in Loveland Chapel on East Campus.

$25,000. When the College was still $600 short of goal at deadline, Marsh, "with some gaiety" according to Doggett, added that last sum. Marsh died soon thereafter, leaving an endowment to the building that now bears his name.

Thus, three of the four major projects that Doggett had included in his 25th anniversary capital fund drive were all funded before the celebration began. The only project remaining was the power plant, and even Doggett had difficulty in finding someone eager to contribute to a boiler room.

A QUARTER CENTURY OF GROWTH

The success of the capital fund campaign set a joyous tone for the College's 25th anniversary celebration, and also happily crowded its agenda—the dedication of Pratt Field, the cornerstone laying at the gymnasium, and the groundbreaking for Marsh Memorial Library.

The invitation to the alumni was informal: "It is the earnest desire of the faculty and the trustees that all former students should return for a glad and happy reunion. This will be 'old home week' in a real sense."

The invitation made the YMCA a part of the celebration: "We believe this week will be one of the most important events of the year in the Young Men's Christian Association" and "Association officers, who are not alumni of the Training School, are particularly invited to be present."

Besides giving the game of basketball to the nation, the College was among the first institutions to popularize gymnastics. Because there were no competing teams at the time, the College's gymnasts staged exhibitions throughout the world.

The College's cooking staff in 1900.

Doggett's best-laid schemes to make the YMCA feel at home almost went awry when, only weeks before the celebration, the faculty and students voted almost unanimously to drop YMCA from the College name. They preferred "Springfield College of Humanics." A trustees committee had recommended to the board that the name be changed to "International YMCA College," but news of the faculty-student vote appeared in the newspapers, with one report commenting that the trustees were expected to adopt the faculty-student suggestion.

Under the circumstances, the trustees did the right thing: nothing. They waited two years until 1912, when most of the voting students had graduated, then changed the name to "International YMCA College." That remained the *official* name of the College until 1954, when the name finally became, officially, what it had been, unofficially, for many years—Springfield College.

The 25th anniversary celebration began with a Sunday fellowship meeting, led by Seerley. More alumni and guests arrived on Monday, and August E. Metzdorf '05, physical director of Springfield public schools, who lived nearby, helped welcome the visitors. Lake Massasoit was the scene of Tuesday's activities. During the afternoon, the classes competed in swimming, single-paddle and four-paddle canoe races, four-oared shell races, water polo, and fancy diving. In the evening, the students took processions of illuminated boats and canoes onto the lake. They were determined to make an even more spectacular scene than the 1909 canoe carnival, which one newspaper called "one of the prettiest spectacles ever witnessed in Springfield."

The more than 500 alumni, students, and visitors who filed into the gymnasium the next morning found it decorated in red, white, and blue bunting hanging from the ceiling. Flags of many nations ringed the hall, and an illuminated front piece contained the school's seal and emblem. Suspended from the gallery were the pennants of every class from 1887 to 1910, and there were graduates present from each of those classes. The first speaker was Thomas M. Balliet, a trustee of the school, former superintendent of schools in Springfield, and founding dean of the School of Pedagogy at New York University.

After a midmorning recess, the College bugler recalled the audience to hear the legendary Gulick, who was escorted to the platform by alumni who had studied under him at the school.

The evening program was opened by the school's glee club and a piano solo by Ballantine's son, Arthur, who twenty years later would serve as undersecretary of the United States Treasury under President Herbert Hoover. For some alumni, the master of ceremonies, and the speaker, part of the program was *déjà vu*. They had been in that same gymnasium at its dedication fifteen years earlier, when then-president Charles H. Barrows introduced Q. Stanley Hall, president of Clark University. As Barrows now introduced Hall once again, he referred to the great progress made since 1895.

Rev. Walter Rauschenbusch of the Rochester Theological Seminary, who had been a popular lecturer at the College, received from alumni and students a rousing cheer, "which he acknowledged heartily," according to a contemporary account. Alumni of the first ten graduating classes were seated on the platform during the address.

After the alumni luncheon, a band led the parade of classes, as more than 150 alumni carrying class totems and banners marched to the old athletic field, where the gymnastics team gave an exhibition. The varsity defeated the alumni in baseball and in tennis.

The evening program began with the gift to Doggett of an oak gavel, handmade in Panama by one of the workers helping to build the canal. W.S. Whitbeck '09, a YMCA worker in Panama, made the presentation. Rev. George A. Coe of Union Theological

A dormitory room at the turn of the century in what is now the Administration Building. It was home for four young men who believed that there was no limit to school spirit.

Organizing a school band was Professor Frederick Hyde (seated), who taught the classics.

FOR OLD SPRINGFIELD.

Written and Composed by F. S. HYDE.

the far-shin-ing wa-ter, Where wind

Al-ma Ma-ter, There sounds thy pr

Seminary, who had just finished two years as president of the Religious Education Association of America, was the speaker.

After that, seniors contributed to the night's bonfire by offering class papers, and, as flames leapt twenty-five feet into the air, there was a grand war dance and songfest to end Thursday's program. (Students were law-abiding; they had an outdoor fire permit signed by the city's assistant chief, Burton Steere.)

Class Day exercises ended with the seniors singing, "We're Going to Leave Old Massasoit."

In addition to the twenty-one graduates, thirteen alumni qualified for degrees. Honorary degrees were given to James Naismith and to the College's founder and first president, David Allen Reed. The ceremonies concluded with advice from James Stokes of New York.

William Orr, school trustee, Massachusetts deputy commissioner of education, and former principal of Springfield's Central High School, was master of ceremonies at the gymnasium. McCurdy laid the cornerstone and G.J. Fisher spoke. Into the cornerstone box went the report of the 25th anniversary from *The Sunday Republican*, the source of much of this account of the celebration.

Librarian Jacob T. Bowne, who had served as a College officer longer than anyone else, was guest of honor at the library groundbreaking. L. Wilbur Messer of Chicago turned the first spadeful of earth, and Ballantine spoke.

Herbert Lee Pratt could not be present for the dedication of his gift, but his letter was read by Professor Berry. Students wearing Greek costumes trimmed in the school's colors came onto the field as the glee club began singing an ode composed by Frederick S. Hyde, who taught the classics.

"The pageant embodied many of the more picturesque attitudes of athletes, both ancient and modern," according to *The Republican*, which listed putting the shot, throwing the hammer, drawing the bow, pitching, delivering and batting, hurling the javelin, shooting, fencing, wrestling holds, and a flying wedge in football. Director of this athletic pageantry was G.M. Caskey '10, tutor in physical education.

THE CAMPUS CONTINUES TO EXPAND

"The observance of our 25th anniversary gave us an opportunity to rededicate ourselves to the great aims of the College. I think I may call these my happiest administrative years." So did Doggett write thirty years later, having already written that judgment in deeds.

Since Herbert Pratt had been unable to be present for the dedication of his gift, the athletic field, Doggett arranged a ceremony at the field's gates when Pratt next visited Springfield. (Throughout his lifetime, Pratt made certain that he paid all costs of the facility that bore his name, even buying pioneering versions of motorized equipment for its care. He paid for the covered grandstand that served the College for many years and then, when the old grandstand was due to be replaced, he treated students and neighbors to a spectacular fire on a June night in 1959.)

Doggett also delayed the dedication of the new gymnasium until Pratt could attend, and that decision proved to be wise indeed.

Pratt seems to have enjoyed himself immensely at the ceremonies. The main speaker was the principal of Phillips Academy at Andover, Rev. Alfred E. Stearns, a grandson of the Amherst College president who so influenced the Pratt brothers, and, like Pratt, an alumnus and a trustee of Amherst.

News accounts note that Pratt presided "gracefully" and that he had made a hit with the audience by his witty introduction of Gulick. Pratt must have been pleased when Gulick paid tribute to Edward Hitchcock, the Pratt brothers' mentor at Amherst.

Before turning the keys over to Doggett, Trustee William Orr made some pointed hints about the need for a swimming pool. The target may have been a wealthy New Yorker who had paid all the costs of educating at Springfield College a young Japanese man to head the Kobe YMCA. That wealthy visitor was even invited to speak at the dinner that day at Woods Hall.

If the hint missed its target, it hit home with Pratt, who agreed to pay for the pool, and wanted it named for McCurdy. Although slighting references would be made later about his pool, it was a wonder when it was built. Contemporary accounts explained that the new pool would have continuous filtration, so that the water would not have to be constantly replaced, as in other such facilities. In the judgment of *The Sunday Republican*, this deserved a two-column photograph of Pratt and a three-column photograph of the pool on the front page.

James McCurdy joined the faculty as one of Gulick's assistants in 1895. He succeeded Gulick as head of physical education in 1900 and remained on the faculty for forty years.

McCurdy attracted George Affleck to become a physical education instructor at the school. Many years later, Affleck ascended to the post of department head.

At its dedication, Pratt said he felt right at home there because the swimming pool reminded him of an oil tank. No one in that audience needed to be told that Pratt was president of Standard Oil.

For all the attention to the continuous filtration at the pool, it was the ventilation system at the new gymnasium that won the greatest attention. Orr had called attention to this system at the dedication: "The humidifier and the fans for forcing in fresh air and for exhausting foul air guarantee that this structure, devoted to the gospel of good health, will not itself constitute an offense against fundamental conditions of bodily vigor."

The system was designed to "wash" stale air and restore its oxygen levels for recirculation, thus assuring pure air while saving on heating bills. McCurdy and Affleck saw the need for scholarly research on the subject, and so they did a ten-month study of the operation. They proved that the system could introduce into either gym 200 cubic feet of fresh air per minute for each student even if the gym were filled to its capacity. That was seven times the requirement set by Massachusetts school building authorities, but, as the professors pointed out, a person doing physical exercise needs seven to ten times the oxygen of a person at rest.

Several seniors, guided by the two professors, did chemical analysis of the "washing" water and of the recirculated air, and their research reports were made available to other colleges and to companies designing ventilation systems.

The American Society of Heating and Ventilating Engineers sent its twenty-member Committee on Tests to observe the system. Professor Affleck utilized his class—brought them into West Gymnasium and detonated powder flashes filling the entire room with smoke, which the system removed in less than four minutes.

If the architects and consulting engineers had come a little sooner, they could have seen another unusual sight—a student work party. These events were well known on and immediately off the campus, but the engineers from some of the country's biggest cities might have marveled at students digging by hand for nine hours to prepare the way for their library.

Seniors, insisting on seniority, went first and removed the trees and roots, and left the easier digging for the underclassmen the next day. Those maintaining that a Springfield College education leads to wisdom may wish to believe that mature altruism prevailed.

In keeping with tradition, students removed stumps, cleared a road, and dug the basement for Marsh Memorial, which would serve as the College's library for fifty years.

Some earlier buildings on campus had been designed by talented students and faculty, but the library was the work of Edward Lippincott Tilton, then of Boring & Tilton, which had won the Paris Exposition gold medal in 1900 for its U.S. Immigrant Station on Ellis Island. Tilton designed more than sixty libraries for U.S. military bases, as well as many public and college libraries. At the time the library was being planned, Tilton was designing Springfield City Library, a project handsomely assisted by Andrew Carnegie. Tilton later designed the Science Museum and the Museum of Fine Arts within the City Library Quadrangle.

As the College library took shape, it still had no name. The announcement that Edward W. Marsh of Bridgeport had died, leaving a share of his estate to the College, made no reference to his contributions to the library. Marsh had insisted that he not be identified, and Doggett honored that wish even after the donor died. The library was not named Marsh Memorial until his widow assented.

The Springfield Union noted that the dedication of the library would begin "what future historians will note as a new era in the course of the development of the International YMCA College." The selection of the twenty-seventh president of the United States, William Howard Taft, to deliver the dedicatory bore out that prediction. The facts that he was late (car trouble) and that a chair collapsed under him at the Doggett home did not detract from the success of the day. Visitors included librarians from collegiate and public institutions, YMCA executives, major donors, and alumni. The College's Dramatic Club ended the day's ceremonies with a production of Aristophanes' *Frogs*, for which Professor Hyde had composed incidental music.

Doggett laid the first brick in 1912 to begin construction of the new library.

Dedicated on October 18, 1913, Marsh Memorial served as the College's library until the opening of Babson Library in 1971. The featured speaker at the dedication of Marsh Memorial was the 27th president of the United States, William Howard Taft.

Early sports teams
(left to right): baseball,
field hockey, soccer,
ice hockey

DAYS OF INNOCENCE AND JOY

Although planning and financing new buildings took much of Doggett's time and energy, and the openings of these buildings generated the greatest excitement on campus and off, there were other factors helping to make these the president's "happiest administrative years."

The College was finding new ways to reach out to other communities. The "Pleasant Hour" programs were actually the students' idea. These were one-hour programs each Sunday afternoon to which any boy over age ten was admitted free. Stereopticon slides were the usual visual aids, but the students promised that, for one program, there would be a motion picture machine with a qualified operator. At each session, there was a brief talk by a Springfield College student. *The Springfield Union* noted: "N.W. Fradd, captain of the 1911 basketball team and tackle on the football team, spoke on 'Fair Play' and had the attention of every boy every second of the time." These programs became so popular that they had to be moved to the gymnasium, and tickets issued to prevent overcrowding. All any boy had to do to get a free ticket was to ask any student.

The College also reached out to a collegiate neighbor when the University of Massachusetts (then Massachusetts Agricultural College) at Amherst decided in 1909 to introduce physical education. Its president chose Dr. Percy L. Reynolds, who had graduated in 1903 from Springfield College, to be the founder of that program. Reynolds had received a medical degree from University of Georgia Medical School and had served two years as director of physical education at the University of Maine.

A Springfield College outreach that was to benefit millions of Americans began on a day in May 1910, when Doggett and Edgar M. Robinson '01, a YMCA boys' work secretary, went to see William D. Boyce, a Chicago newspaper publisher who was trying to organize something similar to the Boy Guides of England.

Robinson sufficiently lifted Boyce's pessimism so that the publisher handed him a check for $1,000 and promised two similar monthly checks so that Robinson could pursue his plan to bring together all the organizations interested in boys' work to form a national scouting program.

At the YMCA's summer school at Silver Bay, New York, of which Doggett was principal and Robinson director of boys' work, Ernest Thompson Seton conducted a two-week experimental scout camp that summer.

Boyce's pump-priming checks having been exhausted, the International Committee of the YMCA loaned Robinson the funds to pursue his plan at no charge for the rest of the year, even though he favored an organization totally independent of its contributors, including the largest, the YMCA.

While Robinson had been a student at Springfield College and a resident of the Springfield YMCA, that association named its first boys' work secretary, but when Robinson became the first secretary for boys' work on the International YMCA Committee just after finishing at Springfield College, there were only 30,675 boys enrolled in all associations. In his twenty years of leadership, the number grew to more than 200,000, and, as a member of the world committee staff at Geneva, he took three trips around the world to promote boys' work. In 1927, he succeeded Eugene C. Foster as honorary (because he accepted no salary) head of the Boys' Work Department, and recruited L.K. Hall to the staff.

For their work in pioneering the Boy Scouts of America, that organization later awarded its highest honor for service to boyhood, the Silver Buffalo, to both Doggett and Robinson. Hundreds of Springfield College alumni have served as professional and volunteer leaders in the organization those two men helped to found.

Doggett initiated another kind of outreach, and it was to involve more women with the all-male institution. The president recorded his view on coeducation: "I believe young men and young women can be educated effectively either in coeducational colleges or in separate colleges, but I am convinced that co-instruction is always desirable. It gives a fine quality to a men's school to have cultivated women on its staff."

Carolyn Doggett, the president's wife, taught literature and music appreciation, using her own extensive collection of recordings. Wives of other faculty members also taught at the College, and Professor Hyde involved more and more women in his musical and theatrical performances.

Carolyn Doggett, who had been dean of women at Washburn College, married Laurence Doggett on October 3, 1894.

In newspaper society sections, there were reports of meetings, teas, and receptions of the "women's board" of the International YMCA College. The wives of the Massachusetts chief justice, the owner of the city's largest department store, a prominent bank officer, and a well-known industrialist and civic leader poured tea, while their daughters poured punch.

One newspaper noted that "the pretty light frocks of the women and the white flannels of the men made a festive and altogether charming picture." That was in describing a program at which an alumnus spoke about his work in Hong Kong, the glee club and senior quartet sang, canoe races were held on the lake and, of course, the president spoke to the 250 women.

The event that drew the largest number of Springfield neighbors was the annual illumination night on the lake. When, during the 1909 commencement week, five seniors decorated their canoes and had a water parade, they started something. The next year's parade of illuminated canoes had been intentionally extravagant to honor the College's 25th anniversary, but the event had grown in size and popularity each year. Newspapers would run the King Street trolley schedule for the convenience of the hundreds, later thousands, of Springfield residents who would find a place on the banks of Lake Massasoit to watch the canoes. Each year, students would call it the best ever, and the local newspapers usually agreed.

The Springfield Union threw away all caution and declared that the 1914 night was "far superior" to any other. Included in that one was the Second Regimental Band playing from a huge float in the lake, and a seventy-five-canoe "S" in red fire.

Newspaper accounts also noted that no one had been hurt during the exercises, and commended the safety precautions. It was in the water sports events during the daylight hours that the lakeside crowd was horrified to see a man, who had rowed from the opposite shore to get a better view, fall into the lake and disappear. After a rescue boat crew pulled him out and revived him, the students threw him high into the air and back into the water. In those times, college students always loved to fool the townies!

The year 1914 had other distinctions. John D. Rockefeller gave the College $50,000, the gymnastics team completed its longest tour in history (4,000 miles), and the College's dramatic club, directed by Professor Hyde, played to an audience of 1,200, filling Court Square Theater downtown.

The College graduated its largest class to date, fifty-seven, and Doggett was twice pleasantly surprised. At commencement dinner, Chevalier William L.F.C. Van Rappard, representing Queen Wilhelmina of the Netherlands, conferred on Doggett the Order of Orange-Nassau. Then, the alumni presented him with a check for $3,500 for a tour around the world, which had been approved by the trustees.

Two weeks later, Gavrilo Princip killed Archduke Francis Ferdinand of Austria as he drove through the streets of Sarajevo in the Bosnian mountains, and changed the course of history. Doggett never specified the exact beginning and ending of his "happiest administrative years," but the termination date had to be June 28, 1914.

Originally built by Gulick, the house that stood near the corner of Alden Street and Wilbraham Avenue was purchased by the College and became the President's home. In the years after World War II, the building became the Student Union.

THE TOLLING OF THE BELL

The incoming students, 134 of them, met Chief Massasoit, heard words of wisdom and warning, were dunked in McCurdy Pool, and served cider and doughnuts.

The date was September 21, 1914, less than two weeks after the First Battle of the Marne had driven the German armies back from their position twenty-five miles from Paris.

The trustees kept their attention not on the Marne, but on the Massasoit. They approved plans for a 200-man, $175,000 dormitory to be built east of Marsh Memorial, overlooking the lake, to be called Alumni Hall. They received the report that the new power plant was operating, all buildings were connected to it, and that the College had acquired the Gulick house, near the corner of Wilbraham Avenue and Alden Street, to be the president's residence.

Doggett had already met with the faculty and reminded them of President Woodrow Wilson's statement that the United States was neutral in the conflict. (When McCurdy commented that he would like to knock the Kaiser's head off, Doggett indicated his agreement, but he also must have had thoughts of his beloved Leipzig.)

Before the school year was out, Doggett presented to the trustees his five-year plan, which foresaw a 400-man student body in a four-year instead of a three-year course, requiring the new dormitory and other facilities. The country work program to prepare men to serve YMCAs in rural sections was started, and the College began working on plans to have one year of that study conducted at the University of Massachusetts (Massachusetts Agricultural College) at Amherst.

Frank Seerley, one of Gulick's assistants for several years, began teaching advanced courses in general and genetic psychology in 1895. Later named dean, he remained at the college for thirty-seven years.

The trustees voted to hire an instructor in business administration by September 1917, but referred to appropriate committees McCurdy's suggestion that a summer school be started, and that alumni be charged a fee when placed in a job. Professor Hyde was given a fall-term leave of absence to study music in New York City.

The trustees approved the president's proposal to invite all YMCA-employed officers in Massachusetts and bordering states to a conference at the College in May, and to invite all YMCA-employed officers in the country to come to the College in 1916 or 1917.

The fifty-two-man graduating class followed the traditions of the grave decorating and the canoe illuminating, moved the play back to campus, built the Class of 1915 sidewalk, and paid tribute to Dean Frank Seerley for his twenty-five years of service to the College. The speaker at the graduation was the Rev. Harry Emerson Fosdick, who strongly supported President Wilson's determination to keep the United States out of the war, and said that the conscience of the world was massing against war and for universal peace.

However, when classes resumed in the fall, the war seemed closer to the campus. As Dean Seerley called the role of names and addresses, there were few foreign countries represented, only one Australian and a few Canadians. All others were from the United States, the largest proportion of United States students in the College's history.

At the graduation of the Class of 1916, the portrait of the first Springfield College alumnus to be killed in the war was placed on the speaker's table and decorated with British flags. He was Harry Whiteman '13. Among the graduates were seven Canadian men who left the next day for military service. Although the tone of many of the commencement week activities was at least serious, news accounts tell of the humorous skits of Canadian Corporal Frank G. Armitage of the Class of 1916. He became a captain, and was awarded the British Military Cross for bravery under fire.

WAR OVERTAKES SPRINGFIELD

On April 16, 1917, International YMCA collegians turned their backs on baseball and track long enough to play the first interclass basketball game, in which the Juniors seemingly defeated the Seniors, 31-30.

Not until the players had gone to the showers and the dormitory did the scorers discover their error. It had been a tie game, and both sides agreed that it would be replayed as soon as possible.

On that same day, the U.S. House of Representatives passed, and President Wilson signed, a declaration of war against Germany.

Many Springfield College men—Australians, Canadians, English, French, and others—were already in the war, but now it was also the Americans' war. On campus, a rally was held in which the American flag was displayed along with the British and French flags. Students began leaving for military service, and faculty members left to direct YMCA programs for the military.

At commencement time, many of the fifty-eight diplomas were awarded in absentia, since the graduates were already in military or YMCA camp service. Whereas newspaper reports of other graduations told familiar stories of pomp and joyousness, the headline on Springfield's read: "Drops June Gayety."

During World War I, many of the College's faculty and graduates volunteered to direct YMCA programs for the military.

The story explained that the International YMCA College had changed its format to include a war conference as a tribute to five of its alumni who had already been lost in the war. Among the speakers were J.J. Virgo, general secretary of the YMCA in London, and Lieutenant Colonel William S. Pierce, commandant of the Springfield Armory, which would turn out 266,638 Springfield rifles before the war was over. Doggett read the names of the five alumni who had been lost in the war, a practice he was to follow at annual memorial services for many years to come, and always with a reverence that impressed those assembled.

The speaker at the graduation exercises was Rev. Frank Crane, who had left a Worcester, Massachusetts pastorate to write a syndicated column that was then appearing in more than one hundred newspapers.

At the 1917 commencement, many things were different, but some things remained the same. Even while grieving for young friends, they remembered the man who had died fifteen years earlier but whose memory was kept green on the campus. The graduates made their way to the grave of Henry S. Lee.

When the International YMCA at New York chose thirteen men to be YMCA physical directors at military training camps, they included six Springfield College students.

Elmer Berry was appointed to the physical education faculty prior to World War I. During the war, he worked at the College on a crash program to turn out the YMCA workers needed to serve in the Armed Forces.

It would have been seven, but Professor Elmer Berry, who had been offered the post at Plattsburg, New York, decided he should stay in Springfield and work on a crash program to turn out the YMCA workers needed to serve the armed forces.

Those courses started immediately after graduation and lasted only one month. The College ran no less than fifteen of them, training more than one thousand YMCA camp workers.

Arthur Rudman, who had served eight years in YMCA camp work in the Philippines and with the Mexican Expeditionary force, was director. Affleck taught physical education, as did Berry, who also taught recreation, a fortunate addition because many YMCA workers found that directing sports and recreational programs for servicemen was an important part of their work.

The first candidates in this program were, for the most part, young and fit, but later applicants were not so fortunate, and Doggett noted to Hyde that the men were sore and glum. Looking to another side of the triangle, Hyde went to the piano and banged out a war ditty, and "he soon had them feeling 100 percent happier," Doggett later wrote.

In later years, Doggett delighted in meeting those thirty-day-wonder alumni. Once, while preserving his Rotary attendance record by making up a meeting in Florida, he was introduced by John J. Tigert, former United States commissioner of education and then president of the University of Florida, who identified himself as a Springfield alumnus of the thirty-day YMCA camp worker course. (Before coming to Springfield College, he had completed graduate work at Oxford as a Rhodes Scholar.)

During that summer of 1917, Frank Seerley began his tour of army bases in this country, lecturing on sex hygiene, before going to England and France for the same purpose. McCurdy went to France that fall to organize recreational programs for American troops, and his manual on that subject was published in Paris at the end of that year.

When September came, only 135 students appeared for regular courses. Many were waiting their call to military service, and only fifty-five were under draft age. In June, there were thirty-eight graduates, but many were not present to receive their diplomas.

Among those present were W. David Owl, who would serve with the Army before returning to do YMCA work among his Cherokee tribe, and Joseph N. Singh, who would return to his position with the Bombay (today Mumbai), India, YMCA.

There was an unusually large number of alumni and other guests, however, because the 40th annual conference of YMCA-employed officers was being held in Springfield. More than 850 attended, and a dining tent served as a temporary adjunct to Woods Hall. The College's faithful friend, L. Wilbur Messer, told the assembled officers that the YMCA should raise a postwar endowment of $3 million to support the association colleges at Springfield and Chicago.

PEACETIME COMES TO SPRINGFIELD

Doggett believed that the war experience could teach the educators, if they were ready to learn.

Before a special committee of the Massachusetts legislature to study education, Doggett testified that physical education should be made compulsory in all schools, and it should be held outdoors as well as indoors. He also said that the Army's efforts to assign tasks on the basis of aptitude could teach colleges how to admit and guide students. Doggett called the collegiate admissions system "absurd."

However, few people were listening. The special committee's session in Springfield's City Hall was brief and poorly attended. In the streets outside, there were thousands of people shouting, blowing horns, ringing bells, snake dancing, and throwing confetti and talcum powder, and when that ran out, scouring powder. One man fell off a truck and was killed, and a woman was shot when a man using a pistol as a noisemaker got some live ammunition. It was November 11, 1918, and all were celebrating the armistice.

The fact that Doggett managed to get through that swirling mob to City Hall indicates his determination to speak his mind on a subject close to his heart and mind.

The next day, the students joined in a more organized parade along Springfield's Main Street, and one newspaper reported: "The students of the Young Men's Christian Association College sang and trod a determined step."

The step was determined by Capt. Henry L. Chesick, who had arrived less than two months earlier to begin the Student Army Training Corps (SATC) program at the College.

Where Alumni Hall now stands, barracks were erected for 196 men, and the captain and his wife moved into one floor in Doggett's house. Woods Hall was enlarged at a cost of $41,000 to accommodate the additional diners, and the War Department paid twenty percent of the cost. Two weeks after the armistice, the College received an order to demobilize the SATC, and the men were gone by late December. The government eventually paid the College $1.63 per day for each cadet's room and board, bringing its total payments to $42,049, only about $10,000 less than the cost.

On the Saturday before Thanksgiving, colleges all over the country held football games for the benefit of the United War Fund Campaign. The Springfield College team cooperated by defeating the naval base team from the Massachusetts Institute of Technology, 7-0, at Pratt Field.

As the year ended, Doggett could pause to record the College's contribution. About 350 alumni had entered combat service, and twenty of those gave their lives. Their names would be placed on a plaque in Marsh Memorial, and would be repeated on Armistice Day anniversaries for years to come.

Inside the entrance to Marsh Memorial are two bronze plaques donated by the Class of 1920, the first class to graduate after the war. In addition to "The American's Creed," one plaque lists the twenty graduates who died during World War I.

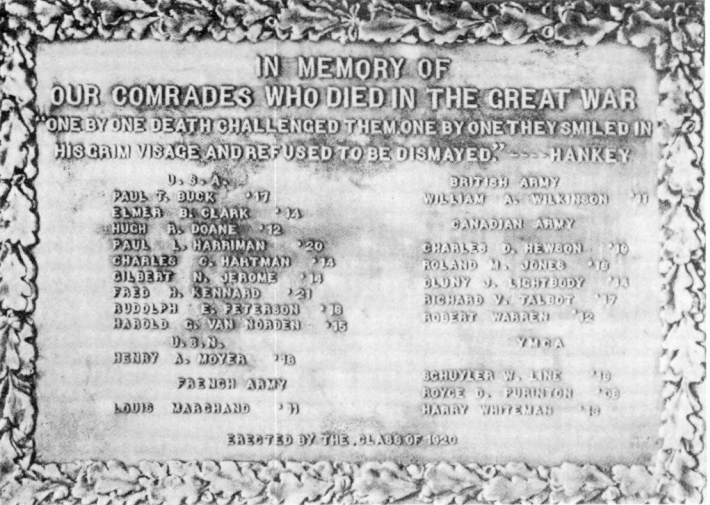

Financed entirely by Herbert Pratt of Standard Oil, Pratt Field was surrounded by an eight-foot-high wall. It was razed in the 1960s. The location is now occupied by Babson Library and Blake Track and Field.

Doggett, ever the optimist, launched a $2 million Expansion and Endowment Fund Drive in 1920. The drive was to settle current debts, fund a dormitory and a science building, and increase the endowment.

Chapter 3

Doggett:
A Return to Normalcy

T he graduating class of 1919 was unique. Every man in it
had served in the armed forces. It was also the smallest
class in years, with only sixteen graduates.

However, the men were determined to do all the traditional things, like throwing fully
clothed seniors into Lake Massasoit, making a class gift (a sundial), and listening to a
commencement speech (by Hamilton Holt, League of Nations advocate, later president of Rollins College).

At that 33rd commencement, there was also something new: the
performance in Woods Hall of an opera, written by Frederick Hyde,
professor of classics, about the burning of the Springfield settlement
by Native Americans during King Philip's War. The title role in *Daphne
of the Colony* was sung by Mrs. Allen Appleton, and Raymond Frank
'18 sang the tenor lead.

Major Ernest M. Best, alumnus and former faculty member who had
supervised the Canadian YMCA's military work, was awarded an
honorary master of Humanics degree. Jacob T. Bowne presented, for
alumni and friends of the College, an oil portrait of Luther Gulick, and
the school's founder was there again to ask the benediction.

President Doggett reported to the trustees that Elmer Berry had been named associate
director of physical education and would begin a summer school that year. (Only forty-
nine attended, but that grew to eighty-six in 1920 and 110 in 1921.) Also, Leslie Judd
and John Brock joined the faculty, and the trustees voted to establish a course in industrial secretaryship.

Thirty of the men who had been in the one-month wartime course enrolled as full-
time students, as did seventy-one of the Student Army Training Corps cadets. The president warned that the dormitory, plans for which had been abandoned because of the
war, was now, more than ever, a necessity. The design was not changed, but the price
was. Inflation had pushed the cost from $175,000 to $500,000 for the two-hundred-
man dormitory.

The trustees adopted Doggett's proposal to seek that sum, and also a College endowment of $1 million. However, applications were already pouring in for September when
enrollment jumped to 344, as compared to the highest pre-war enrollment of 286.

The goal of the Expansion and Endowment Fund Drive was raised to $2 million, and
the local community was asked to start the campaign with $200,000. By the time the
fund drive started on June 22, 1920, gifts or pledges of $108,000 had been received,

Horace Moses, a self-made man and founder of Junior Achievement, became a strong supporter of the College in 1920, running a fund drive to which he contributed $32,000.

and seventy volunteers began a three-day drive to raise the remainder. They came close —$187,062—and promised Doggett they would raise the rest, which they did.

While the local campaign was being organized, the Hampden Hospital in Springfield decided to close and devote its assets to charitable causes. Clifton Crocker, a member of the executive boards of both the hospital and the College, urged that the College be considered. The hospital board decided to give all the assets, $41,784, to the College, which named its health center for Dr. Walter R. Weiser, the last administrator of the hospital.

The fund drive produced another strong supporter for the College: Horace Moses. The self-made man, founder of Junior Achievement and supporter of the YMCA and 4-H, gave $5,000, but later increased his gift to $32,000.

The campaign gave *The Springfield Union* the opportunity to comment: "There is no lack of appreciation here for the pioneer enterprise that the International YMCA College represents, and no lack of good will toward its versatile and energetic president."

A Year of Headlines

Students, neighbors, and many alumni were using the name "Springfield College." The authorized emblem for all varsity sports was a maroon "S" and all student activities were conducted under the name "Springfield College."

Yet, the College's official name was "The International Young Men's Christian Association College."

In 1921, R.J. Conklin, editor of *The Springfield Student*, presented to the trustees a petition signed by 296 students asking that the name "Springfield College" be officially adopted. It was time for another committee, which recommended that the trustees sanction the name "Springfield College," but that the long name be used on stationery and diplomas. That compromise was to last for more than thirty years.

The Springfield Union vigorously supported the idea of a name change with an editorial headed, "Call It Springfield College," without admitting or explaining that the newspaper's own library had, for a full decade, filed and indexed all stories on the College and all stories on American International College together, without distinction.

If Doggett had known this, he might have made an even stronger case when he pleaded unsuccessfully with Chester T. McGown '95, chancellor of the French American College, formerly the French Protestant College, not to change its name to American International College.

There was another change on the campus that year, and many considered it more important. William Ballantine, seventy-two years old, having finished a year's leave of absence, insisted that his retirement be accepted. A lesser man might harbor in his mind the belief that Ballantine had cost the College millions of dollars, but Doggett's mind and heart were filled only with admiration and affection for this professor, whose resignation he accepted with "deep personal regret."

In an unprecedented recognition, two local trustee leaders, Henry H. Bowman and Clifton A. Crocker, co-hosted a dinner for Ballantine at the Colony Club, the former mansion of the late Daniel B. Wesson, partner in Smith & Wesson with the school's early supporter, Horace Smith.

Doggett and about twenty faculty leaders were invited. Ballantine said that he could not have had a richer privilege or a happier life than to be associated with such men in such a cause. "Mental honesty is a spiritual grace of the first order," he said, and offered this wish: "Give us young men who stand on their own feet, look with their own eyes, think with their own brains and dare call their souls their own."

Four days later, the trustees met just before commencement and voted an honorary degree to Ballantine. When it was conferred, Ballantine was, according to a contemporary account, "too overcome with emotion to make a reply."

After retirement, Ballantine continued to reside in Springfield, writing books on religion and articles on nature. When Trinity Methodist Church was dedicated, he joined two bishops in pronouncing the blessing. The Methodist bishop used English; the Episcopal bishop, Latin; Ballantine, Greek.

Of the large number of students who came from Australia, Doggett singled out Leslie James Judd '20 to join the faculty.

The biographies of all three of Ballantine's sons joined his in *Who's Who in America*, and others speculated that might be a record. Henry Winthrop Ballantine was a lawyer, law school dean, and longtime professor at the University of California. Although Arthur played piano at Springfield College in his youth, it was Edward who became the composer, pianist, and music professor at Harvard. Arthur became a lawyer, undersecretary of the U.S. Treasury Department, and a Springfield College trustee. Ballantine died in 1937, in his eighty-ninth year.

At the 1921 graduation exercises, which honored Ballantine, only thirty-seven graduated. But Doggett reassured the trustees that total student population was the second largest in history, that scholarship averages were the highest in history, and that enrollment attrition had been greatly reduced, from an all-time high of fifty-seven down to eighteen.

Doggett also pointed out that the great majority of the students were United States citizens, and cited the post-war recession in Canada as a factor in reduced applications from that country, which sent only eight students. There were nine students from Latin America and the Philippines. The students had shown their international awareness in another way that year: More than 150 of them had gone door to door throughout Springfield collecting for famine relief in China.

Along with Judd, John Brock was appointed to the faculty after the war.

The Class of 1921 had other distinctions. It attracted the largest-ever crowd—more than 5,000—to its illuminated canoe parade on Lake Massasoit. It also modernized the class sidewalk project by renting a concrete mixer and putting in 290 feet of walkway, onto which the Class of 1921 put its mark.

It was during the next year that the College decided that students should henceforth pay one-third of the cost of their education, and so annual tuition was increased from $150 to $185. Students could, however, find more ways to help meet those costs. The College announced that 290 students with College and Student Association jobs had earned $11,756.68 during the three months before Christmas break.

Enrollment that year surpassed 400 for the first time in the history of the school, and the number of students in the YMCA secretarial course exceeded 100 for the first time.

Judd (back row, center) was extraordinarily successful in training gymnasts. His teams gained international recognition and helped popularize the sport in the United States.

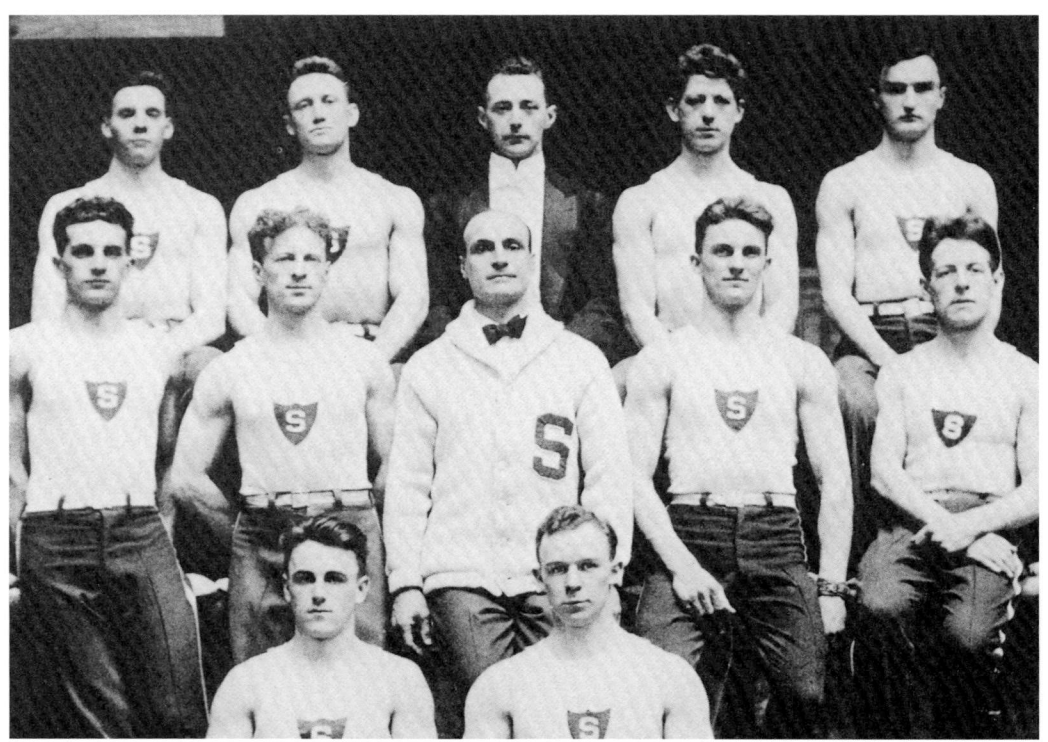

However, because of the increased popularity of physical education in schools, colleges, playgrounds, and the Boy Scouts, as well as YMCAs, James McCurdy foresaw the need for 1,000 physical educators each year, and he believed Springfield College should be prepared to graduate 200 of them.

The Student Association, which had been managing student activities since its formation in 1896 and had an elected, sixteen-student cabinet, decided to give a one-year trial to a Student Congress with ten percent of the student body as members. The freshman class would have ten percent of the members, and the percentage would increase ten points for each year.

All of these developments were duly reported in the public press of the early 1920s, but the news story of the period that received the greatest attention was the expulsion of six students.

One of the expellees was a basketball star. Another was captain of the tennis team. Yet another was prominent in four sports. A fourth was a member of the track team. Although early stories stated only that the men had been expelled for "infractions of college rules and customs," the student newspaper explained that they had been expelled by the faculty for "cribbing."

The student paper commented: "Springfield has high ideals to maintain, higher by far than most colleges, and no incongruous person should be allowed to discredit them and smirch our reputation."

What would be considered a more positive story was the report that the College was ready to erect the first building from the Expansion Fund—an infirmary. It was to be erected either on Wilbraham Avenue northwest of Doggett's house, or on Hickory Street, south of the gymnasium. (The first site was chosen; the second was later used for Cheney Hall.)

Local newspapers noted that Springfield residents would benefit from the new building because larger facilities would be provided there for the work being done by Professor Stacy B. Betzler, who had had such great success in helping Springfield children recover the use of limbs crippled by infantile paralysis.

RELIGIOUS PREJUDICE AND ACADEMIC FREEDOM

Even during his "happiest administrative years," Doggett was beset with what he later called "perhaps the most serious experience during my administration at Springfield" —the theological controversy that threatened academic freedom in the early years of the 20th century.

The curtain-raiser of this drama had been the publication of Rev. Burr's article, "The New Testament," in a school magazine, setting off such a reaction among theological conservatives that Rev. Burr offered to resign.

William C. Ballantine, whose teaching about the Bible alarmed some benefactors, enjoyed the complete support of Doggett during succeeding controversies.

The first act had been Doggett's confrontation with Oliver Morse, who said that he could not continue as the College's fundraiser if William Ballantine continued as Bible instructor. Morse left, but the problem remained.

In 1909, the YMCA-Employed Officers Conference, meeting in Omaha, Nebraska, appointed a committee headed by S. Wirt Wiley to study the problems of the training agencies in Springfield and Chicago.

A year later, James Stokes, the New York philanthropist who had supported the College since its formation, came from his summer estate in Stockbridge to lunch with Ballantine. The meal was digestible, but the Stokes' note that followed wasn't. It contained five questions of faith to which Stokes wanted "yes" or "no" answers. Ballantine suggested a meeting at which the questions could be discussed, but the meeting never took place and Stokes became a strong opponent of the College.

Doggett, who showed his respect and gratitude to Morse even when he was sending him on his way, was not so tolerant of Stokes. Doggett recorded his conviction that Stokes' questions had been ghostwritten, and noted that they showed up again from Judge (later U.S. Senator) Selden Parker Spencer, head of the committee of five named by the International YMCA Convention in Toronto in 1910 to investigate the training schools.

Stokes later met with the College's vice president, F.G. Platt, in New Britain, Connecticut, where Platt was a prominent industrialist and state and local YMCA leader. Stokes asked Platt to remove Ballantine from the faculty and threatened to take the school out of his will if this were not done. (Ballantine stayed, and Stokes was as good as his word; his will left money for the training of YMCA secretaries so long as they were *not* trained at the College.)

James Stokes, a New York philanthropist who had been a contributor since the College's founding, was so troubled by Ballantine's religious positions that he withdrew all support in 1910.

Doggett would not turn the other cheek to Stokes, but instead corrected his grammar. When Stokes wired the school's good friend, Wilbur Messer of Chicago, asking him to "see that Springfield College is evangelized," Doggett noted: "I supposed he meant 'made evangelical.'"

The Omaha committee arrived in Springfield on April 11, 1911, and met with faculty for an afternoon and long evening session. At Ballantine's invitation, the committeemen attended his class the next day.

To help quell the theological controversy, Thomas M. Balliet, a College trustee and dean of the School of Pedagogy at New York University, wrote a report on the school's biblical instruction. It was sent to churches and YMCA leaders throughout the country.

In its report to the 700 secretaries meeting in Cleveland, Ohio, the committee praised the Training School graduates but added that the College's methods of biblical instruction might be proper in a postgraduate school, but were not appropriate in a training school.

The school's trustees had made their own year-long study of biblical instruction, and Thomas M. Balliet, founding dean of the School of Pedagogy at New York University, wrote the report that *The Springfield Republican* published in full. The text filled two full pages, an indication of the importance the newspaper attached to the controversy but also, it must be admitted, an indication of Springfield community leaders' great respect for Balliet—who, as superintendent, had made Springfield's public schools the best in the nation. A press overrun of 3,000 copies allowed the College to send copies of the report to churches and YMCA leaders all over the country.

Although this report won favorable comment from important people and publications, the drama had not yet ended. In 1913, the International YMCA Convention in Cincinnati received the Spencer committee report, which included a requirement that the training school make certain that each instructor be in sincere accord with evangelical standards.

When a motion was made to delete that paragraph lest it lead to a theological inquisition, Judge Spencer took the floor of the convention to attack openly the biblical teaching at Springfield College. B.B. Farnsworth of New York argued that if such a test were imposed on each faculty member, it should also be required of all YMCA employees and board members. However, the school's critics had the votes and the measure passed, 400-294. "This vote was rightly interpreted as a vote of censure," Doggett wrote.

Nonetheless, in the spirit of Christian charity, the convention named a standing committee to create better relations with the training schools by visiting them, studying their workings, and reporting back in three years.

William N. Birks of Montreal was named to head the group, and one of the other four members was William Orr, a Springfield College trustee and an admirer of the man who had written the Balliet report. (The feeling was mutual; while Balliet was superintendent of Springfield's schools, Orr was named principal of its honored high school.)

In 1913, at the request of this committee, the College was host to fifty leading YMCA executives, and four of the five committee members also attended.

When the Birks committee recommended at the Cleveland convention that there be no personal test for faculty members, Judge Spencer protested, and William D. Mackenzie, president of Hartford Theological Seminary, proposed a compromise that the 2,000 delegates adopted without a dissenting vote.

The compromise avoided the personal test and pleased Doggett, who later said that it "did much to allay further theological criticism of the school." Indeed, he saw good from ill wind. He concluded that the College had shown the religious denominations how to encourage cooperation between liberals and conservatives in their ranks.

However, the College had to pay still a higher price for this controversy. Edward S. Harkness, who had been interested in the College and generous to it, withdrew his support because he saw the College as part of the fundamentalist YMCA structure. Lawrence K. Hall, in his biography of Doggett, says that this was "one of his greatest disappointments." During his lifetime, Harkness donated more than $100 million, most of it to other educational institutions.

A problem with less-serious administrative and financial consequences stemmed from the fact that the YMCA, which was open to all evangelical Christians, considered Unitarians not to be Christian and Roman Catholics not to be evangelical.

When the school was about to open in 1885, the city's Unitarian minister had written an open letter to *The Republican* in which he noted that Unitarians were to be excluded from the College and they should not be asked to support it financially.

The exchange of letters in 1885 was duplicated almost thirty years later, when the Springfield YMCA was raising money for a new building. From Rev. Augustus P. Reccord, minister of the same church, came an announcement that no self-respecting Unitarian would contribute to the YMCA and no self-respecting YMCA leader would ask for Unitarians' money.

Only six months after that exchange, one of the country's most prominent Unitarians, former U.S. president William Howard Taft, came to speak at the Marsh Memorial Library dedication and made headlines by defending the College's policies.

In a front-page story, *The Springfield Union* reported: "Voicing highest praises of the YMCA movement and the works of the college, there was a plain disagreement between the views which Mr. Taft expressed and those of Unitarian ministers, the creed to which he gives allegiance. In fact, he openly called attention to this question, taking a side against the clergy of his own faith."

Taft accepted the invitation to speak at the Springfield YMCA lecture series the next year, and said he was proud to be appearing under YMCA auspices. Off the bench, Taft could be a dissenter, however. He invited his wife to the YMCA's men-only lecture and addressed the huge crowd in Springfield Symphony Hall: "Lady and gentlemen."

Even Reccord appreciated the YMCA's work during World War I—so much so that he volunteered to give his vacations or a leave of absence in such service, and the Unitarian minister became YMCA secretary. The times were changing.

In the College's early days, there were Catholics among students from traditionally Catholic countries, and later some American Catholics were admitted, but Doggett explained the problem: "We always had difficulty in placing them after graduation. They were not acceptable to the YMCA; the Catholic schools were suspicious of a man who had been trained in a Protestant institution; and the public schools were generally reluctant to accept Catholic physical directors. The number of Catholics who applied for admission increased greatly, and it became necessary to limit the quota admitted."

Dan Kelly '13, believed himself to be the first American-Catholic graduate at Springfield College. (The College remembers him for another distinction; he was captain of the 1912 football team that lost to Carlisle when Jim Thorpe scored all thirty points to Springfield's twenty-four. Kelly scored the College's first touchdown.)

Immediately upon graduation, Kelly was appointed physical director in the public schools of Holyoke, Massachusetts. When he resigned in 1917 to accept the New York State Board of Education's appointment as physical inspector of the state's public schools, the Holyoke School Board instead voted him a leave of absence in case he wished to return. He later served many years in the athletic department of Harvard University.

The generosity of John D. Rockefeller, Jr., enabled the College to be in a financial position to weather the Depression.

Some of the men enrolled at Springfield College by the Army late in World War I were Catholics, and a few remained after the war to complete the course. This caused the trustees to undertake a study. "It was the opinion of the committee that the small number of Catholics then enrolled did not justify any feeling of anxiety," Doggett later wrote.

Only a few months after that study, the College awarded an honorary doctorate to one of the world's most prominent Catholics who had to overcome strong anticlerical resistance to become head of the French forces, and later commander-in-chief of the Allied forces. Marshal Foch came to Springfield during his American goodwill tour, called on Springfield's Catholic bishop, particularly for his strong support of the YMCA during the war, and received an honorary Doctor of Humanics hood from Doggett.

BARONS AND BENEFACTORS

Whenever a college goes outside of its geographical region asking for money, the potential donors always ask how well the College has been supported by its alumni and its local community. So the facts that the local goal of $200,000 had been met, and that the alumni had gone over the $25,000 mark, encouraged the trustees to launch the campaign in thirteen Eastern states.

Doggett and the trustees started big, asking the Rockefeller General Education Board for $500,000. Officers of the board visited the College, and their report sustained the need for such a sum and praised the institution and its programs. However, they concluded that Springfield College was then a specialized institution preparing men for a particular profession, and the fund supported only institutions for general education. The Laura Spelman Rockefeller Memorial board also turned down Springfield's request, but one of the board members, W.S. Richardson, an alumnus, took the application to Rockefeller himself. The philanthropist gave $50,000 at once, and promised another $50,000 when gifts from other sources totaled $500,000.

At that point the country went into the 1921 recession, but Doggett was eager to press forward anyway. However, Pratt and other committee members convinced the president to postpone the campaign.

To divert his attention from that disappointment, Doggett needed the happy news from his daughter, Ruth. In the home of Captain James S. Summers '11, then head of the British YMCA Training School, Ruth married Clarence Kennedy on May 6, 1921. After a three-month tour through France, Italy, Greece, and Turkey, the newlyweds returned to Smith College where Mr. Kennedy was an assistant professor of art, and Mrs. Kennedy taught economics.

On May 14, 1922, G. Frank Adams died in Springfield, leaving one-third of his estate to the College. He had been connected with the school and its pioneers throughout his lifetime. He had been bookkeeper for Julius H. Appleton, trustee of the Springfield Institution for Savings and the Horace Smith Fund, and vice president of the national bank where Horace Moses was a director.

Not surprisingly, Adams' estate was largely in the stock of Horace Moses' paper company, and of the insurance company that David Allen Reed's father-in-law had founded. One of Adams' relatives recommended to his fellow trustees that the College hold those stocks, then worth $20,000, until the recession ended. They did, and then sold them for $73,200.

The end of the recession also signaled the start of the campaign for the remaining $1,500,000, and a new application was filed with the Laura Spelman Rockefeller Memorial board. Beardsley Ruml, executive director of that board, visited the campus, as did at least two of its board members. At a meeting April 23, 1923, that board voted to give $500,000 to the College if it raised an additional $2 million by July 1, 1928. It should be noted that the vote required the College to raise $2.5 million, which the board members believed to be the minimum needed.

Herbert Pratt gave $125,000 and collected $25,000 each from his brothers, Frederic, George, and Harold. Herbert Pratt's brother-in-law gave $15,000 of the $60,000 raised in Greater Boston for the College. When the campaign stalled with still $800,000 to go, Herbert Pratt made that report personally to John D. Rockefeller, Jr., who gave $150,000 as a personal gift, and another $200,000 which Rockefeller required be listed as anonymous.

At the meeting of eleven campaign leaders in New York on deadline day, the report showed a Greater Springfield total of $400,000, twice the goal, and $250,000 in pledges from alumni.

When all the reports were in, the total stood at $2,409,000. Pratt announced that he personally would guarantee the remaining $91,000 to meet the conditions for the Rockefeller gift. Each of the other committee members agreed to raise $5,000, which they did, and other donors contributed $16,000, leaving only $25,000, which Pratt himself paid.

As donors paid on their three-year pledges, Isabel E. Richardson, the College's assistant treasurer, sent the reports to the Rockefellers, who matched them. When some pledge payments were delayed, the Rockefellers extended the deadline to July 1, 1929, when the entire $2.5 million had been collected.

Less than four months later, on October 29, the stock market crashed, and Doggett wrote simply: "It may be said with confidence that the securing of this Expansion Fund assured the perpetuity of Springfield College and saved it from eclipse during the depression that followed."

Doggett also recalled that, while in New York seeking funds, he would often visit in Trinity Church yard the stone dedicated to the War of 1812 hero, Captain Lawrence, for whom Doggett's uncle was named. The uncle, taken prisoner during the Civil War, died at Andersonville after twice stepping aside to allow married men to be freed by exchange. Doggett bore the uncle's name, albeit with a different spelling. As Doggett stood in front of Captain Lawrence's grave, he recalled his father's injunction to him when he was a boy: "Laurence, don't give up the ship."

Perhaps no benefactor worked harder to ensure the success of the Expansion and Endowment Fund Drive than Herbert Pratt. He personally gave $125,000, collected $25,000 each from his three brothers, and encouraged Rockefeller to support the College.

Pivotal to arranging a tour of Mexico by the gymnastics team was Enrique C. Aguirre, a 1915 graduate. Aguirre served as physical education director of the Mexico YMCA and, later, chairman of Mexico's Olympic Committee.

THE GROWING INTERNATIONAL CHARACTER

Wisely and fortunately, Doggett gave his major attention throughout the '20s to the Expansion Fund, but the postwar period had more problems than financial ones.

Doggett was always sensitive to the concerns of foreign students, and had been stung by the criticism of a friend in Germany who believed that the College had not been sufficiently supportive of a young man from that country.

In 1920, when the College had twenty students from nine foreign countries, Doggett decided that the College needed to have a faculty member be responsible for foreign students. He was able to borrow from the Foreign Department of the International YMCA Committee Frank M. Mohler, a Rhodes Scholar, who had served in Hong Kong for eleven years.

By 1922, Mohler had proved himself, and a way was found to include him in the budget as director of foreign students if he also taught history.

However, much of the College's international emphasis during the '20s was directed by the president himself. When the Latin American Students' Conference was held on campus in the summer of 1923, Doggett invited the attendees to his home and participated in the lively discussions. The conference was covered by the major wire services, which sent daily reports to all Latin American nations. Some of the comments by Latin Americans were so critical of the people of the United States that one local editor commented: "Reference to a number of speeches made by Latin American exponents absolves the conference of any charge of attempting to win the favor of the United States through flattery, for some of the characterizations were not at all complimentary to us."

The first members of the Cosmopolitan Club included students from countries as diverse as France, China, Peru, and the Philippines.

One of the College's greatest international successes of that decade was scored by the gymnastics team. The gymnasts embarked on an 11,000-mile trip that took them through Mexico. In Mexico City, they performed for audiences that included President Plutarco Elias Calles, the mayor of Mexico, the rector of the Mexican National University, and the consul-general of the United States.

President Calles was so delighted with the show that he told the gymnasts he would make physical education a major part of his educational program. With the president at this meeting was E.C. Aguirre '15, physical education director of the YMCA in Mexico, and later chairman of Mexico's Olympics Committee. It was Aguirre who, during a visit to the campus in 1924, began the arrangements for the gymnastics team's Mexican visit.

President Calles was so pleased with the visit he told the gymnasts they would be transported free of charge on Mexican railroads.

On its return from this seven-week trip, the team was received at the White House by President Calvin Coolidge, who shook hands with Coach Leslie Judd and each member of the team, some of whom later expressed amazement at the power of the President's handshake. (No one explained how arrangements could be made for this White House visit, but Herbert Lee Pratt and Calvin Coolidge were classmates at Amherst College and served together on its board of trustees.)

The team returned to Springfield, performing an exhibition at the University of Pennsylvania and an alumni-sponsored show in Trenton, New Jersey, and arrived at

Posing for a photographer in 1920 was a group of international students from China, Portugal, and the Philippines.

One of the most successful trips for Coach Judd's gymnasts was to Mexico in 1925. Performing here in a Mexico City gym, the team was hailed by the country's president, who provided free transportation on Mexican railroads.

Union Station to a greeting by the Springfield College Band, first formed in 1922 by Harry L. Malette '23. Backing up the band were the president of the College and 400 students. A squad of police led the parade down Main Street to City Hall where College, city, and Chamber of Commerce officials greeted the team.

The gymnasts returned to the campus for a banquet, followed by a basketball game (Springfield College 36; Boston College 22), and a dance. All that after 11,000 miles!

The Joy of Effort, by
R. Tait McKenzie

The Doggetts made their own contribution to the College's internationalism. After commencement in 1926, the Doggetts took that world tour that had been so long delayed. Doggett, who had taken part in Sherwood Eddy's American seminars in Europe, found there was one aboard his ship. He attended "some rabid lectures on war guilt, pacifism, and race problems while Mrs. Doggett stayed on deck and read *The Private Life of Helen of Troy*." (Was he implying that she had made the better choice?)

In Helsinki, Doggett attended the nineteenth conference of the World Alliance of the YMCA and, at the Olympic site in Stockholm, saw R. Tait McKenzie's *Joy of Effort*.

He was in the League of Nations when Aristide Briand welcomed the German delegate. For Doggett, it was "a moment of international ecstasy. I felt as if the Kingdom of God had really come on earth. But where was America?" He included those words in his special correspondent's report in *The Springfield Republican*. The Doggetts sailed for home on his sixty-second birthday.

STUDENTS AGITATE FOR CIGARETTES AND FRATERNITIES

When Doggett returned to his presidential duties at the beginning of 1927, "he found all in good order, and no crisis awaited his attention," according to his biographer, L.K. Hall.

Indeed, the news continued to be good. On one of his first days back in the office, Doggett received a call from Edwin H. Robbins, a Springfield land developer, who owned ten lots adjacent to College property. When Doggett had purchased six acres on Hickory Street two years earlier, he said the College needed even more land for "outdoor classrooms," the name he had given to athletic fields. He now hoped that Robbins was ready to sell. The news was even better. Robbins was ready to donate. Not since Jacob Gerrish had given the twenty-acre Gerrish Grove across the lake had Doggett had such a satisfying property transfer.

Doggett said the Robbins gift would permit the construction of at least two more athletic fields, and the president even mentioned the possibility of a stadium some day.

Another property transfer was not so welcome, but it did help to solve a persistent problem at the heart of the campus.

The city of Springfield decided that it needed a municipal golf course and, because it appeared that the College was not making much use of Gerrish Grove on the south side of the lake, that might make a good course. Doggett's response was friendly: "We should be pleased to have the golf links in the vicinity, but we are deeply concerned

To enable students to find summer jobs at boys' camps, a two-week camp training course was conducted at the end of the freshman year.

pianist PIPER GABRIEL   COACH JUDD   YAUCH GRUNBERG Mgr. CALL

SCHONHEITER GEHRKE   CAPT. DICKERSON   PRICE EBERHART PE

The gymnastics exhibition team continued to be among the most popular spectator sports at the College. Coach Judd (center, standing) was the constant innovator.

with the possibility of losing our campgrounds." He said it would be a serious loss to the College unless a desirable place could be secured elsewhere on the lake.

A trustee committee was named to deal with the request from the city, but soon the city had another request. It decided that a crosstown boulevard was needed, and it would require a bridge across the Lake Massasoit Narrows. That meant it would have to go through Springfield College land, including the campgrounds. The mayor said that he was asking property owners along the boulevard's route to yield land without charge, and he would ask the same of the College.

Doggett suggested that the city might give something in return for a broad swath through the campgrounds, and suggested the closing of part of Alden Street. The chairman of the Board of Public Works (BPW) said "impossible," and the College gave the land anyway. The BPW did decide to reverse two of its previous decisions: to abandon the Hickory Street loop that passed through the College, and to build an extension from Wilbraham Avenue to Hickory Street. When a street is abandoned, the abutters take possession to the center of the road, and because Springfield College owned both

Posing for a yearbook photograph is the 1928 ice hockey team. The squad practiced on frozen Lake Massasoit.

sides of the Hickory Street loop, the College came to own the roadway which, until the 1990s, started opposite Babson Library and proceeded through the campus.

Doggett's foresight may have made him realize the great future value of those changes, and there was one more advantage: Because the proposed crosstown boulevard made the remaining land useless as a campground, the College sold that property for residential development and moved the campground to East Campus, which it had acquired mostly from the estate of an old Springfield family, whose members could once walk across the width of the city without ever setting foot on anyone else's land.

The crosstown boulevard that the College's gift helped make possible is now Roosevelt Avenue, and the General Edwards Bridge at the Lake Massasoit Narrows connects to land given by the College.

If it was too early to tell about the value of these land transfers, the College could rejoice that the $2.5 million campaign was proceeding well, and that its first fruit, Alumni Hall, was under construction.

However, Doggett was wrestling with what he considered the greatest problem then facing the College, and he decided that he would present it to the trustees at the fall meeting.

Perhaps some others saw this coming, because there were hints. One came that spring when Doggett returned from a YMCA conference in New Jersey and was asked by a *Springfield Union* reporter to comment on the student poll, released in his absence, which indicated that about half of the Springfield College students smoked cigarettes, and some wanted to allow smoking on campus. "There are always agitators who want something," the president replied.

Although that atypical response might have indicated that the subject was closed, Doggett pursued it diligently. Five weeks later, the College announced that the ban on smoking on the campus would be continued, and that if any senior were known to be a smoker off-campus, the College would make that fact known to any prospective employer.

The College did not comment on the student request for a "smoking room" in the new, fireproof dormitory, but it did not have to. The all-campus smoking ban covered it. The College also said that the statement that almost half of the students smoked was an exaggeration. It released the poll statistics: 205 smoked, 236 did not, and 90 did not respond.

The College also said that its smoking ban applied even off-campus for all freshmen, so long as they were wearing green caps (September to spring.) Ernest M. Ford, gifted editor of *The Student*, saw hypocrisy and wrote: "Either Springfield students do smoke or they do not smoke; and a tradition that forbids them to smoke in public and winks its eye at 'the cigarette behind the Powerhouse' is a poor tradition."

It is possible that Doggett also knew about the movement on the campus to establish fraternities, which he strongly opposed. That referendum was not held until 1929, and was restricted to upperclassmen who were thought to be less interested in fraternities, but the vote was 191-70 in favor of the referendum.

Although L.K. Hall, then acting dean of boys' work, was the faculty representative on the five-man committee that the Student Senate authorized to determine student preferences about fraternities, neither Hall's book nor Doggett's mentions the fraternity or smoking polls, the results of which obviously disheartened Doggett.

ALUMNI HALL: BEAUTY AND USEFULNESS

Doggett could more happily direct his attention to Alumni Hall, fast taking shape on the handsome site where the ugly World War I barracks had been. "Architecture has a ministry to the soul of man," Doggett had written before Marsh Memorial Library was built, and now the budget for Alumni Hall allowed him to add beauty as well as usefulness to the campus.

The success of the Expansion and Endowment Fund Drive enabled the College to construct a new dormitory, Alumni Hall (seen here from the rear), in 1927.

The College had also retained Frederick Law Olmsted, Jr. and John Charles Olmsted of Boston to design the landscape for the dormitory as well as for the whole campus, including future construction.

Even before the building was opened, the terrace at its rear was used as a stage for *Physical Education Symphony*, music composed by Professor Hyde and performed by the freshman class under Professor Brock. It was "an expression of the growth of civilization, both as neuromuscular and social development," according to the program. It included interpretive dancing of primitive man and a Colonial gavotte. (For this, the College imported four singers, girls from Springfield's Technical High School, chaperoned by Ruth Evans. Evans was to return twenty-five years later as the first director of physical education for women at Springfield College.)

When darkness came, so did the illuminated canoe parade and five thousand visitors who saw, during intermission, gymnasts twirling clubs with battery-powered lights.

After the graduation of ninety-six men, the last all-male summer school convened with 140 students. At graduation exercises for the summer students, Colonel Benjamin Franklin, chairman of the trustees' executive committee, made the announcement that women would be admitted the next summer to all classes, including those for the coaching of track, baseball, and basketball.

All through the summer of 1927, the Alumni Hall project continued; it was ready for dedication in the fall. Its architect was George C. Gardiner—who, after graduation from Massachusetts Institute of Technology, had studied in Europe for three years before opening his office in Washington, D.C. Gardiner had come to Springfield in 1892 to join his father's architectural firm, which he headed after his father's death. Gardiner served as chairman of the Springfield Planning Board from its formation in 1921 until his death in 1930. His design, both interior and exterior, was distinctive.

Ted Shawn, a nationally recognized dancer and teacher, conducted classes at the College for several years. The dance company he founded, Jacob's Pillow, is located today in Becket, Massachusetts, and Shawn is considered by many to be the father of modern dance in the United States.

Standing in West Gymnasium surrounded by its elevated running track, basketball hoops, and gymnastics apparatus is a 1927 physical education class.

The handsome foyer was named for S. Richard Carlisle, a local trustee who had started the building fund campaign with a contribution of $10,000.

When John M. Kirby had invited Doggett to dine with him on the Springfield-to-New-York train, it had cost him $5,000. (Doggett loved to tell the story that Kirby had agreed to give the same amount he had just paid for a new Oldsmobile, and that was $5,000.) That was for Marsh Memorial; for Alumni Hall, he came back with twice that amount to outfit a science laboratory in the basement of the new dormitory. (Kirby had worked his Wilkes-Barre dry goods store into a ninety-six-store chain, merged it into F.W. Woolworth Co., of which he became vice president, and gave a fortune to build Kirby Hall of Civil Rights at Lafayette College in Pennsylvania and endow the Kirby Chair of Civil Rights there.)

Although the new building was the center of attention at its own dedication, the program, directed by Harry G. Webster, chairman of the trustees' property committee, had some distinctions, including tenor solos by Paul Samson.

At the trustees' meeting that same day, Doggett reported on the plans to establish a graduate school at Springfield College and to help launch a YMCA training school in Geneva, Switzerland, under Elmer Berry. Doggett said sixty students had transferred to Springfield College from other institutions, and that the number of applicants for the College's physical education department doubled the maximum number of openings.

That led the president to the thing that was troubling him: "I think I may say that, impressive as our financial needs appear to be, the most important problem before the College at the present time is the assimilating of its large student body to Springfield College ideals."

The president noted that, academically, the students were the best in the College's history. However, their religious training was quite different. "In previous years, students came to us with a scientific and dogmatic religious training, much of which had to be unlearned.... Students now come with a very limited religious training."

He spelled out the problem to the trustees: "Student devotional meetings have pretty largely disappeared. Chapel with us has always been voluntary, and we have, I believe, one of the best assemblies in New England, but a considerable portion of the students do not attend."

"Devotion to the professional ideals of the College, to chapel, and to voluntary religious effort seems more difficult to maintain than formerly," he added.

Doggett promised that the College henceforth was going to be much more selective in admissions. He promised a strenuous effort to make certain the College admit only those men ready to accept Springfield College ideals.

The stock market crash, which demonstrated so dramatically the wisdom of Doggett's great work in the 1920s to assure the College's future, also solved the problem that was so worrying Doggett in the thirty-second year of his presidency and the sixty-seventh year of his life. With the Depression came new problems, which must have reminded Doggett of some of his earliest days of struggle at Springfield College.

SHATTERED DREAMS: THE DEPRESSION

The vote of the trustees to launch a $4.5-million Semi-Centennial Fund Drive was taken only two weeks before the stock market crash. Therefore, its failure is not surprising. What is surprising is its measure of success.

Of the total goal, $2-million was to be in legacies. A committee headed by J. Berg Esenwein, an expert communicator who ran a correspondence school in Springfield, edited a monthly magazine for authors, and taught public speaking at the College, succeeded in having $300,000 written into wills for the College.

The other $2.5-million was to be in gifts, and Doggett was able to report to the trustees meeting in June 1930 that John D. Rockefeller, Jr., had pledged $250,000 if $2-million in cash had been collected by July 1935. He also agreed to pay $12,500 a year toward the expenses of the College and of the campaign.

The mortgage on Alumni Hall was burned, and the 1930 graduation play was presented in beautiful Carlisle Foyer. Herbert Lee Pratt was saluted on completing twenty-five years as a trustee.

If there was any sad note in 1930, it was that William B. Kirkham was retiring. For ten years at Springfield College, he had taught biology, which he had done previously at Yale, from which he held a doctorate. However, it was as freshman dean, running through battle lines to bring hot dogs and encouragement to freshmen during flag rushes, that he was most popular. After retirement, Kirkham gave his hilltop estate in Springfield to the Red Cross, but continued to reside in the city and, at his death almost forty years later, named the local science museum as the eventual beneficiary of a million-dollar trust.

Central to the success of the Semi-Centennial Fund Drive was the support of John D. Rockefeller, Jr. Shown here is a check for $355,215.27 from a Rockefeller foundation.

The scriptural title of Rev. Henry Sloane Coffin's 1930 commencement speech contained an undetected irony: "And it came to pass after a while that the brook dried up." On that same day, U.S. President Herbert Hoover announced that he would sign the Hawley-Smoot Tariff Act, which set off a sequence of retaliatory European tariffs, war debt suspensions, world trade declines, and a worldwide depression.

However, the first indication that Springfield College students were beginning to feel the effects of the economic turndown came in response to the Carnegie report on subsidized collegiate athletics.

Springfield College decided it would no longer hire 100 upperclassmen at seventy-five cents an hour to assist coaches, and the announcement noted that this income, however small, was the margin that some students needed to remain in college.

There was other evidence that money was getting tight. The 1931 illuminated canoe carnival on Lake Massasoit drew an all-time-high audience of ten thousand. People were looking for free entertainment, and the College was putting on the best show in town. They even saw a winning float by one of the greatest scholars who ever taught at Springfield College. Not all of the 10,000 may have understood Peter V. Karpovich's satire on the College departments—physical, secretarial, county, foreign, industrial, and boys—but the students and faculty knew, and the judges gave it first prize in the humor category.

Despite the hardships of the Depression, Doggett directed the construction of the Pueblo of the Seven Fires on East Campus. The Pueblo allowed the College to offer more instruction at the eighty-acre East Campus. Here, a biology class studies plant life found in the nature preserve.

Heartley "Hunk" Anderson, football coach at Notre Dame, was hired for the summer school faculty that year, and his assistant, John Chevigny, took his place when Anderson became ill. (Anderson's predecessor, Knute Rockne, had taught at Springfield College's summer sessions in 1923 and 1925.)

It was not until 1932 that the College began to feel the full impact of the Depression. Even then, the graduating class was the biggest in history (143), and the College would later report that more than seventy-five percent of them had found employment.

At commencement, Alumni College was introduced, and a memorial service included the name of David Allen Reed for the first time. The College's founder had endured a deep personal loss when his son-in-law, Congressman William Kirk Kaynor, was killed in a plane crash as he was returning from Washington, D.C., for a Christmas visit to the family in 1929. Funeral crowds, including a large delegation from the House of Representatives and Senate, overflowed Hope Church, and Doggett served as an honorary bearer for the trustee who had helped host the Alumni Hall opening ceremonies only two years earlier. (The Congressman's son, Allen Reed Kaynor, after a distinguished career, retired from the College's faculty in 1984.)

David Allen Reed died in the spring of 1932, having just made his last donation to the College. Reed's final contribution came in the form of the cement blocks for the construction of the Pueblo of the Seven Fires on East Campus by E.M. Robinson, Ernest Thompson Seton, and many students and other volunteers. Reed owned a company that *made* cement blocks.

The Pueblo's large meeting room, known as Post Lodge, was decorated with symbolic Native American murals painted by Wo Peen, a Pueblo Indian. The mural here is entitled "The Buffalo Dancer."

When Doggett noted that salaries might have to be cut, professors made generous voluntary contributions to help. About $12,000 came from 240 residents of Springfield.

Doggett could not be selfish, even for his College: "This is a time when resources of our friends are sadly depleted, when appeals for relief of unemployment must have first consideration, but it is also a time when the character-building agencies for youth are needed as never before."

One of the College's friends whose resources were sadly depleted was Horace Moses, who successfully rebutted two rumors (one that he had been sent to a mental hospital; the other that he had killed himself) and said he was glad he had given his money away while he had it. He did not stay down long; his largest philanthropies were yet to come.

The endowment fund raised through the 1920s saved the College, but dividends from it fell sharply. The YMCAs that had been supporting the College could not maintain the level of giving; they were having trouble meeting their own expenses. Tuition payments fell $55,000 in arrears. The College continued to lose money on the Geneva school, and the summer school became a liability.

The College released several employees, and made cuts totaling twenty percent in salary and wage levels. Two long-suggested changes were finally made, not because they were seen as wise, but because they were seen as money-saving: One was to admit women; the other was to establish a Division of Arts and Sciences.

David Allen Reed had successfully petitioned the Massachusetts General Court to make the School for Christian Workers coeducational as soon as it had separated from the International YMCA Training School. In his valedictory address in 1895, Charles A. Martin suggested that the training school do the same. No one seconded the motion.

Carolyn Doggett taught at the school for thirty years. At her death in 1932, many paid tribute to her services to the College and influence over its students. Wives of other faculty members sometimes taught courses. Shirley Jackson, who had been a concert singer, was hired as the resident hostess of Alumni Hall. Doggett also had his women's board, whose members—wives and daughters of prominent local families—poured tea and punch. Such were the early roles of women at Springfield College.

Doggett was of the opinion that two coordinate institutions under a joint administration would be preferable to a coeducational institution. However, to help with the budget, the College decided to admit a limited number of women. Considering the rationale and the reluctance, it is not surprising that the experiment was less than an overwhelming success.

Springfield College had long offered a so-called General Course, in which students could enroll until they decided whether to join either the physical education division or the YMCA secretarial division. In 1932, faced with declining enrollment, the College established an Arts and Sciences Division, with Hartley Cross '23, who had a doctorate from Clark University, as director. Physical education, allied sciences, and the pre-medical program were included in a division called Natural Science, and youth leadership programs for the YMCA, Boys' Club, Boy Scouts, and other such agencies were included in the Social Science Division.

Even with a popular and able professor as its leader, the new division struggled to survive. A child of necessity, born of the Depression, it had few friends, and one of the most determined of them, Britton C. McCabe '27, was among the most junior of the faculty, having been named in 1930.

Members of the other divisions saw Arts and Sciences as an attempt to turn Springfield College into a second-rate Amherst, and even the president indicated that its students should transfer into one of the "real" divisions by the end of the sophomore year.

In the year the new divisions were instituted, enrollment fell below the 500 mark, and the Geneva school collapsed, a great disappointment to Doggett.

However, for the president, there was happiness, too. In 1934, after the death of his first wife, Carolyn, he married Olive Dutcher, professor of Biblical history and literature at Wellesley College. Less than a year later, on the advice of his doctor, Doggett presented his resignation, asking that it become effective "preferably on January 1, 1936, when I will have passed my seventy-first birthday, and in any case not later than August 1, 1936, when I shall have completed forty years of service."

After the death of his first wife, Carolyn, in 1932, Doggett met Olive Dutcher, a professor of Biblical history and literature at Wellesley College. They were married in 1934.

Doggett wearing the insignia of the Second Order of the Red Cross bestowed by the Estonian Government.

Massasoit

SOPHOMORE CLASS

Massasoit

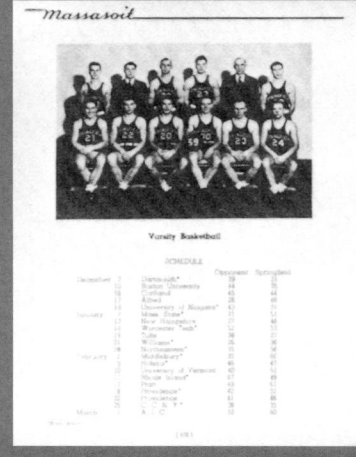

Varsity Basketball

SCHEDULE

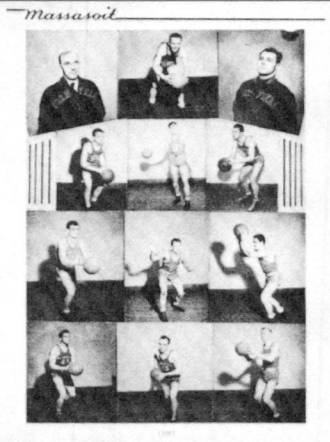

Massasoit

massasoit

VARSITY
EXHIBITION TEAM

massasoit

Varsity Exhibition Team — 1939-1940

PUBLISHED BY THE JUNIOR CLASS OF SPRINGFIELD COLLEGE AT SPRINGFIELD, MASS.

THE ★ SPRINGFIELD

Massasoit
1941 ★

Building for the
FUTURE

IN THE SERVICE OF OUR COUNTRY

To Springfield men in the service,

Chapter 4

Best: An Era Ends and Controversy Ensues

When Laurence Locke Doggett retired after forty years as president of Springfield College, he did not fade away.

With Olive, his new wife, he began a twenty-six-nation world tour visiting alumni groups. In that same year, Theodore Roosevelt, Jr. presented Doggett with the Boy Scouts of America's highest honor for service to boyhood, the Silver Buffalo.

Dean Albert Zachariah Mann, a Methodist clergyman who had been on the faculty of Garrett Biblical Institute when Doggett recruited him in 1932 to head the College's town and country department, was named acting president.

The trustees may have been thinking of "acting" as "holding temporary rank," but the evidence indicates that Acting President Mann thought of it more as "moving to action." Less than a month after being named acting president, Mann initiated a broad study of the College's future. He mandated that programs for high school guidance directors, for registered nurses wishing to qualify for a degree, and for community center staff members be considered, adding that the College might go fully coeducational.

Mann named a twenty-person advisory committee, including judges from several states, to help design a program for law enforcement, prison, and probation officers.

Even off the campus, it was noted that the acting president was active indeed. The headline bank on the *Springfield Union* story of Mann's call for action stated: "Mann's Tenure in Present Post Is Unknown."

That remained unknown for months, while from the campus came word that Springfield College would graduate its first woman, Dorothy M. Audette, and two men, Chester R. Seymour and Ronald Lippitt, who had established the highest academic records in the College's first half-century.

The alumni returned in record numbers, partly because this was, after all, the 50th commencement. They called it a jubilee, and among the celebrators were such worthies as Amos Alonzo Stagg. Although he was to the world the Grand Old Man of Football, he had been the Grand Young Man of Baseball at Springfield College after pitching Yale to championships. (He also played in the world's first public basketball game, between the Springfield College faculty and students, and scored the only basket for the losing professors.) At the reunion, he posed with his Springfield College classmate and catcher, William Ball.

The great majority of the graduates had studied under President Doggett, and he was a guest at the alumni party. The trustees contributed to the celebration by voting to designate Doggett as president emeritus.

Albert Z. Mann came to the College in 1932 from Garrett Biblical Institute. When Doggett retired in 1936, Mann was named acting president.

Ernest Best '11, an alumni trustee and general secretary of the YMCA in Canada, became a finalist against Mann for the presidency. Best was the eventual choice of the trustees after a lengthy and public debate.

President as letterman: While a student, Ernest Best '11 was captain of varsity lacrosse and varsity soccer.

Professor Hyde, who was retiring after making Springfield College men sing and laugh as they learned English literature for almost thirty years, was also an alumni guest.

The Tarbell Medallions for distinguished service had been chosen by a committee that included Edward Tarbell himself, George Affleck, and Ralph Cheney, among others. They had picked the president of the alumni association, Herbert S. Smith '06, and Ernest Best '11, who greeted fellow students and many younger alumni who had been his students during his faculty years preceding his departure for YMCA service in World War I.

The alumni had elected Best as their representative on the Board of Trustees, and some alumni and some trustees began to see this man, general secretary of the YMCA in Canada, as a successor to Doggett.

Within a few months, it even appeared in public print that the search for a new president had narrowed down to Best and Mann.

Best saw it this way: "Some of the physical education staff remembered my efforts to upgrade the school academically and morally when I was a student, 1908-11, and teacher, 1913-16. They were afraid I would 'down-grade' physical education and turn the college into a liberal arts school. One senior physical education professor undertook a campaign among the local trustees and alumni against my nomination and in support of Mann. It now became a struggle between 'pro and anti YMCA' for control of the college."

There were few references to alumni influence in the selection process, but the Tarbell Medallion and alumni trustee designation clearly indicate that many graduates favored the idea of having a fellow alumnus head the College.

Faced with all of these crosscurrents, the search committee for the new president failed to reach consensus and referred the matter back to the trustees without a recommendation.

This caused well-publicized delays and decisionless meetings of the board. Not until October 9 did the trustees finally select Best. The announcement said that Mann had withdrawn his name from consideration and had been named dean.

Actually, the contest had been decided on a split vote after Clifton A. Crocker, Springfield resident and Holyoke industrialist, stepped out of his role as chairman to announce he would vote for Best.

Soon after the selection, three prominent local trustees resigned, but other trustees denied the report that they had quit because the pro-Best trustees had agreed to pay the new president more than had been paid to Doggett.

Best later gave his own explanation for the trustee resignations. He said that the three "resigned on rumor that I was soft on Communism and because I was a foreigner (Canada)."

The next day, the president-elect and acting president met with forty of the College's forty-four trustees at the Colony Club in Springfield, and then announced together that the new president would receive the same salary as had been paid to the president emeritus. (They did not announce the salary: $9,000 a year plus $1,000 for rent and entertainment.) They said there had been no dissension on the board on that subject.

The resignations and retirements of eleven faculty members were interpreted as more aftershocks of the selection controversy. The conflict also registered on Best's own tension barometer: his stomach ulcers.

Confidence rose on and off the campus when the trustees, meeting in New York City, named three locally respected members—Clifton A. Crocker, YMCA Secretary Blake A. Hoover, and Attorney Julius H. Appleton—to the executive committee. Appleton, still in his twenties, was in the third generation of his family to support the College. He bore the name of his grandfather, one of the College's earliest benefactors.

The College had started to replace bad news with good news, and that was only the beginning. Many friends came forward to help the College and its new president.

PRESIDENT BEST: THE TURBULENT YEARS

At President Best's inauguration, he cited a "final urgent need for a new attack on publicity for the College." He said: "This is an international institution and we need more national and international publicity to make the College as unique in the public mind as it really is to us who know it."

His inauguration itself helped meet that need. He was the guest of honor at three banquets—in Springfield, Boston, and New York.

At the Springfield dinner, Best told the mayor that the fact that a city patrolman couldn't give directions to the campus spoke well for the behavior of the students but not for the College's public relations program.

However, the banquets themselves were public relations triumphs.

Smith College President William Alan Neilson was the main speaker in Springfield. In Boston, it was Karl Taylor Compton, president of Massachusetts Institute of Technology. Arranged with the help of such loyal Springfield friends as Herbert Lee Pratt, president of Standard Oil, and Cleveland E. Dodge, president of the International YMCA Board, the New York dinner had as its presiding officer John Huston Finley, who had been president of no less than three colleges and universities before becoming editor of *The New York Times*.

However, even when Best put his best foot forward, Springfield College's physical education professors felt it on their toes. His call for better publicity concluded: "It is an error that the intellectual value and work of the College is being submerged in our publicity by the activities and skills which are publicized so highly." The physical educators read that as a criticism of sports-page coverage of athletic achievements.

In his inaugural address, the new president had said he had not accepted the job to do away with the College's physical education emphasis, calling that "a false rumor, widely circulated." Nonetheless, it was the physical educators who most keenly felt Best's criticism of "academic inbreeding."

All eighteen members of the physical education faculty had graduated from Springfield College, and only a few had advanced degrees from other institutions. Best adopted a policy that no Springfield College graduate would be eligible for faculty appointment unless he held an advanced degree from another institution.

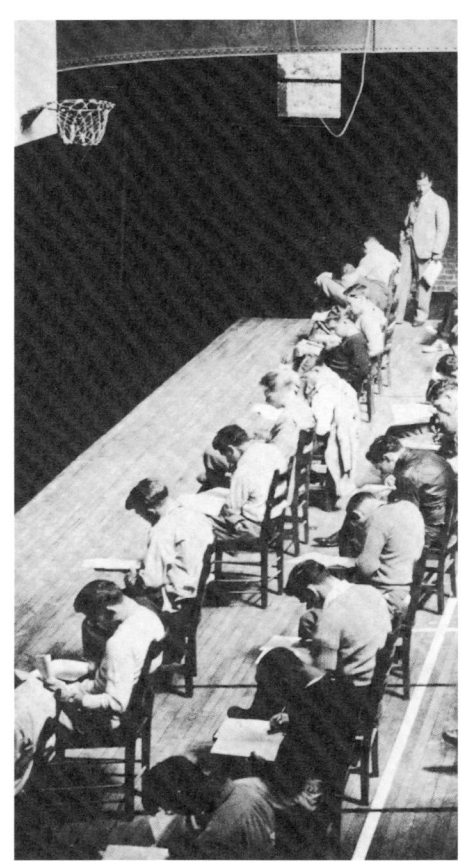

While controversy buffeted the campus as Best pushed faculty changes, classes and exams continued. Here, students are shown taking an exam in the West Gymnasium.

Best always contended that he did not create a breach between the president and the physical education department, but that the breach had existed since 1895, with Doggett on one side and, on the other, Gulick and later McCurdy. Best repeated the comment of Mrs. McCurdy to Mrs. Doggett: "We really have two colleges. Your husband is head of one, and Mac is of the other." Best added: "There was a great deal of truth in this."

After Best introduced the "no inbreeding" and the retirement-at-sixty rules, the faculty ranks were quickly thinned. Elmer Berry, one of the eleven faculty members who left soon after Best's arrival, objected that the College announcement made it appear that he was retiring, whereas actually he was quitting.

Best said that three of them had been fired. When students complained about the faculty changes, Best invited them to submit queries. About seventy questions were submitted, and Best responded that all of the faculty members who were leaving would be replaced, that class size would not be increased, and tuition would not be raised.

A week later, Best announced that the entering class would have better academic qualifications than previous classes because the College would admit only 160 and more than that number of applications had already been received.

All of these faculty departures and the resulting exchanges were covered by the public press, and Best was back on the front page the week after the trustees voted to start building the president's house.

Best told the city he would not start construction until the city closed the Lake Massasoit beach on Springfield Ice Company land near the campus.

Actually, Henry Lee had started the city's first playground on College land at Lake Massasoit, at Burr's suggestion. Dave Polland '02, was its first director, and Lee probably paid him. Doggett persuaded the War Department to delimit the use of its target range on the lake so that it could be of more use to the public.

However, it was the ice company that had allowed the city to use its land for a public beach for more than twenty years. The city now asked if the College would provide a substitute beach.

When that proposal made no progress, city officials asked Best why the College didn't buy the property. Best's publicized answer was that the Springfield Ice Company was trying to get too high a price for the land.

Less than two months later, the Depression came to the College's aid. A federal court approved under the bankruptcy code the transfer of forty acres of land from the Springfield Ice Company, and the immediate sale of that land to Springfield College for $52,000.

The College became owner of the troublesome beach, but Best then announced that the president's house was not going to be built anyway; the bids were too high.

Best began his presidency with a call for better publicity, but the local publicity about faculty departures, student questions, and the townies swimming in Lake Massasoit hardly answered that call.

However, when he was being congratulated on the vitally important acquisition of those forty acres, he generously gave the credit to Doggett who had worked for that goal.

Also, he promised the city that the College would provide an even better beach for public use.

Best scored yet another local public relations coup. S. Richard Carlisle, who had resigned from the Board of Trustees when Best was chosen, returned to the board, was elected chairman of its executive committee, and participated with Harry G. Webster, local trustee, in the arrangements for the land purchase.

The war in Europe and Asia seemed very distant from the tranquil Springfield College campus. Members of the 1940 freshman ice hockey (top) and lacrosse teams would soon find the College transformed by World War II.

THE WAR YEARS

Although Best's tenure lasted less than a decade, it was filled with some of the most difficult years the College had faced to that point.

Best seemed to turn problems into opportunities, as when he convinced the Civilian Conservation Corps to use trees felled during the 1938 hurricane to build ten cabins at the College campground. When the Connecticut River rose during that storm, the College housed the inmates of Hampden County House of Correction in the gymnasium for a week. (The prisoners had used the same facilities during an earlier flood, causing one campus wag to refer to the second visit as an alumni reunion.)

Best's decision to extend the teacher education department and to take over management of the summer school, formerly directed on the Springfield College campus by Boston University, were wise. He put both under the direction of Raymond G. Drewry, who had earned a doctorate at Columbia University, taught at the University of California at Los Angeles, and served as dean of College of Puget Sound, where he had formerly directed the summer and evening schools.

The education and summer programs sustained Springfield College during the World War II years.

The effect of that war was felt early with the departure of foreign students as soon as war began in Europe. The president pressed forward with his citizenship papers so that he could comment more freely on United States foreign policy.

Meetings on campus in which there were calls for no arms shipments to any participants, and assertions that most students believed that the United States should stay out

To demonstrate their support for the war effort, the College's students led a series of blood drives. On occasion they marched to Springfield City Hall.

of the way, were minimized in Best's understatement: "In the College faculty, we had half a dozen convinced pacifists, and a small but vocal group of students, both pacifists and conscientious objectors."

Whatever the state of mind of the campus before December 7, 1941, the Japanese attack on Pearl Harbor that day changed it forever, as it changed so much else. Programs that had seemed so important before that date seemed too trivial to consider after it. The capital drive, postponed because of the Depression, was a war casualty, and Best formally released John D. Rockefeller, Jr., from his provisional gift.

The campaign to build the Memorial Field House had been launched in the fall, and had $20,000 in contributions and $22,000 in expenses when it was halted on December 7.

Although the government first announced that it would not use any college campuses for training, it later decided to utilize universities that could accommodate at least 500 men.

When that cutoff was reduced, Springfield responded that it had facilities for 500. When the government accepted and said 500 air cadets would arrive in May, the College had to double the capacity of the cafeteria, infirmary, and dormitories. Contractors and

Among the military units to be based on the campus was the 323rd Army Training Detachment. Even the McCurdy Pool became a training estation.

Part of a total fitness program devised by Charles F. Weckwerth (right, standing with coat) for the Army Air Corps was an obstacle course adjacent to Pratt Field.

labor unions cooperated, and the prisoners at the Concord, Massachusetts reformatory built 250 bureaus, tables, and chairs for Springfield College rooms.

Best was faced with another problem when the air cadets unexpectedly left after eleven months and moved to a southern location. After conferring with the trustees' executive committee, the president notified faculty and staff that all salaries would terminate on July 1, 1944.

Drewry was retained as dean and director of teacher education, extension courses, and the summer program. Best tried to keep John Pond, who had engineered the prison furniture and other deals, but he left to become purchasing agent for the Manhattan Project at the University of Chicago.

Noting that the Drewry programs were operating, Best warmly contradicted reports that the College was "closed for the duration of the war." He blamed the reports on those who believed that a college died when its competitive sports schedule stopped. Even the larger war had not ended his campus skirmishes.

Best next offered the campus to the Navy for a convalescent hospital, but several interviews in Washington were unsuccessful.

UNITED STATES NAVAL CONVALESCENT HOSPITAL

As he was leaving the Navy building, Best recognized the name "John R. Agnew" printed on a door as the name of a Springfield physician with offices about two miles from the campus. Dr. Agnew, who had been called into Navy service, was cooperative. He called the admiral, and went with Best for the interview. Two weeks later, Navy inspectors were on campus. Best agreed with them that the Old Dormitory was a fire-trap, and the Navy and the College shared the cost of cutting it down to a two-floor administration building.

College neighbors who had watched the arrival of College freshmen every September for years saw a different sight on September 22, 1944, when a special train came in from the naval hospital in Chelsea, Massachusetts with the first 150 patients who went into makeshift hospital rooms in Alumni Hall.

When this contract ended in the summer of 1946, the Navy left campus buildings greatly improved. They also left expressions of satisfaction, which didn't hurt the later campaign to persuade the Navy to give the College one of the huge drill halls at Sampson Naval Station near Geneva, New York.

In what Best called a great victory over red tape, the building was dismantled, brought to the Springfield College campus, and reassembled as a field house. Best credited Francis Oakley, the College's business manager, for the victory.

President Best greets Captain J.S. Rooney of the Naval Convalescent Hospital.

The government also established a Naval Convalescent Hospital at the College in 1944. On September 22, 1944, a special train came in from the Chelsea, Massachusetts, Naval Hospital with the first 150 patients, who went into hospital rooms in Alumni Hall.

By 1949, when this aerial photo was taken, the campus had added the Memorial Field House (center) and removed some of the military training facilities. However, some World War II barracks remained (right) on property where the first Basketball Hall of Fame was later constructed. Another change was the removal of the top three floors of the Administration Building by the government during the war.

Paul M. Limbert, elected president in 1945, earned a divinity degree from Union Theological Seminary and a doctorate from Columbia. Here, he addresses a College convocation in 1948.

Chapter 5

Limbert: The Post-War Years

Ernest Best was determined that the College community would not have to endure another fully publicized, long-lasting battle over the presidency, and so he groomed his successor for years.

At his installation, Best had invited Paul Moyer Limbert of Columbia University to moderate a symposium of scholars.

In 1938 Best announced the appointment of Limbert as visiting professor of education at Springfield College. Limbert joined the Springfield faculty full-time the next year, and became both a professor of education and director of fieldwork, maintaining his close relationship with the YMCA locally, nationally, and internationally.

Limbert was born and raised in Pennsylvania, and was graduated from Mercersburg Academy and Franklin & Marshall College. During World War I, he served as an Army first lieutenant, and then with the YMCA. After the war, he earned a divinity degree at Eastern Theological Seminary in Lancaster, Pennsylvania, and served a pastorate in Pottstown, Pennsylvania, while earning another degree at Union Theological Seminary in New York City. He taught religion at Franklin & Marshall and, after earning a doctorate at Columbia University, became an assistant professor and later an associate professor of education at the teachers' college there. It was from Columbia that he came to Springfield College.

The Springfield community as well as the campus came to recognize Limbert as a leader. Mayor Roger L. Putnam appointed him in 1942 to the Planning Commission. Limbert became a director, later president, of the Greater Springfield Council of Churches.

His wife, Anna E. (Myers) Limbert, assumed board responsibilities with the YWCA, Dunbar Community League, Children's Study Home, Wesson Hospital Auxiliary, and others.

Limbert took a World War II leave of absence to work with the National Council of the YMCA in New York, and also served on the faculty of Union Theological Seminary during those years.

At the June 1945 meeting of the Board of Trustees, Julius H. Appleton, the board chair, read Best's letter of resignation, which would become effective fourteen months later, after he reached the College's compulsory retirement age. At the same meeting, the trustees and corporators unanimously endorsed the recommendation of the Committee on Future Personnel that Paul M. Limbert be the next president.

Best had invited Limbert back from New York City the previous day to confer the only three master's degrees granted that year. (There were only twelve bachelor's degrees awarded, eight to women.) The president continued his policy of keeping the flag flying.

The exercises were held in the auditorium of Marsh Memorial Library, with the president giving the commencement address and conferring a special diploma on Emily Abbey Gill for her contributions to higher education. A Ludlow High School sextet sang, a violinist presented two solos, and Rev. Fred G. Bratton, the professor whom some saw as the new Ballantine and others saw as magician and humorist as well as scholar, gave the benediction.

This meeting was held less than a month after the surrender of Germany. Two months later, Japan surrendered, and American men started flooding back to resume their interrupted lives.

Limbert completed his work in New York City by year's end, and returned to Springfield College in January to reorganize the faculty for the return of the veterans.

When the day came to assume the presidency, Limbert was in Germany, one of ten educators chosen by the U.S. Department of State to evaluate the educational program of the U.S. military government there.

THE POST-WAR BOOM

More than eight hundred students entered or re-entered the College in September 1946; 425 of them were freshmen.

Neighbors answered appeals to help house them, and the College accepted the invitation of Alden Street Baptist Church to use its building, formerly the Alden Street School, for classrooms.

(The president was only a little less crowded. In Berlin, he shared a room with Rev. Reinhold Neibuhr, and they shared a bathroom with two other members of the ten-man American educational mission.)

At Springfield College, some traditions had to be abandoned. Postwar shortages made it impossible to obtain the green beanies for 425 freshmen, but the frosh were required to keep off the Senior Walk, between Woods Hall and the Administration Building.

Another tradition was revived when John Bunn, director of athletics, announced that local youngsters under the age of twelve would be admitted to home football games for

The drill hall at Sampson Naval Station in Geneva, New York, was given to the College and became the Memorial Field House in 1948.

The former Navy drill hall was dismantled and reconstructed at government expense on campus. The College's only obligations were to construct the foundation and to equip the building with utilities and other essential items for use in the gymnasium. The Memorial Field House was the focal point of the physical education program for thirty-one years.

The Memorial Field House was used for intercollegiate games. A portable wooden floor was used for basketball games. In addition, major social events were held on the dirt floor of the Memorial Field House, such as this 1951 commencement dinner.

nine cents. He said that a section of the bleachers would be reserved for them, and Springfield College students assigned to them as cheerleaders.

This did, indeed, revive the city's "Knothole Gang," because American International College and the local professional football team later announced they would follow Springfield College's lead to allow children to attend the games for a nominal fee. No federal admissions tax applied to any ticket under ten cents.

Because so many war veterans were just beginning college, freshmen were allowed to play varsity sports that year, which helps explain why there were more than two hundred candidates for the football team. (There may have been another explanation. Football candidates came two weeks early, giving them a chance to bargain for accommodations on or off the campus.) Within a week, Coach Ossie Solem said that he had pared the squad down to seventy-two candidates.

Philip W. Breaux '38, program secretary for the Springfield YMCA, invited seventy-eight YMCA secretaries from Massachusetts and Rhode Island to a two-day conference just before the students arrived, giving alumni members the chance to greet professors coming for a three-day faculty institute. They would certainly know the College's division directors—Thornton Merriam, Seth Arsenian, Arthur Esslinger, Charles Weckwerth, Raymond Drewry, and Peter Karpovich—and Britton C. McCabe was returning to the faculty after several years as a biologist with the Massachusetts Division of Fisheries and Game. However, for the first time since the College was founded, new appointees outnumbered returning professors, 30-28.

Another tradition had to be altered. There was no venue large enough on the campus to accommodate the student body, faculty, and invited guests, and so the installation of the new president was held in Springfield's Symphony Hall.

Although Springfield College had no building large enough for a presidential inauguration, or for any all-college meeting, help was on the way—from Sampson Naval Air Station in New York.

Thanks to "Oakley's victory over red tape," to use Best's words, Sampson, New York's huge drill hall was cut into parts and moved at the Navy's expense to the Springfield College campus, where the College reassembled it on a new foundation.

Alumni had already been raising funds for a memorial to their members who fought and died in the war, and the new structure was designated the Memorial Field House. A plaque listed the names of forty-six Springfield College students and alumni who had died in World War II.

During commencement week of 1947, Oakley presided at the field house ceremonies, and Norman S. Loveland, president of the Alumni Council, assisted Limbert in laying the cornerstone. Loveland was already making provisions for a College chapel, but only a few knew that. The attention of the alumni would more likely be turned to those of their number who died during the war, or perhaps to two people who reminded them of the school's earliest days. The oldest class represented there was 1891, and that by Willard S. Richardson, who had proven so helpful to the College in soliciting funds from John D. Rockefeller. One of the 109 newest alumni, from the Class of 1947, was Allen R. Kaynor, grandson of the College's founder, David Allen Reed. An honorary degree was conferred on Frank Stanley Beveridge, whose name later would be memorialized on the student center.

It was during that first year of Limbert's administration that Hosaga was formed under the guidance of a young instructor in mathematics and physics, F. Edgar Hubbard. This organization for the study of Native Americans of the Plains and reproduction of their dress and dance admitted members for life. Thousands of people in many states witnessed Hosaga performances.

When it came time for the 1948 commencement, fortunately, the Memorial Field House was ready. It had been planned to hold the ceremonies outdoors, but a downpour gave the field house its first commencement exercise, and 1,500 guests were grateful.

At that time, Limbert compiled a report, "Two Years in Transition," and two years later, another entitled, "Two Years at Capacity." During that period, more students appeared each September than had been anticipated at budget time, and so the College operated in the black.

Enrollment reached a peak of 1,465 in 1949, the year Springfield College granted degrees to three couples, wives receiving their degrees along with their husbands. These were genuine degrees, and were in addition to certificates Limbert introduced that read: "This is to certify that Mrs.—, whose unselfish love and devotion have made her husband's education possible, receives this humble acknowledgement for service and sacrifice, in witness thereof we have awarded this certificate." Limbert signed each of these certificates.

Traditions continued throughout the 1950s, from wearing beanies, to good-natured punishments for a poor freshman, to a tug-of-war between classes.

One of the College's longstanding co-curricular organizations was Hosaga. This student-run group studied the customs and lives of the Native Americans of the Plains. It also performed for schoolchildren and community clubs.

85

Trustees voted in 1951 to make the College coeducational. Abbey Hall, the gift of Emily F. Abbey Gill of Springfield, was ready as the College's first women's residence hall.

Many of these married couples lived in Lakeside Village, the pleasant name given to a collection of barracks the government provided for the housing of married veterans, today the site of Lakeside Residence Hall. It had been stipulated that these had to be torn down within two years, but the number of married veterans applying to Springfield College remained so high that the government extended the deadline on the sixty-five apartments.

It was at the beginning of 1950 that the College received word of the murder of Robert F. Conklin '21, former librarian and head of the English department. He had gone to the University of the Philippines as a U.S. Department of State Fulbright professor, and was killed by spearsmen of a tribe in Northern Luzon.

Conklin's appointment as librarian had been one of Limbert's first, made during the president's work in Germany. Conklin succeeded Georgina Carr, who had come to the College as Bowne's assistant when Marsh Memorial was under construction, and succeeded him in 1923. After her retirement and Conklin's appointment, Doris Fletcher was named as a new assistant at the library, and she succeeded Conklin as librarian in 1950.

During the 1950 commencement, 3,650 folding chairs were placed in the Memorial Field House, and another eighty guests were accommodated in Marsh Memorial Library. The latter were the preschool-age children of graduates, and a committee of students' wives ran a nursery for them during the ceremonies. As the number of graduates increased, Limbert resisted suggestions to abbreviate the diploma-presenting process. He said he wished to give a diploma to and shake the hand of each graduate—a tradition that is still followed to this day.

It was at the trustees' meeting during that commencement week that it was voted to make the College coeducational. Abbey Hall, the gift of Emily F. Abbey Gill of Springfield, was ready to receive them, and other alterations in locker rooms, shower rooms, and the like were ready when the first women—entering freshmen and transfer students—arrived in September 1951.

Until 1951, all honorary degrees conferred by Springfield College had been master's degrees, but, in that year, three honorary doctorates were awarded.

The Springfield Union described the first presentation: "An aged man came forward on the stage and in a soft, slow, but steady voice said to Dr. Limbert: 'It is my privilege to present Dr. George J. Fisher for the honorary degree of doctor of science.' Then was the applause richest and broadest. The man was Laurence L. Doggett, president emeritus, participating in commencement fifty-five years after his first one as College leader."

President Emeritus Doggett (left) receives the second honorary doctorate degree ever awarded by Springfield College. Making the presentation at the 1952 commencement is President Limbert.

Doggett's biographer, L.K. Hall, did not forget that Fisher had not been sufficiently supportive of Doggett during the Ballantine controversy, but Doggett did not record it. For the first honorary doctorate ever awarded by the College, Doggett presented "a gifted leader, administrator and interpreter of the highest Christian ideals," George J. Fisher.

A year later, in 1952, Doggett was back to receive that same doctorate from Paul Limbert, who told the 474 graduates: "I am going with you." That summer, Limbert left the College he had served for thirteen years, six as president.

When the Office of Institutional Research at Limbert's own alma mater, Franklin & Marshall College, did a study of the nation's 867 four-year, private, primarily undergraduate institutions to determine which had sent the most graduates on to doctorates in education, it discovered that Springfield College led the nation with 347 between 1920 and 1980, the period chosen for the research.

Even before the study was reported in the scholarly journals, Springfield College learned of it through its faithful corporator, Paul Limbert, then living in retirement in Black Mountain, North Carolina.

52 SPRINGFIELD COLLEGE

SENIOR CLASS

AQUATIC CLUB

BARBELL CLUB

The Junior Class Presents

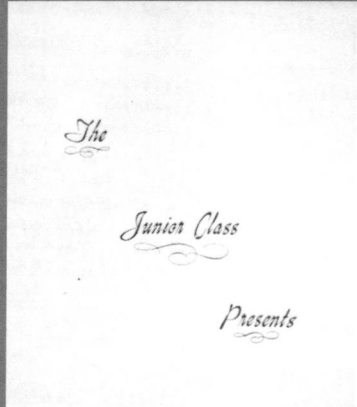

THE MASSASOIT

SPRINGFIELD COLLEGE
SPRINGFIELD MASSACHUSETTS

'55

COSMOPOLITAN CLUB

INTERNATIONAL RELATIONS CLUB

SCOTCHMAN

Administration and Faculty

PHOTOGRAPHY CLUB

SIGMA THETA PSI

Chapter 6

Stone: The Halcyon Years

At the June meeting, the trustees set August 31, 1952, as the effective date of President Limbert's resignation, and named Dean Thornton W. Merriam, then fifty-eight years old, to "serve temporarily as active head of the College … until a new president is duly elected and commences his duties."

Attorney Julius H. Appleton, chairman of the Board of Trustees and chairman of the committee to select a new president, said that a recommendation for the presidency might be made to the trustees' meeting in December. Merriam had come to Springfield College in 1945 from his position as director of training in the National YMCA's Army and Navy department.

He had succeeded Dean Mann after Mann left to assume a position at the Methodist-affiliated Hamline University in St. Paul, Minnesota.

A Maine native, Merriam graduated from Harvard University and earned a doctorate at Columbia University. He taught at Western Reserve University, now Case Western Reserve University, and Northwestern University before being named to the National YMCA post.

Merriam served as acting president for a full year, during which he had to focus his attention, somewhat reluctantly, on finances. He wished fervently "to conserve and develop an enterprise whose ends are spiritual, intellectual, and profoundly social," but realized that this took money. He hesitated to use bookkeeping terms to describe educational programs and almost apologized when he had to do it. When he referred to "better-paying courses," he noted that he was using an "out-of-place" phrase.

The College had achieved an excess of revenue over expenditures (Merriam referred to them as "gains") in 1948, 1949, and 1950, but then big GI Bill veterans classes were replaced by smaller classes of non-veterans, and 1951 and 1952 showed deficits. At the end of 1952, Merriam presented a budget that projected a $40,000 deficit—or in Merriam's phrase, "on the wrong side."

The trustees were hearing a story they had heard before, but Merriam introduced some new material. He presented them with a chart showing the source of dollar-income at Springfield College and at George Williams College in Chicago, which was also known as an "association college." The chart showed that Springfield College was relying on tuition for 80 cents of each dollar, contrasted to 49.5 at George Williams College. Endowment income at Springfield College provided a higher part of the dollar, 6.1, than at George Williams College, 3.7, but recurring contributions provided a whopping 37.6 at the association college in Chicago, but only 5.4 at Springfield College.

When Stone arrived, he was temporarily housed in Alumni Hall. On the door was a sign: "Donald C. Stone, Freshman."

89

Merriam saw one bright spot in that picture, and his name was Calvin J. Martin '34. After thirteen years of professional service with local YMCAs, Martin had returned to take charge of alumni activities. Merriam noted that Martin found some time for fund-raising and gave him considerable credit for increasing contributions during the previous year to the highest total since 1931.

Merriam also told the trustees: "I think it is evident that a new president is urgently needed. The analysis (of College finances) says something very important as to the kind of leader whom we need."

When that leader came, his first actions were directed to the budget and to the long-range financial needs of the College.

Merriam was closely connected to two tributes to Doggett. The dean presided over the 1952 commencement at which Doggett received the honorary Doctor of Humanics degree. Doggett's death at the age of ninety-two came during another interim presidency, and Merriam, dean of the College, served as bearer at the funeral service held in Carlisle Foyer on November 16, 1957. Charles Weckwerth, who made the funeral arrangements, was also a bearer, along with Leslie J. Judd, Erastus W. Pennock, Britton McCabe, and R. William Cheney. Calvin Martin, Fred G. Bratton, and Attalah A. Kidess were the ushers. Officiating clergyman was Right Rev. Charles F. Hall, Episcopal Bishop of New Hampshire, who, in his student days, had lived in the Doggett home. At this last tribute, Doggett's closest associates gathered in one of his favorite places on the campus.

The Springfield Republican, for which Doggett had served as special correspondent to the Pan-American Conference in Lima, Peru, in 1938, and at other times, editorialized: "Those for whom history reserves the most kindly and affectionate remembrances are the builders. It is in that role that Laurence L. Doggett deserves to be remembered."

When Merriam reached the age of sixty-five in 1959, the trustees invited him to retain the deanship for a post-retirement year, and he retired the next June. He had been active in the community during his Springfield College years, serving with the YMCA, Planned Parenthood League, Western Massachusetts Heart Association, and American Civil Liberties Union, and was the highest Republican vote-getter when Springfield elected all Democrats to the school committee in 1957.

Immediately after retirement, the dean received a three-year grant from the Jacob R. Schiff Charitable Trust to study racial conditions in ten Southern states. The study was made for the Southern Area Council of the YMCA.

While on that project, Merriam also assisted thousands of Cuban exiles from the Castro regime. Manuel Diaz, a Springfield College graduate who had been supervisor of physical education in Cuba, served as Merriam's interpreter and later headed an International YMCA for Cubans in Florida.

Upon his return to Springfield, Merriam was named professor of economics at Western New England College, took a year off when he was eighty years old, and then resumed teaching. When he was eighty-seven, he made headlines by joining the walkathon to support the Equal Rights Amendment. It was not a difficult assignment for a man who walked six miles every day anyway, but it did take him away from his task of chopping two cords of firewood.

STONE: INTERNATIONALIST AND MANAGER

When Donald Campbell Stone arrived in the spring of 1953 to become president of Springfield College, there was no president's house and he was temporarily housed in Alumni Hall until he could find a family home in the city.

He found his room in Alumni Hall by the sign on the door: "Donald C. Stone, Freshman."

After the family had settled at 240 Norfolk Street, a few feet east of the campus, President Stone arrived one day with a spade and thirty English ivy plants. Assisted by two daughters (Nancy, a Wellesley student, and Elizabeth, who would enter Mount Holyoke in the fall), he planted the ivy at Memorial Field House, Abbey Hall, and a few other locations. He said the ivy had been brought from the Holy Land by a Methodist bishop who planted it at the Methodist Memorial Church in Washington, D.C. Stone, a trustee of the church, took slips from the ivy, and nurtured them at his home in the Spring Valley section of the capital.

When the Stones transplanted them to Springfield, the new president explained that a college is defined by its many buildings with creeping ivy on the outside and creeping professors on the inside. "When I came to Springfield, I found the creeping professors in abundance but not much of the creeping ivy."

The new president had said that he enjoyed the campus sense of humor illustrated by his door sign, but the creeping professors may have been less amused by the Stone sense of humor.

Stone came to the presidency through a career that combined public administration with academic scholarship. After graduating from Colgate University in 1925 and completing a master's program at Syracuse University, he became assistant to the city manager of Cincinnati, where he did graduate work at the University of Cincinnati. When he was named to the staff of the Institute of Public Administration in New York City, he did postgraduate work at Columbia University. While serving as director of research of the International City Management Association, he was a research associate at the University of Chicago.

Stone went to Washington in 1933 as executive director of the Public Administration Service and, six years later, began his nine-year tenure as assistant director of the Bureau of the Budget.

He served as an advisor to the United States delegation to the San Francisco conference where the United Nations was formed, and was named to the nine-member Standing Committee on Organization of the United Nations. He was also a member of the conference that organized the United Nations Economic and Social Council (UNESCO) and was a member of the first United States delegation to UNESCO.

When Congress adopted Secretary of State George C. Marshall's plan for economic assistance to Europe in 1948, Stone became director of administration of the Marshall Plan agency, and was serving as special assistant to Harold E. Stassen, director of the Mutual Security Administration (MSA), at the time Stone accepted the Springfield presidency.

Dean Thornton W. Merriam, who came to Springfield in 1945 from a position as director of training in the National YMCA's Army and Navy Department, served as acting president from 1952 to 1953.

Like other Springfield College presidents, Donald C. Stone (right) learned that one of his most dedicated trustees and advisors would be Julius H. Appleton, who later served as an honorary trustee and presidential advisor.

In recognition of his contributions to the College, Coach Leslie Judd was honored in 1953 with the renaming of West Gymnasium as Judd Gymnasium. Later, when Judd Gymnasium was renamed the Ruth Evans Gymnasium to honor the College's first director of women's physical education, the entire complex was renamed Judd Gymnasia to honor the pioneer in gymnastics.

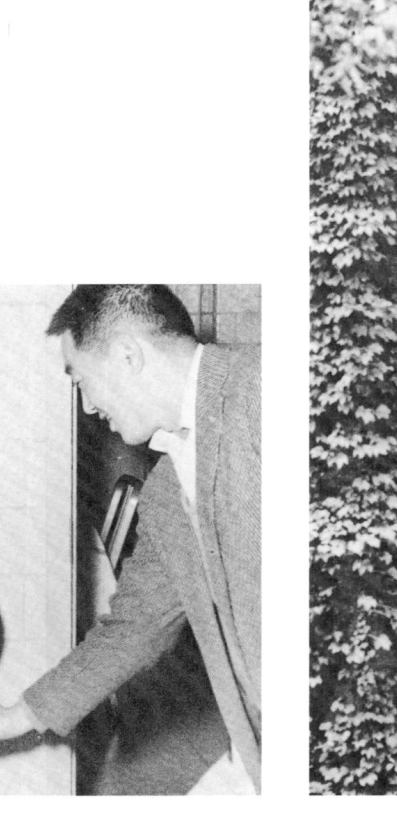

An international student from Japan majoring in recreational rehabilitation works with a young boy at Monson State Hospital in 1957.

The new president had to readjust dramatically his focus on postwar problems. He had been a designer and administrator of plans to restore Europe, and Congress had provided $6-billion for the first year of that effort.

For Springfield College, the postwar era had overcrowded the campus with 1,465 students, about ninety percent of whom were receiving GI Bill financial support. As veterans completed their education, the College's student population dropped to less than a thousand, including more than a hundred women, at the beginning of the 1952-53 school year. By the time Stone arrived, attrition had reduced enrollment to 900, sharply reducing income and increasing the foreseen deficit.

While still living in his freshman room at Alumni Hall, Stone presented to the trustees an eighteen-point plan to cut expenses (one was to deduct $500 from the president's pay when he flew to Europe for an MSA project in September) and a twelve-point plan to produce additional income. Those plans eliminated the projected deficit, and substituted a surplus for the year of $131.

Continuing to stress the College's international character, President Stone helped attract students throughout the world. Here, two students from India (at left) learn about the culture of the Native Americans of the Plains.

In that first report, Stone told the trustees that the fund for a residence for the president exceeded $25,000. He added: "It will be desirable to get this structure erected at an early date in a central location on the campus, so that we will have a gathering place for faculty and students, and for visitors to the college whose interest we wish to gain."

However, he decided the College should not spend money for a president's house until other needs were met, and the Stones and their four children remained in the small house on Norfolk Street, the two older girls sleeping in the attic when they returned from college.

In addition to the accumulated deficit, there was also a debt of more than $120,000 remaining from the loans made to the College to complete the Field House and Abbey Hall, to remodel East Gym for use by female students, and, in Merriam's words, "to prettify the dining room in Woods Hall in deference to the girls and for the refinement of the boys."

The College's East Campus took on increasing importance as both an educational and recreational resource.

Yet, Stone endorsed the plan to increase the mortgage on Abbey Hall to build a wing for the accommodation of fifty additional female students. He projected plans to increase female enrollment to 262 undergraduates and thirty-five graduate students within four years. He also said he would seek to make the College's connections with the YWCA as close as those with the YMCA. Appropriately, the trustees completed the changeover of the College's official name to Springfield College in 1954, so that "International Young Men's Christian Association College" would not appear on the diplomas of the young women who had just entered the College, although the elimination of that corporate name pained Doggett.

Stone was invited to speak at the centennial celebration of the World Alliance of YMCAs in the city of its founding, Paris. Emphasizing the international character of the College, its president made his thirty-third visit to Europe to speak at the convention. In that same year, he was elected to membership in the Department of International Affairs of the National Council of Churches.

Stone received national attention when he called on American colleges to adopt a policy of scholarships on the basis of need, not athletic ability. He proposed that all colleges treat coaches as faculty with tenure rights, rather than as short-term contractors. The physical education faculty took no exception to his proposals, probably because Springfield College had always followed the policies Stone proposed. (The teacher-coach philosophy had been originated by Gulick at Springfield College and by R. Tait McKenzie while he was director of physical education at the University of Pennsylvania.)

There may have been some raised eyebrows when Stone's plan to preclude athletic scholarships included a provision that all grants be made by faculty committees, on which coaches would not be represented.

Support among Springfield's teacher-coaches was eroded even more when Stone proposed to the trustees that physical education majors constitute less than one-half of the total student population.

President Stone (second from left) poses with the honorary degree recipients from the 1956 commencement. To Stone's left is Olive D. Doggett and, next to her, Massachusetts' newly elected junior senator, John F. Kennedy, who delivered the commencement address.

Stone remained president only four years, leaving in 1957 to become founding dean of the Graduate School of Public and International Affairs at the University of Pittsburgh. By 1962, students of his were in eighty nations, and he and Mrs. Stone undertook a three-month tour to visit them and educational institutions that had become affiliated with his program. He retired as dean in 1969, but remained as professor another five years. In retirement, he and Mrs. Stone moved to Pittsburgh, where, in his eighty-first year, he wrote *Making Intergovernmental Administration Manageable*.

Stone's internationalism was so obvious that it has often been stressed in referring to his contributions to Springfield College. What was less obvious was that this man, who identified himself as "a professional bureaucrat," was truly a prudent steward.

Although the designation "Stone Age" was applied to his tenure in the earliest months after he shaved $260 from the budget by eliminating free meals from Freshmen Orientation, he proved that the College could be kept in the black. Just weeks before he left for Pittsburgh, the College could announce that it had passed the $2 million mark on the way to the $3 million development goal he had set.

Stone also helped trustees overcome an unbecoming modesty with these words: "We need to be less modest in asking for support. I can think of few educational and welfare programs where as much mileage is secured from a gallon of gas as at Springfield."

Interim President Wesley F. Rennie (left), an avid golfer, presents a trophy to George R. Hamilton '58.

LEADERSHIP BY BENIGN NEGLECT

Two months after Stone's resignation, Wesley Frederick Rennie assumed leadership of the College, but as interim, not acting, president.

Rennie was not to be a candidate for the presidency. He was sixty-four years old, and had retired a year earlier to Osterville on Cape Cod after thirty-three years of professional service with the YMCA, including with the World Alliance.

Born in Michigan, educated in Illinois and Washington, Rennie worked for the Seattle YMCA for fourteen years as its general secretary. In 1947, he became associate general secretary of the World Alliance of YMCAs in Geneva, where Limbert was general secretary.

Rennie seemed to like the looks of the campus when he first saw it, particularly its lakeside site, and said that he intended later to make a tour of its buildings.

As unfamiliar as he was with the College, he knew about its marketplace. As he said: "I'm new at this field in a sense, but at the same time, I've had long experience in the fields that these youths are preparing for."

In his first press interview, Rennie said he hoped the faculty would take a more active part in the community, but stop short of politics. He said he did not think faculty members should run for public office.

That comment, which appeared in the *Springfield Daily News* under the sub-headline, "No Politics," seems a strange one to have been made while Dean Merriam was involved in a hotly contested race for the Springfield School Committee.

The fact that Rennie's former superior in Geneva, Paul Limbert, had won election to the same school committee and then was chosen by the Republican caucus to be its chairman made Rennie's "No Politics" comment even more puzzling.

The people on the campus who identified him as the man who added golf to Springfield's curriculum may have intended that as only a faint compliment.

Rennie was frequently absent from the campus, and it does appear that he treated some problems with benign neglect, but the system seemed to work. Also, the trustees clearly wanted an interim president to hold the ship steady and not to become deeply involved in the College's administration, and Rennie did as they wanted.

During Rennie's one-year tenure, students were asked to decide whether they would assess themselves $10 a year to help support the proposed Beveridge Center. The students were told that the assessment would continue for as long as seven years, and that it would not be imposed unless the proposal passed by at least a two-thirds vote. If it did not pass, construction of the center would be delayed until another $50,000 had been raised, bringing the building fund to the necessary $425,000. Students voted for the assessment, 651-43.

About a month later, Julia Buxton, a trustee of the College and treasurer of Buxton, Inc., said that she and her family would give the College $150,000 to endow the Buxton Chair of Physical Education. It was the College's first endowed chair, and the first chair in physical education in the United States.

Rennie's comments on those two events are unrecorded. Dean Cheney announced the students' vote, and Vice President Carlton Harrison and Dean Merriam joined Julia Buxton for the gift announcement.

A year later, Rennie was back on the campus to chair a four-day seminar on "Rapid Social Change—Implications for the YMCA." Rennie was then lay chairman of the Commission on Areas of Rapid Social Change of the National Council of Churches. Rev. Glenn Olds and faculty members participated in the Rennie-chaired symposia.

On page eleven of the November 1957 Springfield College *Bulletin* appeared the following notice, printed beneath a slightly melancholy recent photograph of the subject:

> Laurence Locke Doggett, President Emeritus of Springfield College, died at his Longmeadow home on November 13, 1957. President of Springfield College from 1896 to 1936, he was to celebrate his ninety-third birthday on December 22.
>
> He guided the destinies of his beloved College for forty years and his interest in College affairs and its Alumni remained undimmed during the twenty-one years following his retirement.
>
> During his administration he had the satisfaction of seeing the College enrollment rise to over 550; of raising an Endowment Fund of over $1,000,000; of developing the course of training from two years of specialized training in religious work and physical training to a standard four-year course with full recognition in the academic world.
>
> Funeral services were conducted in Carlisle Foyer on November 16 by the Rt. Rev. Charles F. Hall, Episcopal Bishop of New Hampshire.

The interim president did not attend Doggett's funeral in Carlisle Foyer, but was present when the trustees introduced Rev. Glenn Olds as the new president.

President Emeritus Doggett and his wife, Olive, shortly before his death.

Olds (back to camera) attracted new programs to the College for a new generation of students, including some of the first Peace Corps and Job Corps training programs.

Chapter 7

Olds: The Youthful Orator

The trustees committee charged with finding a new president received 124 applications, requested detailed credentials from fifty-three candidates, interviewed fifteen of them and chose Rev. Glenn A. Olds, director of Cornell University's United Religious Work.

Olds had been educated in his native Oregon, ordained into the Methodist ministry, and awarded a Yale University doctorate. At age thirty-seven, he was the youngest incoming president since Doggett had arrived in 1896 at the age of thirty-one.

Olds had become head of the Cornell center the year before the death of its founder, John R. Mott, a Cornell alumnus and the man who had tried unsuccessfully in 1894 to recruit Doggett to help start the World's Student Christian Federation. Mott later became chairman of the World's Committee of YMCAs and was awarded the Nobel Peace Prize in 1946.

The multimillion-dollar building to house the Cornell program that Olds headed was a gift of Myron C. Taylor, U.S. President Franklin D. Roosevelt's personal representative to the Vatican.

Olds was a masterful orator, as more than 2,000 guests, including twenty-six college presidents, learned on the last day of October in 1958, when he delivered an address, "On Becoming Authentic," at his installation. The program included a symposium by four visiting scholars, an augury of the Olds administration.

YEARS OF BUILDING AND SOCIAL CONSCIENCE

Even before he was inaugurated, Olds asked the city of Springfield to close Alden Street to through traffic.

To make the proposal more palatable to commuters between eastern suburbs and downtown, Olds offered College property for the widening of King Street and the redesign at Middlesex and King near the site the College was leasing for ninety-nine years to the Basketball Hall of Fame.

The city's survey showed that the closing of Alden Street would triple the traffic on King Street and overload its western exits, and so Alden Street was to remain a heavy-traffic thoroughfare through the campus.

While the city was counting cars, Olds was studying the College's governance structure. At the first trustees meeting after his installation, Olds presented a reorganization plan with trustee-corporator committees on public affairs, business affairs, student affairs, and educational policy (later renamed academic affairs), with corresponding commissions of

At thirty-seven, Rev. Glenn A. Olds was the youngest incoming president since Doggett assumed the post at thirty-one. An ordained Methodist minister, he held a doctorate from Yale.

As the enrollment of women increased, the College constructed Appleton Hall and linked it to Abbey Hall, the first women's residence hall. The new dormitory bore the name of one of the most prominent families in the College's history. Julius H. Appleton was a founder and his grandson, Julius H. Appleton, served longer than anyone as a trustee and presidential advisor.

College administrators, faculty, and students. He proposed that committee chairmen join the board officers on the executive committee. The Olds plan was adopted.

The new administration moved for another change that had been predicted more than a half-century earlier. When the College was marking its 25th anniversary in 1910, Ralph L. Cheney predicted that the College would one day offer a bachelor of arts degree. It was fifty-three years later that Olds led a delegation from Springfield College to the Massachusetts Legislature to seek such authority. Such degrees were first awarded in 1964.

Olds continued to press forward with the master plan for new buildings. Only weeks after accepting the key to the $460,000 Beveridge Center, named for the Westfield industrialist who had been the largest donor, Olds started a cross-country trip to find a matching gift for a $50,000 Kresge Foundation gift for a classroom building. The matching gift was actually found in Springfield when Clarence and Grace Schoo added $50,000 to their previous gifts, and the building was named after them. Today the totally renovated building is known as the Schoo-Bemis Science Center.

Self-liquidating loans from the federal government allowed the construction of new residence halls—Massasoit, Lakeside, Reed, and International.

As the College looked forward, it also glanced back. At the dedication of the residence hall named for David Allen Reed, the eighty-three-year-old daughter of the school's founder told the audience: "My first remembrance of the School for Christian Workers is crying on our front steps because father had read his resignation as pastor of Hope Church, as the school required his efforts."

The last building Olds dedicated at Springfield College also recalled the College's earliest days. Appleton Hall was named in honor of the late Edward Allen Appleton, whose father, Julius, helped start the school, and whose mother, Helena S. (Allen) Appleton was a cousin of the founder. Edward Appleton's widow, Leirion Appleton, donor of the building, was age ninety-three at the time of the dedication, at which she spoke.

Olds saw far beyond bricks and mortar. Some of the first Peace Corps training programs were conducted at Springfield College. Its director, Sargent Shriver, was so pleased with the results that, when he became director of the Office for Economic Opportunity, he contracted with the College to conduct the first Job Corps training programs in the country.

The Department of Labor also contracted with the College to train managers of youth opportunity centers and of Counselor Aide University Summer Education (CAUSE).

When Attorney General Robert F. Kennedy projected an experimental halfway house for youthful prisoners, the U.S. Bureau of Prisons contracted with Springfield College to operate the test facility at the Brooklyn Central YMCA. All of the five original staff members were Springfield College graduates.

President Olds was a masterful orator, as more than 2,000 guests, including twenty-six college presidents, learned on the last day of October in 1958, when he delivered an address, "On Becoming Authentic," at his installation.

Olds also looked closer to home. He authorized a one-year study by a committee headed by Professor John Brainerd to map the future use of the eighty-one-acre tract known as East Campus.

Olds strongly encouraged students to make decisions for themselves and endorsed the results warmly—or sometimes lukewarmly. After his campaign to close Alden Street failed, and after the blinking signal was removed as illegal, the students tried their hand at the problem.

They flagged down cars and handed the drivers a printed notice: "We are sorry for the inconvenience you have been caused while driving on Alden Street today. However, it has become necessary to dramatically point out the fact that motorists constantly take liberties with the speed limit on Alden Street. We hope no further action will be necessary. [Signed] Students of Springfield College."

The president allowed Dean R. William Cheney to handle the complaints from people who said the students were acting like children, or acting like policemen. Police were kind enough to point out that the students broke no laws because they never blocked the roadway.

Mandatory retirement of faculty drew more student reaction than the Alden Street speeders. When the academic dean declined to renew two post-retirement contracts, some students threatened to strike. At a special meeting of the Student Council on March 1, 1962, some students argued that a strike would only hurt themselves and their grades, and proposed instead a one-day boycott during which students would attend only the one class scheduled by one of the unwilling retirees. In front of hundreds of visiting students, the council passed that proposal, 11-4, with three abstentions.

Naismith stamp issued by the U.S. Postal Service to honor the inventor of basketball.

The students arranged to have the class moved to Memorial Field House, where more than 1,000 listened to the lecture. Olds lauded the "dignity" of the huge class, and praised students for their "orderly, thoughtful tribute" to the two retirees, but pointed out that the faculty had voted for compulsory retirement at the age of sixty-five and he would not intervene.

If Olds applauded two other student actions, he did so privately. Early in his administration, the Student Council endorsed a Student Progress Committee recommendation that the College declare "off limits" two cafes within walking distance of the campus.

Later, after hearing a report from the College physician, the Student Council voted, 13-2, with one abstention, to ask the College to ban the sale of cigarettes on the campus, if a student referendum endorsed the council's recommendation.

Olds, the first president to live in the Doggett Memorial President's House across from the football field, never served alcoholic beverages or stimulants such as coffee or tea there, and he did not smoke.

THE 75TH ANNIVERSARY

During the second year of the Olds administration, the College marked the 75th anniversary of its founding.

The ceremonies more closely resembled those of the 25th than of the 50th, which had been restricted by the Depression and dominated by Doggett's retirement.

Olds (standing) introduces the panel discussion on "The Role of the Whole Man in a Divided World," at the College's 75th anniversary program. Special guests for the program included Aldous Huxley, Margaret Mead, and Norman Cousins.

The 75th anniversary, like the 25th, came during a period when enrollment and physical plant were expanding, and the College could look off-campus to consider the larger issues of the day.

As the 25th had brought scholars to the campus, so did the 75th. Trustee Carl Smith chaired the committee planning the celebration, which brought to Springfield College on October 21, 1960, Aldous Huxley, Margaret Mead, and Norman Cousins to consider: "The Role of the Whole Man in a Divided World."

Massachusetts Institute of Technology Professor Huston Smith was moderator of the day program, which featured Huxley, Mead, and George Williams College Dean Arthur Steinhaus; Cousins was the evening speaker. All classes met that day in the Memorial Field House, and the public was invited. More than 2,000 were in attendance to hear Cousins, even though the final Richard Nixon-John F. Kennedy presidential debate was on television that night.

The alumni homecoming, intended to help mark the 75th anniversary, was not quite so successful, when warm rain washed out the field hockey games, ice skating party, and obstacle race on Lake Massasoit, and the West Point wrestling team broke Springfield College's ten-match winning streak. But the College defeated Long Island University in the game James Naismith invented.

A new President's House was completed in 1958 and dedicated in 1959, and was the family home to Olds, Locklin, and Falcone while they served as president. The house later served as an Admissions Center, and was demolished in 2002 to make way for the current President's House.

Just released from jail in Florida, Dr. King speaks at the 1964 commencement.

President Olds (front row left) with 1964 commencement honorary degree recipients, including (back row left) Rev. Dr. Martin Luther King, Jr., who received an honorary Doctorate of Divinity.

MARTIN LUTHER KING COMES TO SPRINGFIELD COLLEGE

On June 14, 1964, a young civil rights leader named Rev. Dr. Martin Luther King, Jr., was set to receive an honorary Doctorate of Divinity from Springfield College and deliver the commencement address. But just 24 hours before his scheduled appearance, Rev. King sat in St. John's County Jail in the state of Florida for refusing to leave a segregated restaurant in St. Augustine. Meanwhile, Springfield College made plans to broadcast the speech from Rev. King's jail cell if he couldn't make bail.

Neither Rev. King's arrest, nor the anonymous FBI telephone calls warning President Olds not to let King speak, nor the threat made to Olds by a would-be donor to cancel a planned $1 million gift to the College if Rev. King did speak—none of this would deter history. Rev. King did make bail. He did speak, and he told the Springfield College graduates "to be involved participants, and not detached spectators," and to "remain awake through a great revolution."

According to *Springfield Union-News* columnist Tom Shea, writing years later, "King was eloquent that afternoon, stating how we all must learn to live together as brothers or perish together as fools. He also said he stood on the Springfield College campus with a deep sense of appreciation for all the College had meant to the cultural and humanitarian life of the nation and the world."

The following day, Rev. King spoke to another institution of higher education—Yale University, in New Haven, Connecticut.

The Olds family—President Olds, wife Eva Belle Olds, daughter Linda, and son Glenn—was the first to live in the new President's House, starting in 1958.

President Olds speaks at the dedication of International Hall in October 1964.

By the way, the College did lose that $1 million bequest. Olds later told the story of his visit to the potential donor, as reported by columnist Shea:

"As soon as I entered his study, I could see his face was twisted in rage. He was livid. I'll spare you his language and his name. He tore up his will in my presence. He didn't think Springfield College was the kind of institution that would honor a person like Martin Luther King. I told him it was."

WHIRLWIND PRESIDENCY COMES TO AN END

In considering new ideas, Olds could exude enthusiasm and yet exercise caution. His announcement that Springfield College would be the "land-based arm" of the University of the Seven Seas prudently included the stipulation that the agreement would cover only academic offerings, not financial or administrative commitments.

Yet, Olds could not hide his lively interest in the idea of a ship with 500 students and thirty-five faculty members sailing 21,000 miles to twenty-six ports in a semester. He endorsed it as an "imaginative, sound, and exciting educational project."

The idea of opening a Springfield College satellite campus in Hong Kong came from Edwin E. Bond '26, chairman of the Board of Trustees and executive director of the USO. Back from a two-month tour of the Far East, Bond urged the College to consider such an extension. Paul Limbert, who had just retired as executive secretary of the World Alliance, told the trustees of the Alliance's interest in the proposed center for the education of YMCA secretaries for thirteen countries in Asia. Olds heeded Limbert's words of caution, and the Springfield-Hong Kong connection was put on hold.

Olds' enthusiasm could invest not only ideas but individuals. It was Olds who persuaded Art Linkletter to fulfill the dream of his youth by coming to Springfield College. Inspired by Springfield College graduates at the San Diego YMCA, Linkletter had enrolled at Springfield College, but the Depression intervened. More than twenty-five years after he would have graduated, Linkletter stood in the Memorial Field House to receive an honorary Doctor of Humanics degree from Olds.

In his class of honorary doctors, Linkletter was surrounded by Ronald Lippitt, Dean Merriam, former President Limbert, and Leland J. Kalmbach, president of Massachusetts Mutual Life Insurance Company. The next year, Linkletter was elected a trustee and began his voluntary service as the College's interpreter, promoter, Work Week foreman, master of ceremonies, money-giver, and money-raiser. The Olds enthusiasm seems to have gained in translation.

The "youthful orator" makes a point to his audience.

When Olds became president, tuition was still only $725, and the trustees had voted for only the second increase in five years, to take effect in 1959.

The record-high budget was $1,755,000, and the new president would see the first $2 million, the first $3 million, and the first $4 million budget. Enrollment had been on a gentle rise for four years and stood at 1,172. In 1962, it rose to 1,472, breaking the all-time record set during the post-war peak in 1949. The 1962 enrollment included more than 400 women, and the students came from thirty-four states and sixteen foreign countries.

Meanwhile, Olds saw other records fall. He saw tuition rise over the $1,000 mark, and faculty members exceed 100 for the first time. In his last year as president, total gifts from all sources exceeded $500,000.

Olds had been at Springfield College five years when *Sports Illustrated* magazine did a major story on the College, and offered this view of its president: "Olds is somewhat of a human whirlwind, forever dashing off to this meeting and that while cooking up new projects by the dozens. When faculty members once complained that neither they nor he could possibly keep up with all his schemes, Olds explained his bouncy administrative approach in sporting terms: 'You must think I have a lot of rubber balls up in the air, but I have rubber bands attached to each one.' "

Olds resigned the presidency effective July 1, 1965, to become executive dean of the State University of New York, with responsibility for developing international programs for students in the system's fifty-eight colleges and three universities. He explained to 450 Springfield College students why he decided to take this new opportunity, and they gave him a standing ovation.

In 1968, Olds became special assistant to Richard Nixon for policy and manpower development, and later U.S. representative to the United Nations Economic and Social Council with the rank of ambassador.

A year after four Kent State University students were killed by National Guardsmen during an antiwar demonstration in 1970, Kent State named Olds to be its new president. In 1977, he became president of Alaska Pacific University in Anchorage.

Olds, our eighth president, died in March 2006, just one week after Locklin, the ninth president.

Value is a difficult phenomenon to discern, but when does the minutia become realized and separated from relevant substance?

this book to the late Dean of Students,
R. William Cheney
who gave his life
to the job of helping mankind
over the pitfalls of life.
As an Alumnus of the College,
as a professor,
as an administrator,
and as a friend,
he was truly
THE modern man of Springfield

GOLF

SKI CLUB

Chapter 8

Locklin: A New Era Begins

After a faculty and trustee group had interviewed a candidate for the presidency, a professor said to the nominee: "You impress me as having a better comprehension of the philosophy of our College than anyone else in the room."

That view was shared widely enough to make Wilbert Edwin Locklin the trustees' unanimous choice from among no less than 300 applicants, and he was inaugurated on April 30, 1966, in the month he reached age forty-six.

He had graduated in 1942 from Johns Hopkins University into the Army Air Corps and World War II. At war's end, he became assistant director of admissions at his alma mater, leaving in 1947, when he became vice president of the National Bureau of Private Schools. That was the year he married Maria Osterwald.

Two years later, he became an account executive with a New York investment house until returning to Johns Hopkins as assistant to the president, Milton S. Eisenhower, in 1955. Locklin served in that role for fifteen years, and in the last five also served as vice president of the university.

The trustees' unanimous choice from among 300 applicants and nominees, Wilbert E. Locklin became the College's ninth president in 1965.

On the day he was selected by the trustees, Locklin could enhance his knowledge of the College's Humanics philosophy of spirit, mind, and body by simply looking around the campus and its outposts. On the day of his appointment:

- Three Springfield professors and fifteen of their students were in British Guiana (now Guyana), staffing a resident camp for youth leaders, helping to run a demonstration camp for underprivileged children, and teaching sports skills.

- Springfield basketball coach Edward Steitz and ten players were on the third day of their sixty-two-day, 33,000-mile, nine-nation tour sponsored by the U.S. Department of State. They gave 111 clinics attended by 80,000 people, and played twenty-six games, winning them all, before 65,000 fans. They played on dirt courts, and on the mahogany-floored Olympic Stadium in Tokyo. They traveled by air, rail, bus, taxi, rickshaw, pony wagon, camel cart, ferry boat, and elephant.

Among the senior faculty members under President Locklin was Edward S. Steitz, athletic director and president of the Amateur Basketball Association of the United States.

- Trainees from all New England states were on the campus to learn techniques of dealing with economic and social problems of disadvantaged youth. This month-long program was sponsored by the U.S. Department of Labor and the Massachusetts Employment Service.

- About eighty recreation specialists were in the middle of their three-week Job Corps staff training program on the campus, the first in the nation. Another group of 370 would arrive the following week to begin a three-week session. The U.S. Office of Economic Opportunity had contracted with the College to train all of them.

- Reuben B. Frost, director of the College's division of health, physical education, and recreation, was preparing to leave for Olympia, Greece, as the first U.S. representative to the International Olympic Academy.

- The U.S. Department of State announced that Rev. Thich Minh Châu, a Buddhist monk and rector of the Van Hanh University in Saigon, Vietnam, would visit Springfield College the next week as part of his study tour of American universities. The College said the rector would also meet with Nguyen H. Bang, also of Saigon, a student at the College.

- The College announced that a professor and twenty-one students would leave for Europe at summer's end for the first Springfield College Seminar Abroad.

- As if representing both the alumni and trustees in this initiation of a president, veteran Trustee Edmund T. Malley '27 went to Longmeadow Country Club after the trustees' meeting and hit a hole in one.

It was a normal day for Springfield College and a primer for the new president.

TURNING PROBLEMS INTO OPPORTUNITIES

At the September 1965 meeting at which the trustees elected Locklin, they also authorized the administration to seek bids for a $450,000 natatorium.

When those bids were received, Locklin had his first major problem. The subcontractor's bids alone were substantially higher than the cost estimate, and a consultant hired by the College to predetermine the cost confirmed the bad news, giving an estimate of $883,000.

The problem was not only financial, but also diplomatic. It had been Trustee Art Linkletter who had initiated the idea of building a new natatorium, making a few quips about the "McCurdy bathtub." (Did anyone mention that William F. Yorzyk '54, who trained in that "bathtub," was the only American male swimmer to win a gold medal at the 1956 Olympic Games in Melbourne, Australia?)

The students were infected by Linkletter's enthusiasm for the project, and 1,000 of them raised $25,000 in a Work Week. Linkletter responded by donating his Beverly Hills estate to the College, which sold it to musician Henry Mancini for more than $250,000.

At the December meeting, after the College had accepted the students' labor of love and Linkletter's gift, trustees agreed that there could be no turning back. They also agreed that the McCurdy pool, built a half-century earlier for 165 male students, was totally inadequate for the more than 1,500 male and female undergraduates on the campus in 1965. The trustees raised the building budget from $450,000 to $850,000 after Locklin agreed that $33,000 could be shaved from the project.

Locklin was the right person to hold the press conference to explain all of this to the public. When he was asked how the earlier estimate could have been so wrong, he said he didn't know, as he had been on the job only two months.

Before the month was out, the College added 5.3 acres and five buildings to the campus with the purchase, for $239,000, of the Western Massachusetts Electric Company property. Actually, the College was buying back property it had sold to the public utility about a half-century earlier.

In the spring, even before Locklin was inaugurated, ground was broken for the natatorium. The 3,000 people who attended the inauguration ceremonies on April 30, 1966, in the Memorial Field House saw the new building taking shape next door. In the

The natatorium, completed in 1967, was named in honor of Art Linkletter, who donated his Beverly Hills estate to help finance the building. Besides serving as a teaching facility, the Olympic-sized pool has been the site of regional and national championships.

With enrollment of 1,500 students, the dining accommodations in Woods Hall were sorely overtaxed. A new dining commons (above) was opened in 1968 and later named in honor of Dean R. William Cheney (left) and his father, Dean Ralph L. Cheney. It was totally renovated in 2005.

academic procession were representatives of 374 American colleges and universities, including thirty-two presidents. Massachusetts Gov. John A. Volpe and Springfield Major Charles V. Ryan brought greetings. The address was given by Milton Eisenhower, president of Johns Hopkins University and Locklin's mentor for ten years. In his first official act as president, Locklin conferred an honorary Doctor of Humanics degree on Eisenhower.

The thousands of attendees not only saw the natatorium under construction; they also heard about it. At the ceremony, Locklin departed from his text to announce that he had received word of a federal grant of $273,278 for the natatorium, leaving only $125,000 to be raised.

At the dedication of the building in the fall of 1967, Norman C. Keith, chairman of the Board of Trustees, read a telegram from Trustee Paul G. Benedum of Pittsburgh doubling his earlier $25,000 donation and putting the fund drive over the top. Linkletter, for whom the natatorium was named, responded by defeating Charles E. "Red" Sylvia, the College's renowned swim coach, in a 50-meter crawl-stroke race. At the time, rumor had it that Locklin had gently suggested to Silvia that he not win the race with the major benefactor.

The campus' next major project was already underway and breaking records. It was a $950,000 food service facility, with a circular dining room 124 feet in diameter. Private dining rooms for faculty, staff, and guests were included in the design by Alfred P. Casella of Agawam. The building was completed below budget and ahead of schedule, and opened in the spring of 1968, before trustees had approved a name for it. It was only later that it was named in honor of the two Deans Cheney—Ralph L. and his son, R. William.

One of the factors making possible the rapid construction of the dining hall was the fact that its size and its site had been predetermined by the College's long range plan, adopted in 1963 and updated at the beginning of 1967. The plan also determined that the football field would be relocated to a site between the natatorium and the Basketball

Trustee Paul G. Benedum of Pittsburgh was a significant supporter of the College. He doubled his $25,000 donation to put the natatorium drive over the top. In 1970, the Benedum Foundation gave a $250,000 grant, and the trustees voted to name the new athletic field for Benedum.

Among the most influential trustees was Art Linkletter, the television and radio celebrity who could not attend Springfield College because of the Depression. Linkletter directed three capital campaigns and hosted numerous dedications, dinners, and shows for the College. He served as honorary chair of the 2002-2008 campaign.

Hall of Fame then under construction; that a $2 million library would be constructed; that a new dormitory would be erected across from the natatorium; and that the four largest buildings purchased from the electric company would be transformed into a classroom building, a student health center, an arts building, and a theater.

While the dining hall was under construction, the trustees approved plans for a $1,434,000 residence hall, which was being built when President Locklin, speaking to a Greater Springfield Chamber of Commerce Breakfast Club meeting in Cheney Hall, announced that the College was ready to proceed with the new athletic field, which would include one of the largest artificial turf surfaces in the world.

Of the $7.3 million needed for all these projects—completed, being constructed, or contemplated—$3.6 million had been funded by federal loans and grants, as well as private donations, but the remaining $3.7 million would have to be raised from private sources.

The campaign for those funds began four months later at a dinner that had to be moved to a Chicopee convention center as responses from invited guests surpassed the capacity of the restaurant for which the program had been planned.

Norman Keith, board chairman, introduced Massachusetts Mutual Life Insurance Company Board Chairman James R. Martin, chairman of the local campaign with a $1-million goal, and Art Linkletter said that his national campaign would be ready to go as soon as the local $1-million was raised. Actually, he hadn't waited. He told the 800 guests that $611,000 had already been pledged.

STUDENT UNREST COMES TO SPRINGFIELD

The next problem to confront the College was not foreseen in the long range plan, nor were there precedents to guide the president and deans in resolving it.

In February 1969, a list of nine demands was presented to President Locklin by a group of black students. In response, the College made available additional scholarship funds for black students, approved a black studies program, hired additional black faculty members, and sent letters of acceptance to fifty black applicants to enter the College in September.

In addition, the student committee planning freshman orientation agreed to set aside one day for black orientation.

On May 10, a group of black students submitted more demands, including one that those demands be endorsed in writing by the president and faculty. President Locklin and an overwhelming majority of the faculty declined to sign and, two days later, twenty-six black students and one white student occupied the Administration Building. They left voluntarily the next day, and Dean of Students John J. Costello said a Faculty Hearing Committee would determine whether College regulations had been violated.

In a show of support, the Springfield *Student* newspaper covered the black student demonstrations of 1969. The article pictured here spoke of a petition circulated by the Committee of Concerned White Students. The petition asked that "the punishment of 300 hours assigned to the black students be abolished, and that all of the black student demands issued last spring be met to the satisfaction of our black students. Failure to do so will result in appropriate actions as decided by the undersigned."

On May 23, a full-page advertisement appeared in *The Springfield Daily News* in which the trustees reviewed the events and endorsed the administration's actions. The trustees paid for this advertisement themselves, and used no College funds.

Although there was later evidence that some national donors were reluctant to give money to colleges where there had been such incidents, James R. Martin, chairman of the Greater Springfield phase of the $3.7 million campaign, told the trustees on the very day the advertisement last appeared that the local campaign had already exceeded its $1-million goal.

The Faculty Hearing Committee found that the students had broken College rules, and required them to give 300 hours of voluntary service in the community, a commitment they fulfilled by December 9.

The following spring, forty-nine black students occupied Massasoit Hall and were arrested when they defied a court order to leave. They were found guilty of contempt of court. While the College was conducting its hearing on the Massasoit occupation, sixteen white students took over the Administration Building and, after ignoring the dean's order to leave, were arrested for trespassing.

After hearings, some of the occupiers were suspended and others expelled. Some of the latter exercised the right to apply for readmission after one year.

Although Linkletter acknowledged that such disturbances on the campus had made it more difficult to raise College funds nationally, he noted that people who knew Springfield College best had been remarkably generous.

At the trustees' meeting in September 1969, Trustee Paul T. Babson presented from himself and his wife, Edith, a gift of $1-million, the largest donation in the College's history. "The College provides a distinctive education for young men and women who wish to help other people, young and old, in all conditions of life. We want to continue to be part of that sort of education with this gift for the new library," Babson said. He later told trustees that he and his wife had decided that, instead of exchanging gifts on their 50th wedding anniversary, they would make a gift to the College. The library, of course, bears their name.

A year later, Linkletter announced a gift of $250,000 from the Benedum Foundation of Pittsburgh in honor of Paul G. Benedum, a corporator and former trustee of the College. This was the fourth major gift to the College from this foundation, and the trustees voted to name the new athletic field for Benedum.

Received at the September 1970 meeting of the trustees was the lengthy report of the Springfield College Collegium, made up of thirty-two students, alumni, professors, administrators, and trustees who had met all through the spring and summer to consider ways to improve the College. Many of its suggestions were adopted by appropriate authorities at the College, and even its process had been helpful. For instance, students learned that the College didn't pay its trustees, and trustee members learned that they were referred to by students as "the ones with the neckties."

113

STUDENTS MOVE INTO THE BOARDROOM

The collegium recommendation that generated the most debate among the trustees was the proposal that a student be placed on the Board of Trustees. A companion motion to have a professor put on the board received immeasurably short shrift, but the idea of including a student was the subject of considerable discussion.

Examples and experiences of student trustees in other colleges were cited by both proponents and opponents, but most trustees found the experiences of other campuses in this and other matters inapplicable to the Springfield College case.

After postponed and protracted debate, the trustees voted, and it was a tie. The trustees looked to their chairman, Charles H. Schaaff, for the tie-breaking vote.

Schaaff said he believed in the idea of a student trustee, but he wanted the first trustee to join a board on which a great majority favored the idea, not a board that had decided only on the chairman's vote to accept a student trustee. He asked for more study and a later vote.

This was a favorite topic of discussion in trustee sessions, committee meetings, and coffee-break caucuses, during which the trustees went from division to unanimity. The first student trustee was Peter S. Burdett '72, and he made an impact.

Among Burdett's contributions was the idea of initiating a lecture series named in honor of Peter V. Karpovich, then living in retirement in Springfield.

Karpovich had been a faculty member from 1927 until 1961, and was internationally known for his physiological research and published in more than 130 professional journal articles, many of which had been translated into other languages.

When Karpovich died in 1975, in his eightieth year, his widow suggested that memorial contributions be directed to the lecture series Burdett had proposed and, she said, Karpovich had appreciated. Because of the name it bears and the names of those who have been chosen to deliver those annual lectures, scholars in physical education consider themselves honored to be invited to deliver a Karpovich lecture.

All contributions of student trustees have not been so much publicized, but they have been substantive.

Many other recommendations of the collegium were adopted at appropriate levels of administration, but it was the student trustee issue that caused the only tie vote of recent years, although no trustee could later remember ever voting against the idea.

Allen R. Kaynor, the grandson of David Allen Reed, one of the College's founders, taught psychology at the College from 1947 until his retirement in 1984.

The only other issue that so sharply divided the trustees during this era was the establishment of a pub on the campus, finally decided on a split vote. That came after Massachusetts dropped the drinking age to eighteen, making the purchase and consumption of alcoholic beverages legal for most college students. In Massachusetts and other states that lowered the drinking age, collegians driving to and from off-campus drinking spots were exposing themselves to dangers that many colleges decided could be greatly reduced by the opening of on-campus pubs, which could be rigidly controlled.

For many years, any use of alcoholic beverages was sufficient cause for the dismissal of any Springfield College student. Alcohol was forbidden on the campus, and at Locklin's first dinner for trustees, he had to declare the Doggett Memorial President's House "off campus" so that he could offer a clearly identified, mildly spiked punch.

The same arguments that led other Massachusetts colleges to establish pubs were not so easily accepted at Springfield College. The proposal was long debated, and the trustees questioned administrators, including the dean of students. They could not reach unanimity, but a majority voted in favor. Massachusetts later increased its drinking age to twenty, and the pub lost its special reason for existence.

BUILDING AN ADMINISTRATION AND CAMPUS

At the time that John J. "Jack" Costello '57, the dean of students, faced the problems of the building takeovers and the on-campus and off-campus judicial procedures that followed, he had been in that post less than three years.

Costello had been one of Locklin's first appointments, named at the same trustees meeting (May 1966) at which the president designated the acting academic dean, Paul U. Congdon '44, as the permanent academic dean.

The next year, in 1967, Locklin promoted Scott H. Willson '59 from associate director to director of development. Calvin J. Martin, who had been assistant to President Olds, was retained in that position by Locklin until he named Martin, Willson, and the financial officer, Frank W. Smale, vice presidents in 1969.

Robert B. Palmer '65 became associate director of admissions in 1970 and dean of admissions in 1974.

There is a traditional presidential response if anyone asks why Springfield College has so many of its graduates on its professional staff: "The same reason so many other colleges have so many Springfield professionals on their staffs." However, Locklin did not offer that one; instead, he said that he preferred to promote from within. It might be pointed out that Smale, promoted to treasurer in 1980 when Willson was named senior vice president, is a graduate of Pennsylvania State University, and studied at LaSalle College in Philadelphia and the University of Minnesota, but never at Springfield College.

Instead of exchanging gifts on their 50th wedding anniversary in 1969, trustee Paul Babson and his wife, Edith, donated $1-million to the College for the construction of a library. The four-level structure has 70,000 square feet and room for 225,000 volumes.

At their March 1975 meeting, the trustees voted to establish the position of presidential aide, and Jay Evans, who had graduated from Norwich University in 1970 and later earned a master's degree at the University of Southern California, was named to fill it. He was succeeded in 1979 by Edwin H. Hurley, who held two degrees from Notre Dame University and became assistant to the president in 1981.

Locklin and his team of administrators and division heads met often on the campus, but in the summer of 1978, they convened over a long weekend at a retreat in the Berkshires and took a fresh view of the College's problems and opportunities.

The unusual session was financed in part by a donation from a Springfield family that asked that its gift be used for something that the president of the College wanted very much to do. Later, the president agreed that the agenda had been too full but, although exhausted, the team was more unified as it returned to the campus.

The guiding instrument for Locklin and this team was the Long Range Plan, which projected a full-time undergraduate enrollment of 2,000. (It had been 1,524 when Locklin became president.) With the natatorium and the dining hall completed, Locklin said that the College could now swim 2,000 and feed 2,000, but was not yet ready to house 2,000 or teach 2,000.

Enrollment continued to increase every year, and so the president often had to take the Doggett view and give his particular attention to development, the euphemism for money raising.

Previous fundraising campaigns raised money to pay past debts or to increase endowment, but the $7.3-million campaign was entirely for bricks and mortar.

That meant that the administration, in addition to raising the money, had to give its attention to the planning and erection of the structures being financed.

The federal government was still helping with collegiate housing financing. U.S. Rep. Edward P. Boland of Springfield, a longtime corporator of the College, announced in November 1968 a $1-million Housing and Urban Development grant to help finance a 323-student residence hall, completed in 1969 and named for Luther Halsey Gulick, the father of recreation and physical education in the United States.

The Dana Fine Arts Center was completed in 1971; one of the electric utility buildings was redesigned into the Towne Student Health Center, named for Dr. and Mrs. Richard P. Towne of Holyoke, major donors to the campaign; and five air-conditioned classrooms were provided in what is today called Locklin Hall.

However, the great addition to the campus in 1971 was the Babson Library, a four-floor, brick and concrete structure with room in its 70,000 square feet for 225,000 volumes. At its dedication in September of that year, Art Linkletter announced that the campaign was within $572,000 of the $7.3-million goal.

It most frequently happens that the last ten percent of any development campaign is the hardest to raise, and it was not until the spring of 1973 that Art Linkletter presided over the victory party at Baystate West and thanked the Sara Mellon Scaife Foundation of Pittsburgh, which made the final $50,000 contribution to put the campaign over the goal.

The Blake Track and Field, named for S. Prestley Blake, a founder of the Friendly Ice Cream Corporation, was dedicated that fall, with Springfield College winning the cross country meet that opened it. The facility won praise for its six lanes of all-weather artificial surface. It was built on the site of the old Pratt Field, which had been replaced by Benedum Field, down the street.

One campus improvement that came the next year was unplanned by the College. While installing a large sewer line, the city had to reduce the level of Lake Massasoit by ten feet, exposing junk and debris that had been hidden by the water. Although others thought the prospect ugly, more than 200 Springfield College students saw it as an opportunity.

On an October Saturday, they started at 9 a.m. to clean the lake. The Springfield Park Department furnished trucks, which took away twenty tons of old tires, shopping carts, and automobile parts. The city's Forestry Department sent a crew to remove fallen trees and limbs. The volunteers had planned to work until 1 p.m., but remained until 3:30 p.m., missing the Springfield College-American International College football game at AIC. Springfield College won anyway, 28 to 27.

At summer's end of 1973, Mrs. William C. Bemis gave the College $300,000 to complete funding for the biology building that, until 2006, bore the name of her late husband, a Springfield industrialist. Architect Alfred P. Casella presented convincing evidence that a drum-shaped building would reduce the costs of hallways and of

Benedum Field, with seating for 4,500, had a synthetic surface identical to that of the New England Patriots. Equipped with lights for night games, it served as home field for football, field hockey, and lacrosse. The field was resurfaced in 2007 and renamed Stagg Field in honor of Amos Alonzo Stagg G'91.

electrical and plumbing services, and would provide ideally shaped laboratories and class-rooms. It also provided a handsome addition to the campus. Today the building bears the name Hickory Hall, and the Bemis name has been transferred to the nearby Schoo-Bemis Science Center.

At the 1974 commencement, several threads of College history became interwoven. It was on a modern setting, Benedum Field (today Stagg Field, named in honor of football pioneer Amos Alonzo Stagg '91), and the speaker was the man whose name was on the Art Linkletter Natatorium next door. The College awarded Doctor of Humanics degrees to Enrique C. Aguirre '15, and to Seth Arsenian, the first Distinguished Springfield College Professor of Humanics.

Aguirre, who had arranged the Springfield College gymnastics team's Mexican tour in 1925, later founded and served as president of the Mexican Olympic Committee. Although Arsenian had served as director of admissions and later director of graduate studies, he was most famous as a professor of psychology, in which discipline he held a doctorate from Columbia University.

The field of psychology has had a long history at Springfield College, dating back to Gulick's course in physiological psychology in 1890, the year his protege, Frank Seerley, graduated. Seerley studied psychology at the University of Paris and took over the psychology course previously taught by Gulick and James Naismith. Arsenian was heir to a long tradition. At the commencement, the Award for Innovative Teacher was given to Henry J. Paar '49,

Blake Track and Field, named for S. Prestley Blake (center), a founder of Friendly Ice Cream Corporation, has a rubberized asphalt track. It has been the site of both New England and Eastern track and field championships. With Blake are President Locklin (left) and Ed Steitz, director of athletics.

honored for his curriculum design for introductory psychology.

One of the most welcome, although repetitive, reports about the College that year came not from Alden Street but from Tokyo Gakugei University in Japan. A nine-man team of Japanese physical educators had interviewed seventy-two chairmen of departments of physical education in American colleges and universities to learn which college, in their judgment, had the best undergraduate physical education programs in the nation.

Springfield College ranked first with thirty-five votes, followed by University of Illinois with twenty-nine, University of Oregon with twenty-two, Ohio State University with seventeen, Indiana University with fourteen, and University of Iowa with ten.

GOING AGAINST THE TIDE

At a meeting in San Diego of the American Council on Education in 1974, the thirty college presidents were asked four questions: Did your institution operate in the black last year? Did it maintain enrollment? Did it increase faculty size? Did it increase faculty salaries?

Only one president raised his hand to respond affirmatively to all four, and that was President Locklin of Springfield College. Only 3 percent of American colleges could meet that four-way test.

Two of Springfield's all-time football stars who became College trustees, Norman Keith '34 (right), and All-American Joseph Shields '34 (center), show President Locklin reproductions of newspaper accounts of their Springfield College victories. Keith donated the Keith Locker Room and Training Facility and the Keith Scholarships for the development of leadership through football.

Two years later, when Springfield College's annual budget surpassed $10-million for the first time, total student charges were $3,882, only twenty-six percent higher than they had been five years earlier. If college costs had risen at the same rate as the cost of living, the student charges would have been $4,286 a year.

Financial statistics are of great interest only to mathematics devotees and parents of college-age children, but the announcement by Springfield College in 1982 that it would freeze all tuition and room and board rates at least until September 1984 did command some broader attention.

This decision was made after Dean Palmer told the trustees that about ninety percent of students dropping out of college were citing financial reasons.

Because of record-high assistance from the Alumni Fund and increased endowment income, the College increased scholarship aid, and the faculty and staff accepted limited salary increments so that the budget could be maintained without increasing charges to students.

The trustees were also confident that more students would be attracted to the new physical therapy major and to interdisciplinary studies. More first-year students were choosing to have undeclared majors, and others were attracted to courses preparing students for management of nonprofit agencies.

Although lectures in management of nonprofit agencies had been offered even in Henry Lee's time, Professor Thomas J. Shea devised and promoted a curriculum to better prepare students to deal with the economic problems of human service agencies. This fast-growing program had extensions for non-traditional students. The largest grant ever received by the College for an academic program was the $97,000 given by R.J. Reynolds Industries, Inc., for the Springfield College Institute for Executives of Non-Profit Organizations, a program proposed by Robert W. Van Camp '54, president of R.J. Reynolds Development Corporation and a trustee of the College. The pilot program brought executives from twenty-five nonprofit agencies to the campus during the summer of 1983 to improve their management skills and to help them deal with federal and state budget cuts.

Curriculum changes involve many risks, including financial, and the Harry L. Lippincott Curriculum Improvement Foundation was formed in 1981 to provide start-up costs for curriculum changes proposed by faculty and approved by a five-member faculty committee headed by the academic dean. The fund began with a $60,000 bequest from Harry L. Lippincott '36, a College trustee.

Applications for admission to the Class of 1987 increased 27 percent over the previous year, and the College welcomed 269 men and 266 women, a six percent increase over the entering class in 1982. The freshmen came from nineteen states and six foreign countries, including China and Japan.

Springfield's two-year freeze of all costs was to end in September 1984, and trustees approved increases in room and board and tuition that were to raise total costs of a full-time student on a full-week meal ticket to $7,950 a year, the highest in the College's history but still substantially lower than the average of the country's four-year, private, independent colleges.

While other colleges were reporting a decline in applications through the spring of 1984, Springfield College actually had a 20 percent increase, with many applicants expressing interest in programs that were not available at the College only a few years earlier.

A 1954 graduate and trustee, Robert W. Van Camp proposed a summer institute in 1982 to train executives of nonprofit organizations in management skills. The program attracted agency leaders from throughout the United States.

The East Campus has played a major role in the College's history. The College's summer program for area children, Camp Massasoit, is as popular today as it was in 1943, when children pledged allegiance.

Chapter 9

Locklin: Centennial Celebration

The W.K. Kellogg Foundation agreed in 1976 to fund the Academy for Educational Development's proposal to enhance the long-range planning of American colleges and universities.

The academy, staffed by former college presidents and other academicians, wished to select ten private four-year colleges to participate in separate planning efforts along guidelines set by the academy.

The selection of Springfield College was determined in part by the fact that the College had a considerable and successful experience in long-range planning.

Doggett's five-year plans, including the Olmsted firm's proposal for future campus expansion, were pioneering efforts at long-range planning that grew to modern, all-encompassing form under Presidents Stone, Olds, and Locklin.

Before the first ten-year plan expired in 1972, work was begun on a new plan, with a five-year projection, and it was while preparing for the 1978-82 plan that the College learned of the Kellogg-AED project.

The academy stipulated that each college would assign planning responsibilities to a five-person team that included the president, academic dean, comptroller, elected faculty representative, and an administrative specialist.

At Springfield College, that meant Locklin, Congdon, and Smale, along with the faculty's selection, Emery W. Seymour, Buxton professor of physical education, and the administrative specialist, Calvin J. Martin, vice president for administration, who had been alumni secretary before he became assistant to Olds in 1964.

This team worked in Chicago under the chairmanship of the academy's vice president, John D. Millett, former president of Miami University (Ohio) former chancellor of the Ohio Board of Regents, and one of the country's most widely published educational administrators.

Springfield College's team members were not only learners in that process, but also teachers, who saw justification for what the College has called its "prideful uniqueness" in long-range planning.

In addition to the obvious benefits to the planning process, the Springfield College participation in this Kellogg-AED study also increased the College's recognition among corporation and foundation grants makers.

President Locklin appointed the Centennial Commission and placed emphasis on a fine arts series.

Springfield College's long-range plans, with projections of enrollment, faculty, tuition, endowment, curriculum, and construction, allowed the College to present a clear prospectus to prospective students and potential donors.

Springfield College had a road map with objectives clearly marked and distances computed, allowing it to know where it was going and how to get there.

SAVING THE EAST CAMPUS

On February 28, 1980, Springfield Mayor Theodore E. Dimauro urged the Springfield School Committee to choose Springfield College's East Campus as the site for its new $42-million high school.

"It's the most attractive, beautiful site we could have found in the whole city. We're fortunate to have found it," the mayor said.

The mayor said that the state, which would pay the lion's share of building costs, would not pay anything for land acquisition, but the city could bond for $1-million to buy fifty or sixty acres of the eighty-one-acre site.

"The kind of facility we can build there would make Springfield the envy of every community within fifty miles," the mayor said.

The College community was shocked by the proposal, but more shocked by *The Springfield Union*'s report that the mayor had said that discussions related to acquisition of the property had been going on between city and College officials for about a year.

The mayor had called the president in August, outlined the idea, and asked Locklin to keep the whole matter confidential. The president said that he would inform the board

The College's opposition to a proposed city takeover of East Campus became a major news story. President Locklin made himself available to answer media questions.

leadership, which he did, and the trustees were later informed in executive session. At that meeting, the president and board chairman said that they had both told the mayor that the property was not for sale, and legal counsel explained the principle of eminent domain by which the city could take the property for public purposes.

On the day after the mayor and the city's planning director recommended the site, School Superintendent John E. Deady, a corporator of the College, endorsed it over all other proposal sites. "In a city, when you can find, directly in the middle of the community, eighty acres of land with few apparent problems and difficulties, it's a lovely thing," he said.

That view was not shared by students, faculty, and alumni, many of whom questioned the decision of the administration and board to keep the matter in executive session for six months.

Misgivings on the campus increased when *The Springfield Union* quoted the mayor as telling the school committee that he had talked with Richard C. Garvey, the College's board chairman, about the possibility of a collaborative program on the site, with the high school located on the northernmost thirty acres, leaving fifty acres and the lake for College use. It helped only a little that the mayor said he wished to emphasize that the College was not offering any part of the property for sale, but that the College was sensitive to the city's needs.

One of the committee members, Miriam R. Nelen, said she was pleased that Springfield College was sensitive to the city's needs, and added: "I think we should be sensitive to the College's needs."

The next day, the trustees reiterated their position that the land was not for sale, and adopted a resolution concluding: "We firmly and unanimously believe that we could not surrender any part of the East Campus without severely, perhaps fatally, damaging the institution we are pledged to serve."

The mayor responded by saying: "The land is there and the city has the legal right to take it. I think the trustees are reacting to the negative backlash by the faculty and students."

The mayor may have been referring to the fact that, on March 10, the faculty had voted, 56-0, to ask the Board of Trustees "to do everything in its power to prevent the loss of this valuable educational asset." Later that same day, the Student Government unanimously endorsed the faculty's resolve.

Lake Massasoit long served the College as an educational and recreational resource.

125

Situated at the entrance to East Campus, Loveland Chapel was dedicated in 1981. Besides religious services, the academic chapel was used for trustee meetings, lectures, and campus and community gatherings. It was named for Norman S. Loveland, a 1924 alumnus, and today houses the nationally accredited Child Development Center.

After the lines had been clearly drawn by the trustees' statement and the mayor's reaction, the president asked to speak before the school committee. When he arrived on April 18, he was met by 1,300 teachers there to talk, not about the school site, but their contract negotiations.

"Teachers occupied every square inch of floor space, then stood on chairs or sat on window sills and the tops of book shelves," according to news accounts.

When the teachers had their say and left, Locklin was given the floor. He started by saying that he respected the intensity of the board's problem, and spoke admiringly of the high school, attended by both of his sons, which now needed replacement.

He noted that three hundred independent colleges had failed during the previous decade, and their home cities and towns suffered from the loss. He noted that the colleges of Greater Springfield were the region's fourth largest employer, with an annual payroll of $31-million for 2,825 local residents.

Locklin mentioned some of the things that made Springfield College unique, including the fact that the student body that year came from thirty-nine states and seventeen foreign countries.

He identified East Campus as a National Science Foundation Experimental Ecological Reserve, one of two hundred in the country, of which only twelve were in New England, three in Massachusetts.

He said that Camp Massasoit served children from the area each summer, and that the previous year's 482 enrollees included disadvantaged children sent by the Greater Springfield Council of Churches.

The president said that there had been 87,206 student hours of instruction given at East Campus during the previous academic year, and that a new academic position, East Campus director, was in the 1981 budget. He also said that an academic chapel was being planned for that site.

Noting the city's condemnation of the field house, the city's threat to take East Campus, and the city's efforts to move the Basketball Hall of Fame from the campus, Locklin said that students were asking: "What have we done to be treated so inconsiderately by the City of Springfield?"

Locklin asked, in the name of forty-four trustees, in the name of 300 faculty and staff, 225 of whom lived and voted in Springfield, 2,400 students, 4,400 parents, and 16,500 living alumni, 952 of whom lived and voted in the city, not to take any part of the campus.

"If the school committee is to get it, it will need to take it by eminent domain. Should that be attempted, the school committee is entitled to know that I and my board, and my faculty, students, staff, parents, alumni, and our neighbors will use every legal and ethical means to resist this needless damage to both Springfield College and the City of Springfield," the president concluded.

The committee made no decision, and soon its attention had to be diverted to another problem—the public-school teachers went on strike and remained out for two weeks.

On June 13, Locklin was back before the school committee, urging its members to remove the threat to East Campus.

The president told them that there had been a drop (8.7 percent) in the number of applications for admissions to the recreation department, whereas total applications for the Class of 1984 were excellent. Alumni, upset about the cloud hanging over East Campus, had been less responsive than anticipated to the College's $6.1-million capital campaign. More than 1,400 city residents, all alumni and friends of the College, had signed a petition opposing the seizure of East Campus.

Nelen made a motion to exclude the East Campus site from consideration, and Andrew M. Scibelli, later to become president of Springfield Technical Community College, seconded it. The mayor, who served as chairman of the committee, voted against it and was joined by two other members. The vice chairman and the other three members voted in favor, winning the vote, 4-3.

It had been a bruising battle, and the College did not escape injury. However, there were benefits. The threat to East Campus had brought trustees, administrators, faculty, students, and alumni together in a rare display of total unanimity.

The controversy provided the president with the opportunity to tell the College's story to the school committee, and those presentations were widely covered by the media.

The dispute also forced many people, both on and off the campus, to give fuller consideration to that asset and how it should be used. Treasurer Smale's statement to an on-campus group that the property, if sold, would provide the College with recurring annual income of almost $100,000, emphasized one aspect of its value.

The controversy also underscored for all parties the fact that the city had the right to take property to meet public needs, and that the best defense against such eminent domain procedures was full utilization of it.

There was some more recent history, showing that the College could not have been shocked by the 1980 proposal. Eight years earlier, Educational Planning Associates, hired by the City of Springfield to make long-range recommendations for its school system, published a report stating that the new high school could be located on the East Campus of Springfield College.

Evans Clinchy, author of the study, suggested that the city take fifteen to twenty acres for the high school site, and, in return, agree to close Alden Street as had been so often recommended by College officials for safety reasons.

After publication of that report, the president of the College sought faculty recommendations for better utilization of East Campus. The crisp tone of a Locklin memo to a faculty leader suggests that he was not satisfied with progress: "It is a vexing problem that many are enthusiastic to delineate, but few are proposing ways to resolve." Concluding his memo on East Campus, Locklin wrote: "I continue to pursue a variety of alternatives to the present unsatisfactory arrangement." That memo was written two years before the mayor made his bid to take East Campus.

During his presentation to the school committee, the president had noted that the College budget already provided for a full-time director of East Campus programs, and that the College was proceeding with plans for an academic chapel there.

Norman S. Loveland '24, and his wife, Ruth, had established in 1946 a fund for the erection of a new chapel at the College. After Babson Library was opened and Marsh Memorial was renovated for other uses, a chapel was developed in the large room in Marsh which already contained stained-glass windows. The Loveland chapel fund could not be used for that purpose because it was restricted to a construction of a new chapel.

In the spring of 1979, a bequest from the Loveland estate made it possible to erect a $400,000 academic chapel. Loveland's friends, on and off the campus, noting his long interest in Boy Scouting and the outdoors, agreed that it would be appropriate to locate the memorial on East Campus. An apartment for the East Campus director was included in the Casella plans, and ground was broken in the late summer of 1980. The building, dedicated on May 20, 1981, received heavy and varied use, and made possible the greater use of the whole eighty-one-acre outdoor laboratory. The handsome building, designed to conform to its natural surroundings, had a touch of the traditional in its setting. Today, the building houses the College's Child Development Center.

THE CHINESE CONNECTION

The Springfield School Committee meeting, at which the president of Springfield College was waiting to make one of his "Save East Campus" presentations, was interrupted when the superintendent had to take an important telephone call.

It was from the Massachusetts commissioner of education, asking how he could contact the president of Springfield College at once.

This was a happy coincidence for the College, the commissioner, and the head of the world's largest educational system.

The commissioner's guest, Jiang Nanxiang, minister of education of the People's Republic of China, was determined not to return to China without first visiting Springfield College.

Jiang was a protégé of John Ma, founder of modern physical education in China, and a 1920 graduate of Springfield College. Jiang toured the campus, and in Locklin's office admired a delicate painting, a gift of John Ma's son, Ma Qi-Wei, also a Springfield alumnus, and then vice president of the Peking Institute of Physical Education.

Less than fifteen months later, in Peking (today Beijing), President Locklin of Springfield College and President Zhong Shi-Tong of the Peking Institute signed a two-year exchange agreement. The pact, written in both Chinese and English, provided for exchanging faculty, students, and teaching materials, and planning joint research projects, workshops, and conferences.

Within twenty-four hours of their arrival in China, Locklin and his wife were guests of the minister of education at a state dinner. They spent eleven days in China, during which time the agreement was completed and signed.

After renewing an agreement with the Beijing Institute of Physical Education in 1983, President Locklin celebrates with two alumni, Professor Xia Xiang '45 (left), director of physical education at Tsinghua University, and Beijing Institute President Ma Qi-Wei '49.

The next spring, Springfield College sent its first representatives to Peking—Charles J. Smith, assistant professor of physical education and swim coach, and Lance Lambdin, a freshman from Oklahoma City. The exchanges had begun.

The Locklins returned to China two years later for the contract renewal, after Ma Qi-Wei had become president of Peking Institute. Ma Qi-Wei returned to Springfield College in 1984 to receive an honorary doctorate from his alma mater. (Locklin, who delivered the citation in Chinese, had learned it by rote from a recording made for him by Mrs. Frank Fu, wife of the former director of the Doggett International Center at the College.)

Speaking in English, Ma was several times interrupted by applause, once when he said how proud he was to be a Springfield College alumnus and the son of a Springfield College alumnus, and to be the father of Ma Ning, then a student at the International Academy at Springfield College.

The academy was another result of the Locklins' visit to the Far East. In Hong Kong, Locklin met with YMCA leaders, including Patrick Chung '74, assistant general secretary, to make arrangements for an academy at Springfield College to prepare Hong Kong youths for American colleges and universities.

All sixteen members of the first graduating class were accepted to American colleges, including Springfield College. (One graduate, accepted to nine colleges, chose Brown University.) In 1984, there were thirty graduates.

As a result of the Locklins' 1983 trip to the Far East, the YMCA College in Osaka, Japan, made arrangements to send graduates of its two-year program to Springfield College to complete their education. Nicholas P. Moutis, director of the Division of Health, Physical Education, Recreation, and Physical Therapy, and Kenneth Wall, director of the Doggett International Center, went to the Far East to work out details on programs and studied a proposal for an exchange agreement with the Chinese University of Hong Kong, where Frank Fu G'73 was then associate director of the Division of Physical Education. Today Fu is professor and assistant vice president at Hong Kong Baptist University, and dean of its faculty of arts and sciences. Coincidentally or not, Hong Kong Baptist has a good number of Springfield College doctors of physical education among its faculty.

Although Locklin was quoted as saying that no international exchange agreement of his tenure as president was more important than the Chinese pact, there had been various

To prepare for the Pan-American Games, President Borges (left) of the Venezuelan Sports Federation turned to Springfield College and President Locklin (right). In the center is Frank Fu, an adjunct professor who also headed the International Center.

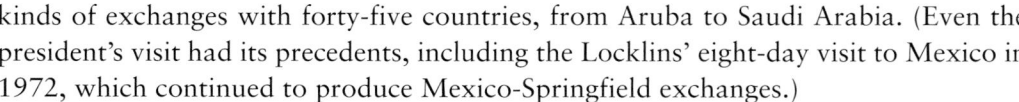

kinds of exchanges with forty-five countries, from Aruba to Saudi Arabia. (Even the president's visit had its precedents, including the Locklins' eight-day visit to Mexico in 1972, which continued to produce Mexico-Springfield exchanges.)

The College's exchange program in Aruba was not with the Netherlands Antilles government, but with the Aruba Sports Union and its School di Deporte, headed by Roy Van Patten '60. Several Springfield College faculty rotated through the Aruba program over the years.

Under the College's Saudi Arabian agreement, seventy-three young athletes came to Springfield College in 1976 to train in cycling, gymnastics, fencing, table tennis, handball, and volleyball for the Pan-Arab Games. (Springfield College had to hire one instructor from outside the faculty—to teach table tennis.)

The Saudi Arabian athletes spent three weeks at a training camp near Montreal, where they could observe the XXI Olympiad, four weeks on the Springfield campus and, on nights out, hours in the shopping malls buying custom-lettered T-shirts to take home to Saudi Arabia.

In the College's earliest days, when keeping the school solvent was a daily concern, foreign students sent by YMCAs paid no tuition, and the College worked with local YMCA officials to provide free room and board. Wealthy American friends of the YMCA often paid all transportation costs.

In contrast, many of the young people coming from foreign countries to Springfield College as it approached its centennial needed no financial assistance.

AN ERA ENDS IN TRIUMPH

On Thursday, May 11, 1979, the Memorial Field House was condemned, ordered closed within twenty-four hours, and then to be razed. The College padlocked the building immediately. The dramatic action by the City of Springfield's building commissioner made headlines and created shock waves.

The president of the College was quoted as saying: "Candidly, it presents us with vexing problems, unique but not insurmountable." He even looked on the bright side: "The good thing is we found out about this two weeks before the end of the school year rather than two weeks before the beginning of the school year."

If the president appeared calm and philosophical, it should be noted that he knew of the problem before the building commissioner did. When the trustees decided that a new physical education building would replace the front part of the old building and would connect to the rear section of the Field House, the president retained an engineering firm to determine the soundness of the old structure.

When that report was made, the president shared it with the trustees' Executive Committee and then with the city. The commissioner used another consultant, but the verdict was the same: The building had to come down. While that was an accurate assessment, some faculty noted at the time that it took a very long time to raze this unsafe structure.

While the wreckers were removing the building, the College began the search for other teaching stations, and the community responded quickly and generously.

In 1976, Attallah A. Kidess (left), retired director of the International Center, and Professor John L. Neumann (right) of the Physical Education Department discuss an educational program for Saudi Arabian coaches and athletes.

With the wrecking ball going through the College's largest and busiest building, the College had to devise a new plan and a way to pay for a replacement. The College had launched a $3.6-million campaign to pay for the partial replacement of the Field House and the modification of the recently acquired electric company's transformer building into a theater arts center.

The Physical Education Complex Task Force, headed by Nicholas Moutis, director of Health, Physical Education, and Recreation, heard proposals from five architectural firms and then cast ballots ranking the presentations.

Alfred Casella was listed at the top of each ballot. Trustee Chairman Richard C. Garvey, Campus Planning Committee Chairman John Gallup, and the president met with Casella to review his presentation, and then voted unanimously to retain him. He agreed to have a final plan ready for the Campus Planning Committee on August 7, and, although it required twenty-six task force meetings in thirty-five business days, deadlines were met. Confident that they would be, the board chairman on July 6 wrote to every trustee urging him or her to attend a special meeting at the Colony Club in Springfield on August 13.

The trustees, who had approved a $3.6-million campaign for a Field House addition and a theater arts center, were told at that meeting that the Casella-designed physical education center would itself cost $5.3-million, and that the theater would bring the total to $6.1-million.

Understandably, several trustees considered that an impossible goal, and noted that the previous campaign had raised only $3.6-million from private sources, and that there was no federal money available for these projects.

A proposal for a partial solution at a lower price was actually moved and seconded. Trustee Art Linkletter then said that we should ask for what we truly believed was needed, and a trustee asked if Linkletter were ready to lead a national campaign for the full amount. The answer made the vote unanimous, and the trustees left with a national campaign chairman and a $6.1-million goal.

At a later meeting, the trustees also approved a departure from their practice of never starting a construction project unless the funding is complete. They agreed that the need for physical education facilities was so crucial that the building must start as soon as possible.

They had two encouragements. A few weeks before the condemnation, S. Prestley Blake, whose major gift in 1972 is recognized by Blake Track, offered to give the College $500,000 if it would raise a similar amount in gifts of $50,000 or more within twenty-one months. After the condemnation, major donors responded so generously to the new appeal that the Blake gift was fully matched in only nine months.

Likewise, the response was encouraging in the local community, where James R. Martin was campaign chairman, assisted by John F. Cauley, Jr., then executive vice president of Friendly Ice Cream Corporation. Only five weeks after the condemnation, Martin, Cauley, and company had exceeded the $500,000 goal by 33 percent, reporting $662,350.

Eight months after the condemnation, the bids were opened, and Locklin's relief still emits from the memo he sent to Linkletter: "Bids are in, and under budget by a few

The $5.3-million Physical Education Complex became a reality because of the success of a capital campaign. S. Prestley Blake (center in lower left photo) contributed $500,000 to the local phase, which was directed by James R. Martin (left), chairman of Massachusetts Mutual, and John F. Cauley, Jr., president of Friendly Ice Cream Corporation. The largest gift to the drive was announced at the dedication by John Cox, president of the Insurance Company of North America (lower right photo), which contributed $1-million.

hundred thousand dollars." The administration resisted the temptation to hedge; instead, it added three more racquetball courts and another teaching gymnasium to the back section, and the president signed a contract with D.A. Sullivan & Sons of Northampton to build the new complex.

The $1-million bequest of Trustee Winston Paul was assigned to the building fund, and, at the end of 1981, the Dana Foundation, which had funded the Dana Arts Center two years earlier, gave $500,000 for the physical education complex. When the building was about half-completed, the Pew Memorial Trust of Philadelphia gave $250,000.

Also in 1981, Trustee Thomas K. Hendrick of Oklahoma City added $500,000 to the $100,000 he had given earlier, and pushed the campaign over the $4.8-million mark.

Recognizing the College's need to use the facilities as soon as possible, the municipal building department issued a certificate of occupancy for the rectangular rear section of the complex while work continued on the domed, circular structure, which the students dubbed "Galactica."

The work schedule had to change because of strikes by roofers and carpenters in the district that included Springfield. Yet, twenty-nine months after the condemnation of the old Field House, in October 1981, its $5.3-million successor was finished.

Linkletter, chairman of the national campaign committee, presided at the ceremonies in the arena named for S. Prestley Blake. More than 100 students—gymnasts, dancers, and musicians—took part in the entertainment.

The program was interrupted to allow Trustee Philip Brown '52, to introduce John R. Cox, president of Insurance Company of North America, who presented his company's gift of $1-million. Newspaper accounts mentioned the "resounding applause." There was good reason for applause—the newly dedicated building was paid in full.

The $1-million gift made the total receipts $5.8-million, still $500,000 short of the goal that the trustees had increased to $6.3-million after it was decided that the electric utility building was not suitable for renovation into a theater arts building, and a new structure would have to be erected.

Linkletter, noting that he had raised money for physical education, which was his special love, said that he would also give something for a facility more closely connected with the way he makes his livelihood. He gave $50,000 for the theater lobby. The other major contribution for the theater arts building was the $100,000 gift by Attorney and Mrs. Julius H. Appleton.

The College learned again that the last ten percent of any fund drive was the hardest to raise, and also learned that, among the friends of Springfield College, it was easier to raise money for a physical education facility than for a theater, even one which would be used for many things, including daily classes.

The trustees, who had allowed the physical education building project to begin even though all the money was not in hand, were not ready to make another exception for the theater building. Locklin, admitting to partiality for the theatrical arts, responded that the experience with the physical education complex showed that it was easier to raise money for a building going up, rather than a building in an architect's sketch.

The president offered another argument. He said that the College was, in effect, breaking faith with friends like Linkletter and Appleton if it accepted their money and then didn't use it for the purposes the donors intended.

With some trustees, his most persuasive argument was the $1,700 proceeds of the students' productions of *Best of Broadway*, which constituted the first contribution to the theater when it was not even an architect's sketch.

Finally, Locklin prepared a worst case presentation showing how the College would pay for the new building even if no more contributions were made, and the trustees' Executive Committee approved.

The new building was erected on a famous—or infamous—site. Generations of Springfield students had complained about the ice company building at the southwestern corner of the campus, and the College had tried unsuccessfully for years to acquire

Constructed on the site of the "old ice house" (inset), the Fuller Arts Center (above) is a multi-purpose structure able to accommodate theatrical performances, musical recitals, faculty lectures, and special events—such as the Centennial Convocation, which attracted this audience. The Fuller Arts Center was totally renovated in 2008-09.

it. A friend of the College, insisting on anonymity, provided the money to buy the building, tear it down, and grass the site. It was on that location that the theater arts building was erected.

Early in 1983, two Worcester, Massachusetts foundations, the Alden Trust and the George F. and Sybil H. Fuller Foundation each gave $25,000 to the theater arts building fund, greatly improving Locklin's worst case projection.

When the frost was out of the ground, construction of the Casella-designed building began and, in the fall, only ten months after the Fuller Foundation had made its $25,000 gift, it agreed to give $300,000, completing the funding for the new facility, still about seven months from completion.

The Fuller gift brought the gift total in the $6.3-million campaign to $6,384,500.

On May 4, 1984, Linkletter was master of ceremonies in Appleton Auditorium of the Fuller Arts Center for a ninety-minute performance by student singers, dancers, and musicians, and by the American National Theater Academy, which had been based at the

College for twenty years. On the next day, at an executive session of the College's trustees, Locklin read his letter of retirement, to take effect June 30, 1985.

Board Chairman William J. Clark, commenting that this was no time for speeches, gaveled the meeting into adjournment. Two days later, Locklin read the letter at a meeting of faculty and staff in Marsh Memorial Chapel.

"Of course, I'm going to miss being president of Springfield College and I do love the job a great deal, but I really love the College more than the job," Locklin was quoted as saying.

Locklin later noted that he would be "on the job" for the next year, until June 30. "If anyone thinks I'm going to be a lame-duck president, they are sadly mistaken," the hard-working president promised.

Soon thereafter, Clark appointed his immediate predecessor, Willis H. Hayes, to chair a trustee presidential selection committee to choose the College's tenth president.

THE FINAL YEAR

If anything, the pace of the Locklin presidency was more intense during its final year. During that meeting of faculty and staff in May 1984, Locklin outlined his major plans for his final year: developing the College's wellness programs, including an International Wellness Conference in cooperation with the Japanese YMCA; finding new uses for the building on Alden Street after the Naismith Memorial Basketball Hall of Fame relocated to its new facility in downtown Springfield; and preparing for a coast-to-coast tour addressing alumni and business leaders about the College's future.

Calvin J. Martin directed the Centennial planning until his death in 1981.

About that future, Locklin summed up his feelings crisply to the assembled faculty and staff in Marsh Chapel: "The future of Springfield College is extremely bright. It is a unique institution with its Humanics philosophy and dedication to training people-helpers. It is fiscally sound. The new academic facilities are paid for and there are no mortgages to burn. Our curriculum is vibrant and constantly changing to respond to the emerging needs of our students."

Another key priority for Locklin in his final year as president was the planning and implementation of the College's centennial celebration. Calvin J. Martin, who had retired as vice president in 1979, directed the early centennial planning efforts until his death in the spring of 1981. Martin and Locklin were the driving forces behind the writing and publication of the first edition of this book.

Hubert Hill, for seventeen years the director of student activities, became executive secretary of the Springfield College Centennial Commission following Martin's death. Other members of the commission included: President Locklin; Charles Weckworth, Distinguished Springfield College Professor of Humanics; Edwin Hurley III, executive assistant to the president; Joseph McAleer, director of public relations, and Keith O'Connor, assistant director; Vern Cox, alumni director; Diane Potter, professor of physical education; and Gerry Davis, librarian. Chairman of the commission was Richard Garvey, former trustee chair, editor of *The Springfield Daily News*, and author of the first edition of this book.

Hubert Hill, retired student activities director, was the Centennial Commission's executive secretary.

Centennial logo.

As early as 1981, three full years before the start of the centennial celebration, the Centennial Commission set out five goals:

1. Focus local, national, and international attention on the Humanics philosophy of the College in its preparation of young people for service

2. Expand and strengthen the College's YMCA heritage

3. Relate other important persons, institutions, and agencies to Springfield College

4. Broaden Springfield College's leadership in higher education and social service

5. Encourage help from local, national, and international leaders in continuing a creative future for the College

The centennial celebration was a year-long affair, and it began, appropriately enough, at the summer Olympics in Los Angeles. The "Olympic Connection" has long been important to Springfield College alumni, faculty, and staff, but the Springfield College reunion at the 1984 summer games in Los Angeles was special, helping to launch officially the College's 100th birthday celebration.

Scott Willson, senior vice president; Ed Steitz, director of athletics and a member of the U.S. Olympic Committee; and Vern Cox, alumni director, greeted members of the Springfield College family at a reception July 27 at the Century Plaza Hotel.

Art Linkletter (second from left) returned to campus in May 1985 to speak at the centennial commencement. Honorary degree recipients included Louise Appleton, a prominent Springfield civic leader whose family has been part of Springfield College since the beginning; and Darryl Stingley, former wide receiver for the New England Patriots, whose football career ended after a tragic spinal cord injury and who then directed his activities toward humanitarian efforts.

Said Cox: "I can't think of a better site than the summer Olympics for our 100th anniversary celebration to receive worldwide attention. Many Springfield College graduates from around the world are now leaders of athletics in their homelands, as well as heads of their country's Olympic movement."

Ed Steitz added this exclamation point: "No institution over the years has contributed more leadership to the Olympic movement than Springfield College," noting that the International Olympic Committee had awarded the College a trophy marking the involvement of its alumni in the games.

The on-campus kickoff and "Springfield College Day at the Big E" both took place in September. On-campus events included a formal ceremony with Locklin, Garvey, and Springfield Mayor (and later Congressman) Richard Neal, as well as a ribbon-cutting, a hot dog roast, fireworks, and an ecumenical centennial folk mass.

In November, Marge Paw, adjunct professor of art, coordinated the "Centennial Art Exhibit" showcasing the work of LeRoy Nieman in Babson Library's Hastings Gallery, as many owners of originals and prints by the premier artist of the sporting world loaned them for the show.

The College commissioned the Springfield Symphony Orchestra to present a collegiate "pops" concert in October, and Linkletter hosted the Gymnastics Home Show at the Springfield Civic Center during Homecoming in November. Solon Cousins, national executive of the YMCA, came to the campus to speak at a special centennial program.

Founders' Day was celebrated on January 28, 1985, the anniversary of the date on which the Commonwealth of Massachusetts granted the College its charter in 1885. To join in the celebration, alumni associations throughout the country held "Happy

As part of its 100th anniversary observance, the College commissioned the Springfield Symphony Orchestra to present a collegiate "pops" concert in October 1984.

Centennial commencement.

Art Linkletter hosted the Gymnastics Home Show at the Springfield Civic Center during Homecoming weekend.

Birthday Socials" during the weekend of January 26-28. The on-campus program featured the first public performance of the "Springfield College Centennial Anthem," written by Gil Vickers, professor emeritus of music education. Accompanied by his wife, Florence, on the piano, Vickers sang the anthem during festivities at the new Fuller Arts Center.

In April, the Hosagas of Springfield College transformed Blake Arena into a Native American village, where visitors experienced the early lifestyle of the Native Americans.

Linkletter returned to Springfield in May to speak at the centennial commencement. Honorary degree recipients included Louise Appleton, a prominent Springfield civic leader whose family has been part of Springfield College since the beginning; and Darryl Stingley, former wide receiver for the New England Patriots, whose football career ended after a tragic spinal cord injury and who directed his activities toward humanitarian efforts until his death in 2007.

The Women's Centennial Committee staged a series of seminars, and the annual Peter Karpovich Lecture was presented that year in Atlanta, at the convention of the American Association of Health, Physical Education, Recreation, and Dance (AAHPERD), which was also celebrating its 100th birthday.

Centennial programming was added to the alumni reunions May 31-June 2. The programming highlight of the four-day weekend was the Presidential Forum in Marsh Chapel—a reunion of four men who had collectively held the office of president of Springfield College for thirty-seven years: Paul Limbert (1946-52), Donald Stone (1953-57), Glenn Olds (1958-65), and Bill Locklin (1965-85). It was a rare moment in the 100-year history of the College.

Reporting on the historic event, *Triangle* magazine had this to say: "Inside, when you saw the four men laughing and posing for the television cameras and photographers in front of the stained-glass windows, you knew this was a historic moment, never to be repeated. People were happy to stand and be able to witness the four presidents of Springfield College grapple with the increasingly thorny issue of the relevance of Humanics at Springfield College in 1985."

Left to right: former Springfield College Presidents Dr. Glenn Olds, Dr. Donald Stone, and Dr. Paul Limbert joined President Wilbert Locklin in the Marsh Chapel for a 1985 celebration honoring the College's 100th anniversary.

At the time of his retirement, Locklin's signature was on the diplomas of more than half of all living alumni throughout the world. Imagine—in thousands of offices, dens, and living rooms in dozens of nations around the globe, one might encounter framed Springfield College diplomas with the familiar signature "Wilbert E. Locklin" at the bottom.

During the twenty years of Locklin's presidency, the College's curriculum had been transformed, new international exchange programs had been inaugurated, and the

College's physical plant had been greatly expanded. The net equity of the College had tripled during Locklin's tenure, as had the College's endowment.

Thanks to two successful capital campaigns, Locklin had been able to add a startling number of new facilities to the campus: the Art Linkletter Natatorium, Cheney Hall, the Towne Student Health Center, the Maroon Building (later named after Locklin), Babson Library, Benedum Field (now Stagg Field), Blake Track and Field, Bemis Science Hall (now Hickory Hall), the Physical Education Complex, Loveland Chapel, and the Fuller Arts Center.

Leaving the President's House following Reunion Weekend in June 1985, the Locklins moved to their own home for the first time in twenty years, at 225 Prynnwood Road in Longmeadow, and continued to enjoy their "getaway" cottage in the Berkshires during the summers. (Locklin had always been a very hard worker, but at 4 p.m. on Friday afternoons in the summer, you didn't get in the president's way when he set out for the Berkshires. By the same token, you steered clear on subsequent early Monday mornings, when he was coming back down the mountain, on his way back to the campus, and his desk.)

Locklin remained "professionally active as a consultant in philanthropy and independent higher education" for many years before his death in March 2006, a week before his predecessor, Glenn Olds.

Centennial banquet in Blake Arena.

The new Allied Health Sciences building was opened during the Falcone years—housing the departments of health fitness, cardiac rehabilitation, movement science, athletic training, and the newly accredited physical therapy program. Before its renovation, the building had been vacant for more than a year, since the Naismith Memorial Basketball Hall of Fame had moved to its new quarters in downtown Springfield.

Chapter 10

Falcone:
East Campus Tempest

rank Falcone's sporty jet-black BMW convertible was
a distinct change from the staid four-door Buick sedan
driven by Locklin. And speaking of changes, the spirited
noontime pick-up basketball games in which the new president
competed—the word is not chosen lightly—contrasted with
the Locklin style of chatting amiably with faculty, staff, and
students over coffee or lunch, or on a convenient campus bench.

Engaging and energetic, Frank S. Falcone assumed the presidency of Springfield College
on July 1, 1985. He was warmly welcomed by a faculty and staff primed for new leadership, committed to strengthening the College in every way, and eager to work colle-
gially in reasserting the mission of the institution.

In his first campus speech, Falcone invited his audience to work with him in guiding the
College into the future. He said he expected to launch a capital campaign "immediately" to strengthen financial aid resources for students, enhance faculty development,
and move beyond heavy dependence on tuitions. And he promised to put financial
resources into programs and people, not bricks and mortar.

The new president was applauded enthusiastically. However, the promises made in July
1985 were to remain largely unfulfilled when Falcone left the presidency amid conflict
some six-and-a-half years later.

The selection of Falcone was the result of an extensive eight-month search. The search
committee appointed to the task, in need of a suitable location to do its work on an
already overcrowded campus, had settled on the northern third of the Marsh Conference Room, overlooking what is now Naismith Green. The space had originally been
partitioned off from what was, at the time, the Graduate Lounge, to provide an office
for the director of graduate admissions. A conference table and some filing cabinets were
moved in, a lock was procured for the door, and the committee began its work.

As one of three finalists, Falcone had withstood the demanding sequence of interviews
with faculty, staff, administration, and trustees. As part of the process, several student
representatives, including the president of the Student Government Association and the
editor-in-chief of the *Springfield Student*, had spent time interviewing the prospective
president on the campus. He had received the standard unanimous vote from the
trustees. He was, as they say, fully vetted.

Frank S. Falcone was warmly welcomed
by a faculty and staff primed for new
leadership, but left the presidency amid
conflict six-and-a-half years later.

The new president was a native of Kenosha, Wisconsin. Falcone was somewhat familiar with higher education in the Pioneer Valley, having received a Ph.D. in history from the University of Massachusetts Amherst. He had earned his undergraduate degree from the University of Wisconsin and a master's in history at the University of Denver.

Filling out the Falcone resume was attendance at Harvard University's Institute of Educational Management and the University of Michigan's Consortium for Political Research.

Before coming to Springfield College, Falcone had served as executive vice president of Pace University in White Plains, New York, and in a number of senior positions at Ithaca College in Ithaca, New York, including provost and assistant to the president.

The Falcones moved into the president's residence on Alden Street less than thirty days after the departure of the Locklins, following the latter's twenty-year residency. Falcone noted that he intended to spend as much time as possible with his wife, Judy; his daughter, Jennifer (at the time a freshman at the University of Massachusetts Amherst); and his sixteen-year-old son, Jeffrey.

In contrast to Locklin, who was age sixty-five when he retired, Falcone was forty-four. He was viewed by many observers at the time as a savvy, personable, high-energy, get-it-done guy with a strong record of administrative successes. He was, people felt, just the man to start the necessary change process, raise some money, and represent the College well. The chemistry seemed to be right, the expectations high.

INAUGURATION DAY

"I am proud to invest you as the tenth president of Springfield College." With those words, intoned by John F. Cauley, vice chair of the Board of Trustees, Frank S. Falcone was formally inaugurated in Blake Arena on November 9, 1985. In attendance were

November 9, 1985: Falcone speaks at his inauguration.

Falcone and John Cauley, vice chair of the Board of Trustees, lead the inauguration processional.

142

more than eighty representatives of colleges and universities, along with a number of alumni, faculty, students, and city, state, and national representatives.

Springfield Mayor (now U.S. Congressman) Richard E. Neal said he took pride in Springfield College because the school "carries the name of this city to every corner of the globe." Raymond A. Jordan, Jr., a member of the Massachusetts House of Representatives, noted that Springfield College had been dedicated to the same purpose for more than 100 years—helping people. And U.S. Representative Edward P. Boland, in whose district the College was located, brought with him "the greetings of the United States of America."

As reported in the *Springfield Student*, the man they came to honor sat solemnly throughout all the preliminary speeches. But when the Presidential Medallion was placed around his neck, Frank S. Falcone broke into a radiant smile.

PRESIDENTIAL UPDATES

At the outset of his presidency, Falcone seemed determined to set an example in fostering good communications on the campus. In an interview with the *Student* in February 1986, he identified three issues on which he said he would focus his efforts at the start of his presidency: running Academic Affairs as a single division, rather than multiple divisions; enhancing the College's relationship with the surrounding community; and improving the quality of student life.

On this latter point, Falcone noted, he would look at "whether we are doing enough, whether we are doing the right things, what we are doing wrong, and try to see if we are living up to the philosophy and standards of this school."

Three months later, in another *Student* interview, Falcone noted concerns about the College's financial situation, saying he would like to increase the College's endowment

When the Presidential Medallion was placed around his neck, Falcone broke into a radiant smile.

Falcone (second from left) with inauguration guests: Richard Neal, then mayor of Springfield; U.S. Representative Edward Boland; Massachusetts Representative Raymond Jordan.

to "do the things we can't do right now. We could enhance the quality of life around here, support programs and people who are really worth supporting, but we just can't go too far in supporting them right now."

Falcone also noted in passing that "fundraising has to become much more aggressive at Springfield College."

Left unsaid by Falcone among all these goals was another goal the new president kept pretty much to himself: to move the College away from its focus on physical education and towards becoming more of a liberal arts institution. As events in other arenas overtook the president, he was obliged to put that matter on hold. When he was succeeded by Bill Bromery in 1992, the issue became moot; Bromery said he was "dead set" against any such change.

Ed Bilik '57 coached more basketball seasons and won more basketball games than anyone at the Birthplace of Basketball.

Bilik's 1975-76 team poses for its yearbook shot, with Bilik kneeling at left in the front row. Current men's basketball coach Charlie Brock '76 is second row center (#40).

PERSONNEL CHANGES

Ed Bilik '57, faculty member since 1959, who coached more basketball seasons (20) and won more basketball games (322) than anyone else at the Birthplace of Basketball, relinquished his coaching duties following the 1985-86 season, but remained a member of the faculty. Not long after that, to the surprise of almost no one, Bilik was tapped to be director of athletics, succeeding Ed Steitz, who retired after a distinguished thirty-three-year career.

Bilik's appointment was just one of several faculty and staff changes during this period. Taken together, the changes served as a foreshadowing of things to come under Falcone.

Paul Congdon '44 stepped down as academic dean after twenty-one years and, following a sabbatical, "stepped up" to return to the classroom full-time on July 1, 1986.

144

Bob Palmer   Paul Congdon   Martin Anisman   Carol Taylor   Scott Taylor

Following a search, Martin Anisman, formerly the dean of the School of Arts and Sciences at Southern Connecticut State University, came to the College as vice president for academic affairs and dean of the faculty.

Anisman left Springfield College in 1989 to become president of Sam Houston State University in Huntsville, Texas. Congdon retired from the College in May 1988.

Around the same time Anisman was hired, Bob Palmer '65—who had served twenty years in various positions in admissions, financial aid, and development—was tapped by Falcone to be vice president of admissions.

Early in the Falcone presidency, what came to be a regular pattern of shifting of personnel was established:

• Carol Taylor '64, associate director of career planning and placement counseling and a key member of the presidential search committee to identify Locklin's successor, was named assistant to the president, succeeding Ed Hurley III.

• Scott Taylor '66, Carol Taylor's husband, who had been director of student activities, was named acting director of alumni affairs.

FALCONE'S FIRST YEAR

Summing up his first semester as president for a reporter from the *Student*, Falcone noted: "I was highly visible on campus and talked to many students, faculty members, administrators, and others to better understand the specifics of how the school operates. I couldn't impose all of my ideas and changes without first knowing what needed to be changed and how these changes could be implemented."

During the summer of 1986, a number of campus offices were moved and/or renovated. Most prominently, the Office of the President was relocated to the first floor of Marsh Memorial from the second floor of the Administration Building, where it had been since before Doggett. The Office of Alumni Relations was relocated to the lower level of Marsh, while the Office of Development, the vice president for academic affairs, and the vice president of administration were assigned to the second floor of Marsh.

In the fall of 1986, as part of his effort to improve campus communications, Falcone instituted President's Breakfasts with students. The *Student* editorialized about "a step in the right direction, as it diminishes the separation between administration and students."

The editorial added: "Perhaps the administration should not only continue the breakfasts with students, but also open the option up to the faculty...."

This Falcone chose not to do, and the implications of that decision would soon become clear as the relationship between the president and the faculty began to deteriorate.

THE ALLIED HEALTH SCIENCES CENTER

In December 1986 Falcone proudly announced that the former Naismith Memorial Basketball Hall of Fame building on Alden Street would become the Allied Health Sciences Center, housing the departments of health fitness, cardiac rehabilitation, movement science, athletic training, and the newly accredited physical therapy program. The renovated building would include eighteen faculty offices, a film analysis lab, a

Renovations in progress: The former Naismith Memorial Basketball Hall of Fame gets a makeover, to be transformed into the Allied Health Sciences building.

computer lab, five large laboratory/classrooms, five conference rooms, and a new research area.

The building had been vacant for more than a year, since the Hall of Fame had moved to its new quarters in downtown Springfield on the riverfront in the summer of 1985. Under the conditions of a long-term lease on the building, ownership reverted to the College. Groundbreaking for a $1.6-million renovation took place in the spring of 1987, and renovations were completed in the fall of 1988.

Falcone initiated a localized fundraising campaign to complete financing for the Allied Health Sciences Building. And he took some steps to prepare for some serious fundraising. He announced the creation of the David Allen Reed Society, an organization named in honor of the College's founder which recognized loyal financial supporters of the College who made gifts of more than $1,000 in a fiscal year. And he proceeded with a search to fill the new position of vice president for college advancement, a position which was soon filled by Joan Patota—who, Falcone said at the time, came to the College with twenty years' experience in higher education development, alumni relations, and public relations.

A DISTINGUISHED ALUMNUS PASSES AWAY

On July 11, 1987, Dr. Tom Waddell '59 died at age forty-nine, following a long struggle against AIDS-related illnesses. Rev. Ken Childs, the campus minister, writing in his *Student* column, described the full scope of Waddell's achievements: "Some will remember him as the best all-around athlete in SC history. He co-captained the gymnastics team, garnered All-East honors in football after a legendary diving TD catch, and single-handedly outscored the entire Amherst track team. At the age of thirty, he took a sixth in the Olympic decathlon. Some will remember him as a dedicated and compassionate physician—volunteering in African and South American hospitals, serving as the ship's doctor in oceanographic expeditions, working in Saudi Arabia, Lebanon, London, and San Francisco. Some will remember him as a symbol of the moral conflicts of the Vietnam era, a physician who volunteered to be a paratrooper but refused to be part of the carnage of Vietnam. Some will remember him as a homosexual who founded the Gay Olympic Games as part of his ... long struggle to dispel homosexual stereotyping and bigotry. But those who knew him best will remember Tom Waddell '59, as a sensitive, compassionate, gifted and courageous human being," Rev. Childs concluded.

Sportswriter and ABC correspondent Dick Schaap agreed with Rev. Childs. Schaap had sought out Waddell and interviewed him extensively. The two men had collaborated on a book titled *Gay Olympian*. Later, Schaap said this about Waddell: "He may have been the most impressive human being I ever met."

The life of this distinguished Springfield College graduate was celebrated in a special service in Marsh Chapel on Saturday, September 26, 1987. Waddell was inducted into the Springfield College Athletic Hall of Fame in 1990.

Tom Waddell '59, M.D., founded the Gay Games, a quadrennial arts and athletic event open to anyone, fourteen years after he competed in the decathlon for the U.S. in the Mexico City Olympics. He was the subject of a book by sportswriter Dick Schaap.

Trio of alumni relations directors: Scott Taylor '66 (served under Falcone), Hal Lynch '41 (served under Olds and Locklin), Vern Cox '44 (served under Locklin and Falcone).

Current incumbent Tamie Kidess Lucey '81 G'82, with eighteen years in the Falcone, Bromery, and Flynn administrations, is the College's longest-serving alumni relations director, and the first woman to hold that post.

ACQUISITION OF THE SCHOOL OF HUMAN SERVICES

By nearly any yardstick, one of the primary milestones of the Falcone years was the acquisition of the School of Human Services (SHS) from New Hampshire College in May 1988. SHS offered opportunities for experienced direct-care workers and mid-level managers in human services agencies to improve the delivery of services to their clients. The school's weekend-college format enabled students to earn the credentials required to gain career advancement within their agencies.

Established in 1976 and based in New Hampshire, the school was accredited by the New England Association of Schools and Colleges and offered bachelor's and master's degrees. The curriculum included attendance at weekend classes, independent study, and completion of intensive group projects.

The School of Human Services had been founded on a business model that required revenues from tuitions to be always in balance with expenditures. Thus, any shortfall in admissions necessitated a corresponding reduction in the school's operating budget. After the school's acquisition by Springfield College, and periodically thereafter, the College's Board of Trustees reaffirmed that business model.

The new school fit the mission and the tradition of Springfield College in a unique way, by focusing on non-traditional students. The "typical" SHS student was a non-white female in her late thirties who had a family and was employed. In reporting the acquisition, the *Student* noted that "most of the school's 700 students have worked an average of eight years in social services, and many of its 1,800 alumni are presently administrators in various state and social service agencies."

148

Despite the natural compatibility with the College's mission, the move was vaguely criticized by some at the time as not being quite "in keeping" with the "image" of Springfield College. In retrospect, however, it's clear that the acquisition of SHS made it possible for the College to provide new mission-consistent opportunities for students throughout the country, and helped to spread the news about the College nationwide and even worldwide.

Since being "incorporated" into Springfield College in 1988, SHS has grown to be the most successful school of its kind, and today it is an integral part of the Springfield College educational portfolio. Now encompassing eleven sites around the country, including the campus-within-a-campus in Springfield, SHS serves about 2,000 students —most of them "non-traditional."

Announcing the acquisition, Falcone said, "Since its founding in 1885, Springfield College has continued to develop programs that respond to the changing needs of society."

THE CHEMICAL FIRE

In June 1988, a hot, smelly chemical fire at Advanced Laboratories, Inc., at the corner of Allen and Walnut Streets, raged out of control for three days. The blaze left a chlorine cloud four blocks wide and two miles long, forcing the evacuation of more than 20,000 nearby residents. This included a few Springfield College students remaining on the campus, who were evacuated to Western New England College, where they remained for the duration. Visibility in the neighborhood was limited to fifty feet. It was called the most serious chemical-related emergency in Massachusetts history.

Commenting on the fire for the media, sophomore Stacey Hall said, "At midnight we were told to evacuate because of a chlorine cloud. We could smell the chlorine really bad when we stepped into the hallway outside our rooms in Gulick. We then evacuated to WNEC, and could still smell the chlorine and see the cloud. It was really gross."

WOMEN'S ATHLETICS: THE 25TH ANNIVERSARY

During the 1988-89 academic year, Springfield College observed the 25th anniversary of women's varsity athletics. It was a joyous year-long celebration, with special programs at Homecoming and Reunion, a film salute in Fuller's Appleton Auditorium, and an art exhibit featuring a Leroy Nieman painting of Olympic gymnast Cathy Rigby.

There was an exhibition basketball game between female faculty/administrators and members of various women's varsity teams; students wore uniforms from the early days of women's basketball, and the game ended in a 56-56 tie. A slide show and pictorial display of "25 Years of Springfield Women's Athletics" was presented in the old Beveridge Center in conjunction with "National Girls and Women in Sports Day." And at Reunion in June, Mimi Murray '61, Diane Potter '57, and Dottie Zenaty '65 were honored for their extensive contributions to women's sports at the College, nationally, and internationally.

Fall 1988: Celebrating "25 years of Women's Athletics" at Springfield College. This photograph, taken before the exhibition basketball game between female faculty/administrators and members of various women's varsity teams, includes, in the first row, the coaches of the first four women's varsity teams at Springfield College: Martha Van Allen (left), head coach of field hockey and assistant coach of basketball; Jone Bush (second from left), head coach of basketball and tennis; and Diane Potter '57 (right), head coach of softball. Also in the front row, third from left, is Dottie Zenaty '65, who, remarkably enough, played on *all four* of those first teams.

THE TOWNHOUSES

During the late 1980s, the College faced a residence hall crunch, causing many first-year students to live in triples (temporarily) and seven residence hall lounges to be used to house students (also temporarily). Falcone moved quickly to remedy the situation, and the result was a new residence hall such as had never been seen on the campus.

Overlooking Benedum Field (now Stagg Field), the twenty Townhouse units, each with eight private bedrooms, could accommodate 160 students. Each unit had a large living room, combination kitchen/dining area, and two bathrooms. And the units were *air-conditioned.*

Residence in the Townhouses was restricted to seniors. The building filled up quickly as soon as it opened in late 1989, following some construction delays. The handsome design of the building added to its appeal.

In a November 1989 letter to the campus community, Falcone wrote, "The opening of the Townhouse project signals a major step towards our goals of accommodating more students on campus and easing the burden that off-campus student housing places on the surrounding community."

The Townhouses, seen from the perspective of Benedum Field (today Stagg Field).

150

In the same letter, Falcone noted that trustees had authorized the purchase of the Standard Electric Time Building (today Herbert P. Blake Hall and the Graduate Annex). "The addition and renovation of this property will allow us to provide as many as 235 additional units for student housing, much-needed space for classroom use, and office space."

EMBEZZLEMENT

In March 1989, the *Union-News* reported that a forty-one-year-old former administrator of the Physical Plant Department (precursor of today's Facilities and Campus Services) had died in his garage shortly after the local district attorney's office came to his home to question him about money allegedly embezzled from the College. Following an internal investigation, the amount in question was determined to be $612,000.

The district attorney's office got involved after College officials specifically contacted the office "with a suggestion that funds were missing from certain accounts" in the physical plant area, the newspaper said. The story of the investigation surfaced when the *Union-News* received an unsigned letter laying out details of the probe.

In April, another *Union-News* article reported that the physical plant director had left a $350,000 estate. In June, the paper reported autopsy results: The administrator "took his own life," dying of acute carbon monoxide intoxication, caused by inhalation of car-exhaust fumes.

PERSONNEL CHANGES: ROUND TWO

Round two of the personnel changes under Falcone took place in September 1989, with the sudden change in duties for Jack Costello, dean of students, and the appointment of Scott Taylor, director of alumni affairs, as interim dean of students. Costello would take a one-year sabbatical, then return as director of student health services and a faculty member. Already a tenured faculty member, Costello described his reaction to the announcement as "surprised and shocked."

CLOSING OF ALDEN STREET REDUX

Every Springfield College president since Doggett has expressed a desire to eliminate— or at least slow down—the fast-moving traffic on the street that bisects the campus. Over the years, proposals have been floated for everything from a complete ban on vehicular traffic on Alden Street to modified plans involving speed bumps, radar tracking, and pedestrian crossings.

Most people believed that the campus would be quieter and safer as a result. But through the years, each time the College proposed any change to Alden Street traffic patterns, the effort was stopped in its tracks by objections from the College's neighbors, who saw it as an unwanted intrusion in their neighborhood.

Jack Costello: "Surprised and shocked."

One can certainly understand the neighbors' preferences in this regard. Still, a succession of presidents has raised the question: Why can't we find a middle ground on this issue?

In May 1989, speaking at his second annual State of the College address in Marsh Chapel, Falcone addressed the issue of closing Alden Street thusly: "I will lay down on Alden Street if that is what it takes to close it. We are looking to have a temporary closing of Alden Street for a few months to study it. I want to see Alden Street closed."

In October 1989, Falcone asked Kateri Walsh, the newly appointed director of community relations who was (and is today) also a sitting city councilor, to conduct a "fact-finding mission" in the community on how neighbors felt about the idea of closing Alden Street. The results surprised no one, least of all Walsh. After a flurry of negative publicity in the local media, the issue was dropped once again, and would be re-examined during the Bromery years.

CAMPUS IMPROVEMENTS

As students, faculty, and staff returned to the campus in the fall of 1989, they noticed several improvements to the look of the campus. As the *Student* put it: "Schoo Hall's once tri-colored classroom walls are now one universal color. Upon entering the Natatorium, we are no longer rushed with the smell of chlorine. Short cuts to Cheney Hall and Fuller Arts Center are now hindered by fences that protect our ever flourish-

Physical improvements in the campus could not mask the growing concern about Falcone among the faculty.

Springfield Student

Volume 104, No. 3   Springfield, MA   Thursday, Oct. 5, 1989

Alums Receive Social Justice Award

James Genasci, Springfield College Professor of Physical Education, and his wife Jean, a teacher/librarian, were recently honored by the New England Methodist Church for their efforts in addressing homophobia and oppression. The Genascis were presented with the 1989 New England United Methodist Award for Excellence in Social Justice Actions, during a ceremony held at Springfield College this summer.

The Award that the Genascis received is presented annually by lay persons whose work to achieve social justice exemplifies the Judeo-Christian justice tradition embodied in the United Methodist social principles. The Genascis, who were nominated by Trinity United Methodist Church in Springfield, were presented the award by Bishop F. Herbert Skeete, the spiritual leader of 124,000 United Methodists in New England.

In 1986 the Genascis founded the Pioneer Valley Chapter of P-FLAG (Parents, Families/Friends of Lesbians and Gays), after their son told them he was gay. In 1987, they organized the Campus Alliance For Equality (C.A.F.E.), a group of students, faculty, and administrators whose goal is to alleviate the fear and oppression of sexual minorities

within the Springfield College Family. Also in that year, the Genascis organized and conducted the first Gayness/Oppression/Homophobia Series of eight seminars held on the Campus. That Series is now in its third year, and will host a presentation entitled, AIDS and the Campus, on Wednesday, October 25 at 7 p.m. in Locklin Hall, room 233.

Membership in C.A.F.E. is open to any member of the SC Family interested in assuaging the homophobia and oppression which occurs on campus, and in society at large. C.A.F.E. sponsors programs in the dormitories, co-sponsors some of the Gayness/Oppression/Homophobia Seminars, and maintains contact with support groups on other campuses. Members of C.A.F.E. also participate in off-campus activities, such as the Rally at the State House in support of the Gay and Lesbian Civil Rights Bill currently being debated in the Massachusetts legislature.

The Alumni/ae Alliance For Equality (A.A.F.E.) has recently been formed to offer support to sexual minority graduates of Springfield College and their allies. Anyone interested in joining any of the organizations, can contact Dr. Genasci in Room 306, Judd Gym, or by calling either 788-3221 or 532-4883.

Concerned Faculty Question Falcone

By Dave Gerome
Associate Editor

Pres. Frank Falcone makes changes and raises eyebrows.

Task Forced To Be Launched

By Natalie C. Corridan
Student Staff

There has been a great deal of talk about the "task forces" around campus, but no real information. This article is designed to clarify some of the rumors.

What exactly is a Presidential Task Force? At the end of last semester President Falcone sent out a letter to the entire Springfield College family. This letter

chairs, Tammy Kidess-Lucey and Patricia Rau, expressed how valuable he students in their group have been in terms of providing the force with priceless insights into situations here on campus. Dedicated students wishing to take part in any of these task forces are greatly encouraged to do so. (Speak up it is the student body's chance to be heard!!)

ing green grass. The traditional 'Snack Bar' became known as 'Le Café' this past year, and now has added a new dimension, 'Le Mini-Mart.' The Astroturf has a new scoreboard and press-box. And the newly paved/fenced parking lots now come fully equipped with guard shacks (and guards!)."

But the physical improvements could not mask the growing concerns among the faculty. "Concerned Faculty Question Falcone" was the headline in the October 5, 1989 issue of the *Student*. Three key issues: reassignment of the dean of students, appointment of a new interim dean of students, and the process of decision making at the College.

EAST CAMPUS AND REEDS LANDING

Every so often in a college presidency, a single watershed event looms so large that it overtakes everything else in importance and becomes a symbol of that presidency. Such was the case with Frank Falcone and his handling of the controversy over the use of East Campus.

The East Campus of Springfield College is a bucolic retreat from the grit and noise of the city and the hustle and bustle of the campus. It includes acres of forest ecosystem, a mile of shoreline on Lake Massasoit, an outdoor fire-pit with seating for 200, a picnic grove, camping facilities, and an authentic southwestern pueblo.

The East Campus Outdoor Learning Center for adventure-based training and development had been established in 1930 "to integrate the advantages of outdoor recreation, individual and group leadership, adventure training, and focused human development." For thousands of Springfield College students, the first experience with East Campus was Freshman Camp. Many students, faculty, staff, and alums considered East Campus "a special place," almost sacred ground.

Perhaps, then, it should not have surprised anyone when, in the fall of 1989, East Campus became, overnight, the centerpiece of an all-campus dust-up rivaled in Springfield College history only by the serious disagreements over theology early in the twentieth century. The East Campus controversy, ultimately, would polarize the College and precipitate the departure of its president.

The first public disclosure of the College's plan for East Campus was the story on page seven of the October 7, 1989 *Springfield Union-News*: The College and Baystate Medical Center had "conducted talks" to construct a "continuing care retirement community" on 23.6 acres of the eighty-one-acre area of East Campus, the paper said. The land would be leased by the College to Baystate for seventy-five years.

It didn't take very long for opposition to the plan to coalesce. Members of the faculty met with the president to discuss the matter. Hundreds of students gathered to hear Falcone describe the plan. The East Campus Coalition was formed, bringing together faculty, staff, students, neighbors, and alumni to "examine the impact" of development of East Campus, identify alternatives, and "develop a Master Plan for the East Campus." The Board of Trustees meeting was picketed. The student association and the faculty voted to oppose the idea. Neighbors, encouraged by some faculty and students, formed "Residents United to Save East Campus."

Falcone listens as Tom Johnson '59, a former trustee, makes a point.

At the time, some said Falcone had been overly "secretive" about his plans to develop East Campus. But a perusal of the *Student* newspaper files tells a different story:

- In May 1988, eighteen months before the first story on the proposed "continuing care retirement community," (now named Reeds Landing) broke in the *Union-News*, the *Student*'s Jeffrey Berk, reporting on a Falcone "update" for students, wrote, "Falcone also said that East Campus will be developed to enhance studies for a nursing and extending life facility."

- In October 1988, Falcone said in a *Student* interview, "We're looking to use part of that site [East Campus] for a health care/life care center, while keeping the mission of the College in mind and maintaining the wooded, rural, quiet aspect of East Campus intact."

- And in May 1989, in another *Student* interview, Falcone noted, "This [center] would bring onto our campus an outlet for our academic programs, a clinical setting for programs."

Curiously, the first formal presentation against development of East Campus did not occur until October 1989, after the article in the *Union-News* had formally broken the news. Professor Tony Maniscalco of the chemistry department presented a series of overheads to about 100 faculty members, and, two days later, to about 500 students. He showed topographical maps of East Campus and indicated where the new facility might be situated.

Soon thereafter, Rev. Ken Childs, the College chaplain, writing in his regular column in the *Student*, called for the formation of a collegium to discuss the subject, similar to the one organized under Locklin in 1970 to consider ways to improve the College.

The plan to develop a part of East Campus did have a few supporters among the faculty. One was Byron Koh, an English professor who had known Falcone since long before the latter was named as president. Koh wrote a strong letter to the *Student* in February 1990, saying, "I support the continuing-care facility on East Campus because it is in keeping with the social service philosophy of Springfield College. It will be a service to a growing segment of our society. Also I support it because it will help students and the college."

The East Campus Coalition summarized the pros and cons of the proposed continuing-care retirement community (CCRC) this way:

The advantages:
1. As enrollments fluctuate, colleges are searching for new sources of revenue to supplement tuition revenue.
2. Other colleges have built similar communities on their campuses, with positive results.
3. The initial payment to be received by the College will become part of the endowment and be used for student financial aid.
4. The proposed facility will provide academic opportunities for allied health majors in terms of fieldwork and internships.
5. Alums will receive preference as residents of the CCRC.

The disadvantages:

1. An invaluable natural area of open woodland will be lost to the College and to the community of Springfield.
2. Academic, co-curricular, and recreational use of the East Campus will be lost to the College and community.
3. The proposed development is inconsistent with the College's stated mission.
4. The designated area for the CCRC is the heart of East Campus.
5. As the main campus has become more congested, more students seek the open space at East Campus.
6. The proposed academic use is limited, and students have similar opportunities in many other facilities in Springfield.
7. This project can be seen as the first nibbling at the property and may set a precedent for more to follow until the land is gone.

Falcone carries his case on East Campus to the campus community with a page-one interview.

By January 13, 1990, after more than a year of discussion, argument, charges, counter-charges, and general turmoil on the campus, it was all over but the shouting—and there was a little of that, including continued letter-writing to the *Student* and talk of a year-long continuous picket in front of Marsh Memorial. The trustees voted 23-9, with six abstentions, to lease a portion of East Campus to Baystate Diversified Health Services for a continuing-care retirement facility—which would become Reeds Landing. The trustees also voted to appropriate a portion of the initial receipts to enhance the remaining parts of East Campus.

Trustees Chair John Cauley said: "For a variety of reasons, chief of which is that we believe this project will be good for the community and good for the College, we agreed to proceed with the lease. Trustees believe the benefits of this project far outweigh the alleged negatives." Cauley went on to say that the trustees were well aware of the "unique value" of East Campus, and that the feelings expressed by faculty, students, alums, and neighbors were earnestly considered.

155

Most observers thought it was unfortunate that the College had to give up part of a place as beautiful and pastoral as East Campus to development. On the other hand, it was certainly true that establishing a continuing-care retirement facility in close proximity to the campus would provide a natural "laboratory" for academic programs and also allow residents of the facility access to College programs.

In the midst of the campus turmoil over East Campus, the accreditation team from the New England Association of Schools and Colleges (NEASC) started and concluded its deliberations and pronounced the College accredited for another ten years.

At a June 18, 1990 meeting, the Springfield City Council unanimously passed the zone change required for the project to go forward.

NEW SENIOR ADMINISTRATION — FALL 1990

As the new school year began in September 1990, there was a new occupant of the dean of students office: Corinne Kowpak, recently arrived from the University of Vermont. There also was a new dean of academic affairs, Adelaide Van Titus, from Temple University, where she had been dean of the School of Pharmacy.

Three months later, Van Titus announced the formation of the Academic Affairs Restructure Committee. This committee's charge was to "conduct an examination of the current structure of the departments and programs in Academic Affairs. Recommend to me a structure for Academic Affairs comprised of clusters of departments and programs with coherent and future-oriented possibilities for academic and disciplinary excellence, research endeavors, and community outreach." This committee's work was to become the basis for the current structure of academic affairs at Springfield College.

THE FINAL DAYS

At the same time the campus was busily preparing for Family & Friends Weekend in 1990, the Faculty Senate voted to investigate what some were calling "gross mismanagement" of the College's financial resources and budget. At the top of the list, according to the *Student*, was an $800,000 budget shortfall, an amount that Falcone had covered with funds from the College's endowment. The faculty also was upset with a disagreement over the amount and distribution method of the faculty's lump-sum salary increases for the coming year.

The words "no-confidence vote" began to be used with increasing frequency, and a number of faculty members predicted a vote at an upcoming faculty meeting. Such a vote, if successful, would imperil what some were calling Falcone's "imperial presidency."

Van Titus scheduled a faculty meeting for October 16 to discuss the issue. A few days later, Falcone met with the faculty. In early November, an all-campus walk-out brought 800 students, faculty, staff, and administrators to the Administration Green (now Naismith Green) for a show of "Springfield College family unity" to provide, in Student Government Association President Stacey Hall's words, "the first real clue to President Falcone that both students and faculty are truly concerned about his lack of communication and leadership." Falcone was said to be "out of town," and the doors to Marsh Memorial were locked by campus police to prevent a takeover of the building.

Adelaide Van Titus joined the College in the fall of 1990 as dean of academic affairs.

In January 1991, in a letter published in the *Student*, Falcone announced that, as a result of his "planned reorganization," twenty-nine staff positions were to be eliminated—fifteen of which were presently vacant and fourteen with employees who would not be rehired as of the end of the fiscal year in May. Falcone cited three external factors in the decision to make staff cuts: "increasing costs of utilities, uncertainty due to the war in the Persian Gulf, and the New England economy."

But the president added, "These planned reductions do not signal a retrenchment and the College is not in a state of financial exigency." He expressed confidence that the fiscal year 1992 budget "will enable us to respond to the unexpected as well as support unplanned opportunities."

THE VOTE OF NO CONFIDENCE

After nearly a full academic year of deliberation and discussion (not to mention years of conflict and turmoil), the faculty of Springfield College filed silently into Locklin Hall, Room 233, on the afternoon of April 17, 1991, and, after some preliminaries, voted "no confidence" in the six-year presidency of Frank Falcone.

In higher education, a vote of no confidence is the most emphatic rejection of a college president that a faculty can assert. This was the first, and thus far the last, presidential no-confidence vote in Springfield College history.

The actual wording of the motion was, "We, the faculty of Springfield College, acting out of deep concern and commitment to the institution we serve, express our lack of confidence in the ongoing presidency of Dr. Frank S. Falcone." The historic vote was 133 in favor, five against, with one abstention.

The meeting was run by Faculty Senate President Paul LeBlanc of the English Department, who, remarkably enough, was untenured. (LeBlanc today serves as president of the University of Southern New Hampshire.)

A week later, representatives of the student body passed a vote of no confidence in the Falcone presidency, 16-2, with one abstention. In the days before the student vote, the Student Government Association sponsored a three-day poll on the issue. The result was 763 in favor of the no-confidence vote, fifty-eight against, with seventy-eight abstaining.

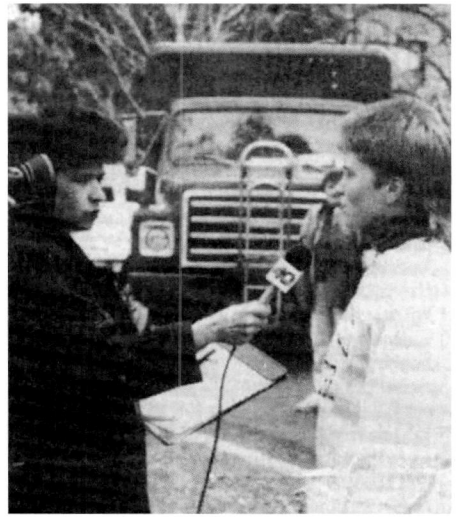

In the midst of all this, also on April 24, Joel Cohen, the sitting Distinguished Springfield College Professor of Humanics, walked deliberately to the podium in Marsh Memorial and somberly delivered the annual Humanics lecture. Cohen's title: "Humanics: Creed vs. Deed." With a bow in the direction of the problems then being faced by Springfield College and the world as a whole, Cohen noted, "This may be the 'best of times' to re-evaluate our propelling philosophy, our heritage."

Scenes from the all-campus walk-out in October 1991.

Cohen's conclusion: "We must, as a cohesive whole, rededicate ourselves to the implementation of Humanics in all of its meanings and applications."

By this time, the controversy had attracted outside attention from local, regional, and national media. Television channels WWLP and WGBY, the *Springfield Union-News*, the Associated Press, the *Boston Globe*, and *USA Today* all covered the story.

Also in the midst of the turmoil, and in celebration of the 100th anniversary of the birth of basketball, Doctor J—aka basketball phenom Julius Irving—spoke at the 1991 commencement exercises.

The *Springfield Student* and local media both covered the vote of no confidence.

Springfield Student

Volume 105, No. 23   Springfield, MA   April 18, 1991

Faculty Votes "No Confidence" in Falcone

By JILL STORMS
Editor

After nearly a full academic year of deliberation and discussion, the faculty of Springfield College voted yesterday afternoon, 133 in favor, in a vote of "no confidence" in 6 year-SC President Dr. Frank S. Falcone. A vote of "no confidence" is the most emphatic rejection of a college president which a recognized body of that college can assert. There were 5 votes against and 1 abstention.

At Wednesday's meeting, faculty members discussed the various options and repercussions of such a vote. Consequently, the following motion was made, "We, the faculty of Springfield College, acting out of deep concern and commitment to the institution we serve, express our lack of confidence in the ongoing presidency of Dr. Frank S. Falcone."

been done so historically.

"I don't dispute that there was a disagreement in this matter," said Falcone. "They (faculty) understood something different than was intended."

According to senior faculty member Dr. Diane Potter, "It's not a misunderstanding, it's a different decision made by the president."

At Tuesday's meeting, Dr. Dietrich Schlobohm stated, "When I came back from Germany in September, I was stunned by the high level of frustration and low morale exhibited by the faculty and around the campus."

Rumors of a "no confidence" vote circulated in early October of last semester when President Falcone and Treasurer Jim Moriarity presented the faculty with the 1990-1991 budget along with a 5% cutback in all departments due to difficult financial

SC And Neighborhood Council Look To Work Together

On March 19, Student Government President Stacey Hall and Dean of Students Corinne Kowpak attended the Old Hill Neighborhood Council meeting at St. John's Church. The residents invited them as a follow up to the discussion of students living off-campus that took place in the Cafe on February 24.

Much of the meeting focused on the relationship between the College and the residents and their "desire for dialogue" as Mr. Watson stated. Spring Fling poses a major concern for the residents. They will not tolerate a situation like last year. Over the next few weeks, the Old Hill Council, which represents the area between Alden Street, State Street, Wilbraham Avenue, and Six Corners, will be pressuring the Springfield Police Department to be less tolerant of infractions of the law, particularly those involving alcohol.

The Council members expressed interest in working with the College in many ways. They would like to be involved with the Lake Massasoit clean-up project, to establish more opportunities for students to do community service, to work with students on voter registration campaigns,

and to utilize more of the College's facilities.

"I think that this meeting was a great beginning for opening communication between the College and the residents, but there are many deep wounds caused by past administrative decisions that must be worked out first," says Hall. Mr. Watson summed the discussion up nicely when he said, "It might seem that we don't want students...It not true. Rather we would like to build a better rapport and work together."

During this academic year, the need for establishing increased communication and better rapport with the area neighbors has taken on an increased importance. The outreach efforts to date attempt to have students gain an understanding of the effect their off-campus behavior has on the community they reside in. Discussion about alcohol violations, noise, damage, theft, and public urination have predominated the conversations at Springfield City Hall, in neighborhood council meetings, and with individuals who have contacted the Dean of Students Office.

As summer waned and September arrived, members of the Springfield College community were rudely jerked back to reality with news on an entirely different subject: The beloved Vern Cox, superb athlete, gifted teacher, talented coach, and part of the campus since 1940, had died from a stroke at the age of 71.

Rev. Ken Childs put it this way in his *Student* column: "It's hard to imagine starting this academic year without Vern Cox. For forty-four years, Vern's handsome smile and twinkling eyes, his gentle presence and humble humanity, were sure signs that the Humanics philosophy, vague and indefinable though it may be, was alive and well at SC."

Over the summer, Falcone had worked on yet another reorganization of his senior staff, in anticipation of the increasing demands of fundraising on his time, he said, and to concentrate more on the areas of enrollment and resources management. In a letter, the new organization was announced:

- A search would be started for a new vice president of finance and administration,

- Once the finance and administration vice presidency was filled, Bob Palmer, currently in that job, would move to the new position of dean of enrollment management,

- Corinne Kowpak, the dean of students, would report to Van Titus, who assumed the additional title of provost,

- Carol Taylor was promoted to vice president and executive assistant to the president and,

- The internal auditors would report directly to the president and the Audit Committee of the Board of Trustees.

After beating AIC, Falcone and players receive the Mayor's Trophy from Mary Hurley, the mayor of Springfield.

Derby Wilson

John Mann

Falcone outside his office with secretary Anne Wierstrom.

Meanwhile, in mid-October, in a dramatic demonstration that life goes on, bulldozers began clearing the proposed site for a permanent two-bedroom, 1,500-square-foot model unit at Reeds Landing. And on the weekend of November 15-16, Springfield College celebrated the 100th anniversary of the birth of the game of basketball. Festivities included the gymnastics Homeshow, the dedication of Naismith Circle in front of the Physical Education Complex, "A Taste of Springfield" in the Benedum Field parking lot, and a football game between Springfield College and in-town rival American International College.

But all through the fall, a series of lengthy, thoughtful letters by political science professor Tom O'Connor appeared in the *Student* newspaper. They argued passionately, relentlessly, for further action on the presidency.

"WELL, I GUESS I'M OUT OF HERE."

In December 1991, John Mann, the immediate past board chair, placed a telephone call to Frank Falcone's office. Derby Wilson, the current board chair, was going to be in town next week. Could the two of them come to see the president for a few minutes on Wednesday?

When Wednesday arrived, the two trustees walked to Marsh Memorial and were ushered into the president's office. The door closed. Some forty-five minutes later, the door opened, the two trustees emerged and left the building, and the door closed again.

After a few minutes, the door opened once more, and the president came out into his outer office and announced to all within hearing: "Well, I guess I'm out of here."

On January 6, 1992, Frank Falcone officially resigned as the tenth president of Springfield College, after six-and-a-half years of controversy and accomplishments. At least two of the decisions he made—to acquire the School of Human Services and to lease a portion of East Campus for development—were criticized at the time. But as the years have gone by, Falcone's decisions—as opposed to the way he went about making and implementing those decisions—have come to be viewed more favorably by many.

Still, in retrospect, the same observation that was made about President Best (1937-46) could also be made about President Falcone: "Although his tenure lasted less than a decade, it was filled with some of the College's most difficult years."

Chapter 11

Bromery:
Healing…and Rupture

When the telephone rang, Bill Bromery—geophysicist, corporate director, and college president—checked caller ID and noted the Houston area code. Must be one of my contacts at Exxon Corporation, he thought. But picking up the phone, Bromery found, on the other end, Derby Wilson.

Walter C. "Derby" Wilson was in charge of the thriving Houston agency for the Massachusetts Mutual Life Insurance Company. More to the point, in May 1991, Wilson had been elected chair of the Board of Trustees of Springfield College.

Now, around the end of 1991, Wilson was calling Bromery to see if he would consider discussing the position of interim president of Springfield College, while a national search was carried on to find a permanent successor to Frank Falcone.

Specifically, Wilson asked Bromery to make a stop in Springfield on his way back to his home in the Amherst hills from the NYNEX Corporation board meeting he was attending in Manhattan.

A few hours later, Bromery pulled into the driveway of the gracious home at 64 Ardsley Road in Longmeadow, Massachusetts. Inside, he shook hands with John Mann, the home's owner and former board chair; Derby Wilson, the current chair; and John Cauley, another former chair.

After some pleasantries, they all sat down in the comfortable chairs in Mann's living room. Before a warming fireplace, they launched into a three-hour discussion revolving around Randolph W. "Bill" Bromery and the presidency of Springfield College.

Reaching out to Bromery made perfect sense, of course. He had quite recently served as interim chancellor of the University of Massachusetts Amherst and interim president of Westfield State College. For the past year, he had been interim chancellor of the Massachusetts Board of Regents of Higher Education in Boston.

In short, he was a highly respected charter member of that elite group of former college and university presidents who are called upon to lend their expertise, temporarily, to institutions with emergency needs.

Bill Bromery was a highly respected charter member of that elite group of former college and university presidents who are called upon to lend their expertise, temporarily, to institutions with emergency needs.

Initial pieces of the College's Facilities Master Plan had fallen into place, including the installation of new Astro Turf on Benedum Field and a repaired roof for the Townhouses.

Recalling that first encounter, John Mann says today, "We had a good meeting. We were all impressed with Bromery's background and experience." There were still some procedural bases to touch, including a final board vote, but it wasn't very long after that meeting in John Mann's living room that Randolph W. Bromery was unanimously elected interim president of Springfield College, effective February 8, 1992.

The task now confronting Bromery was simply stated, but difficult to accomplish: Heal Springfield College.

SOLID-GOLD RESUME

In announcing Bromery's appointment to the campus, Derby Wilson was effusive: "We are extremely delighted to have attracted a candidate of Dr. Bromery's national educational renown to Springfield College. It is a great credit to our fine institution that an individual of Dr. Bromery's stature and experience will be with us as interim president. Dr. Bromery will lead Springfield College forward in the development of our basic Humanics philosophy, and at the same time be part of the...search for a permanent president for Springfield College. The College community will benefit greatly from his broad corporate experience throughout the United States, and his exposure throughout the U.S. will bring a new awareness of our College."

All it took was one glance at Bromery's solid-gold resume to conclude that Wilson was not exaggerating. Bromery enjoyed a national reputation as an engaging educator of considerable accomplishments. It was considered a coup to have him serve as interim president.

The native of Cumberland, Maryland, had more than forty-four years of experience in higher education and government service. After serving in World War II, he'd been associated in many capacities with the United States Geological Survey in Washington, D.C., from 1948 to 1967.

Beginning in 1969, Bromery had served the University of Massachusetts in a number of capacities, including: chairman and professor of geophysics in the department of geology and geography; vice chancellor of student affairs; interim chancellor and later chancellor of the Amherst campus; and executive vice president in the Office of the President.

Bromery had received a doctorate in geology from Johns Hopkins University, a master of science in geology and geophysics from American University, and a bachelor of science in mathematics and physics from Howard University. He'd also been awarded six honorary degrees.

A member of the Cosmos Club, Explorers Club, and Commercial Club of Boston, Bromery had served as president and a fellow of the Geological Society of America, a fellow at the American Association for the Advancement of Science, and a member of numerous other professional societies. His writings had been published in more than 150 professional journals.

Bromery was a leader in the business community as well as in higher education. At the time of his appointment as interim president of Springfield College, he served on the boards of Exxon Corporation, Chemical Bank, NYNEX, and John Hancock Mutual Life Insurance Company. He also served on the boards of trustees of Johns Hopkins University and Mount Holyoke College.

162

As Bromery's arrival was announced, political science Professor Tom O'Connor, continuing his letter writing to the *Student*, shifted his tone: "We all welcome the appointment of Dr. Bromery. . . . As an educator of considerable achievement, his arrival is timely and his talent is sorely needed. . . ."

CONVOCATION

Speaking at the February 7 convocation for the new interim president in Blake Arena, Provost Adelaide Van Titus reflected the feelings of many in the audience: "We welcome you with joy in our hearts and with expectations probably beyond what they should be."

For his part, Bromery was his usual gracious self: "I accept the challenge with humility and also with determination.... I don't want you to lose confidence in where you are now, where you have been, and where you are going to go." Bromery promised his "unwavering commitment and dedication to strengthen the niche that Springfield College has carved out for itself."

Bromery's convocation comment telegraphed his opinions about the idea, espoused by Falcone and others, that the College ought to become more of a traditional liberal arts institution. This Bromery was dead set against.

"I had run into Frank Falcone a couple of times when I was interim president of Westfield State," Bromery recalls today. "I remember telling him that the idea of changing Springfield College into a liberal arts college didn't make sense. In fact, I told him, there were going to be more liberal arts colleges in the country *closing* than there were being born, so you would be rowing upstream." Bromery believed then, and believes today, that Springfield College had established a national reputation in a unique higher education niche, and shouldn't abandon it.

Bromery at his convocation with Tom Wheeler, chair of the Board of Trustees.

Near the end of his remarks at the convocation, Bromery made "a simple request of the campus community" which recalled a longstanding Springfield College tradition—one that had fallen into disuse in recent years: "As we pass each other on the campus from day to day, smile and say hello. I know it may sound corny, but try and see if you do not feel better during the day as you go about your tasks. I predict that small gesture will act as a catalyst in making the institution a better place to teach and to learn. It may even be contagious and infect the new president whom we are about to recruit to lead Springfield College toward our 'shared vision.'"

To reinforce his message, Bromery sent copies of his convocation remarks to the faculty and staff, along with a note expressing his "hope that it will help in setting a tone for our future campus relationships, a tone which has historically existed on this campus. Our relationships should be firmly anchored on trust, honesty, and mutual respect."

Bromery at his convocation with former presidents Locklin (center) and Limbert (right).

Bromery's note went on to stress the importance of addressing that critically important issue, who we are. It read, "It is extremely important for the College to make that determination prior to beginning the search and selection of the next president. The Springfield College family can then tell the next president what we see as the vision of our future. The new president would be expected to accept that shared vision for Springfield College and then to provide the leadership, for the College community, to achieve their goals. The most important component of my brief tenure is to work with the College in preparing to embark on this exciting voyage toward our 'shared vision.'"

THE HEALING BEGINS

As the new interim president began his work, his priority was clear:

Job One was to heal the divisions and the wounds of recent years. In this Bromery made progress. Early on, he took steps to improve communications with all campus constituencies—starting "brown bag" luncheons at which opposing viewpoints were raised and discussed; meeting with student, faculty, and staff leaders to engage in dialogue; developing a plan to write regular letters to the Board of Trustees to keep them informed; and making every effort to make himself visible and available on the campus.

Bromery's visibility on the campus played to his great personal charm and his ease in engaging people in meaningful conversation. He also benefited in this regard from comparisons with his predecessor, who had become less visible in the last couple of years of his presidency. Even though he chose to remain in his longtime family residence in Amherst, rather than move into the president's house, Bromery's visibility on the campus seemed high, at least early on.

IMPROVING TOWN/GOWN RELATIONSHIPS

Another priority for Bromery was to work at improving the town/gown relationships. Over several decades, the neighborhood in which the College is located had shifted from predominantly Irish and Italian to predominantly African American. As the first African American president of Springfield College, Bromery recognized that he had a unique opportunity to improve a relationship that had been slipping in recent years.

One major accomplishment of the early Bromery years in this regard was the establishment and growth of the College's relationship with William N. DeBerry School, an elementary school located on Union Street, a short walk from the center of campus. Early in his presidency, Bromery visited the school and spoke to a number of teachers and students. None of them knew much about Springfield College. Bromery vowed to change that, and a few weeks later there was a Springfield College banner in the main hallway at DeBerry, along with a photograph of Bromery, the College's first African American president.

The first collaboration between the College and DeBerry School was a "reading aloud" program, in which the students, faculty, and staff came to the school and read to students individually. Bromery himself recalls sitting under a tree outside the school on a warm spring afternoon, reading books to DeBerry students. This program was ultimately funded with a small grant and formalized as the Partners Program, which exists today in a much expanded form.

164

The William N. DeBerry School, located on Union Street, is a short walk from the center of campus.

Among the many other community programs started by Springfield College in the Bromery years were Project Spirit, to provide scholarships to Springfield College for deserving local children, and the Sage Program, later folded into the AmeriCorps Program.

A key player in the College's relationships with the community was John Wilson, who today is the College's director of multicultural affairs. Wilson had come to Springfield College as an admissions counselor in the Locklin years, and had been named by Falcone in 1987 to run the new office of minority affairs (today multicultural affairs). Now, with Bromery's interest, the importance and visibility of minority relations were growing, and Wilson saw the opportunity to initiate new programs with the community.

With every year that passed, there seemed to be more College programs with DeBerry School. More Springfield College students, faculty, and staff were making the walk to DeBerry to work and learn, and more DeBerry students were making the reverse trip, too.

However, the College's relationship with the neighborhood was not always positive, as Bromery was to discover. Near the end of his presidency in 1997, just as at least three presidents before him had done, Bromery led yet another attempt to close Alden Street. Bromery's persuasive powers with the neighborhood failed him at that critical juncture, and he was obliged to abandon the effort. Most people on the campus were disappointed with this result, recognizing it as another missed opportunity to transform the campus environment.

These two priorities—healing the campus and improving relationships with the neighborhood—stood out, but Bromery knew the College also faced financial, philosophical, and governance issues, solutions for which were longer term, most likely longer than he expected to remain.

In the spring of his first year as president, Bromery formed the Vision Task Force, to assist with the search for a "president for the 21st century" and "to outline and define the goals of the College encompassing upcoming years."

CHIEFS (AND MAROONS) VS. PRIDE

The College had come a long way since its athletes were dubbed the "Stubby Christians" (because of their size, compared with the Yale football team they played in 1890). But in April 1992, during the course of a *Student* interview conducted by reporter Bryan Hagberg '93, Director of Athletics Ed Bilik '57 made a statement that surprised many who knew the usually traditionalist athletic director. This was the exchange:

> *Student*: There had been some attention focused lately on the nicknames of some of our sports teams. Some people feel that a change should be made, because "Chiefs" is demeaning to many Indian groups. What is your opinion on this issue?
>
> *Bilik*: The native Indian doesn't appreciate being associated and used as a mascot. I believe we have to respect that viewpoint.

Even before the Bilik interview in the *Student*, Rev. Ken Childs, the College chaplain, had raised the issue in his own *Student* column: "It may be time for us to start thinking about a new SC sports symbol. Given the current wave of reassessment of Indian-related symbols, logos, and mascots (Indians, Braves, Redskins, etc.), it might be time to think of an alternative to our own Chiefs."

Bilik's comments and Childs' observations ignited a two-year examination on the suitability, in the 1990s, of the traditional "Chiefs" nickname and mascot for Springfield College sports teams. At the same time, it was felt that having one nickname for the men's teams (Chiefs) and another nickname for the women's teams (Maroons!) created what marketing people called brand confusion.

Displaying his usual smooth blend of humor and sarcasm, Rev. Childs had this to say about "Maroons": "I've always been a little skittish about 'The Maroons,' though; it sounds too much like a bunch of people stranded on a desolate island (marooned for the week). It also lends itself too easily to Bugs Bunny's most caustic insult, 'What a maroon!'"

The resolution for all of this was announced by Bromery in May 1995, coincident with the move to Division III for all intercollegiate sports. After nearly three years of discussion, arguments, committees, open forums, sit-ins, letters to the editor of the *Student*, proposals, and counter-proposals, the decision was made to discard the "Chiefs" and "Maroons" nicknames and use "Pride" for all sports teams.

The original Pride logo, which proved to be short-lived.

The initial reception for the new nickname was decidedly neutral, and the new "Pride" logo featuring a complicated illustration of three lions proved to be a nonstarter. But the brevity of the word "Pride" made it a great headline word, and today the nickname has become second nature to all—as has "Spirit," the College's feline mascot.

THE MOVE TO DIVISION III FOR ALL SPORTS

Another significant decision regarding the College's athletic program was made in early 1993, but was not fully implemented until the fall of 1995. After years of exhaustive study involving the coaching faculty, academic faculty, students, administration, and alumni, it was concluded that the College would switch from NCAA Division II to NCAA Division III for all sports, men's and women's. Division III, it was felt, "best fulfills the needs of our student-athletes," and, Bromery said, represented a better balance between academic interests and athletic pursuits.

Commenting later, Bromery said, "The College has a niche, and athletics is one of the strengths. With the move to Division III, we can begin to schedule schools we should be associated with, athletically and academically." Agreeing wholeheartedly with the decision, Bromery proposed the change to the Board of Trustees, which voted overwhelmingly in favor.

Ken Cerino, the College's sports information director at the time, was encouraged by the change: "Springfield College has operated with a Division III philosophy, playing primarily Division II, with what I like to think have been Division I coaches."

Around the same time, Mimi Murray '61, professor of physical education and former coach of women's gymnastics, achieved national prominence with her election as national president of the American Alliance of Health, Physical Education, Recreation, and Dance (AAHPERD). To this day, Springfield College has provided more presidents to AAHPERD than any other college or university.

Murray, who already had become a key player in winning parity for women's sports through Title IX legislation, delivered the keynote address at the AAHPERD annual convention and visited with President George H.W. Bush at the White House.

REMEMBERING GULICK

As classes began in September 1992, 107 years after the very first class on September 9, 1885, an extraordinary faculty leader was remembered by the College community. Luther Halsey Gulick, who was named to head the physical education department at the age of twenty-three and created the spirit-mind-body triangle, was honored at his gravesite in Springfield's Oak Grove Cemetary by a delegation of seniors and Roland Holstead, director of continuing education. (In later years, efforts were made to correct the common mispronunciation of Gulick's last name to honor the family's preference: It was, according to family sources, "GYU-lick" and not "GOO-lick.")

Mimi Murray '61 with the first President Bush, in the Oval Office. Murray is one of several Springfield College alums to serve as national president of AAHPERD.

EAST CAMPUS REDUX

Meanwhile, at East Campus, Reeds Landing was accepting down payments for residency in the new continuing-care retirement community. A permanent duplex model unit was open for business, and further groundbreaking was imminent.

Rev. Childs, in his regular *Student* column, exhorted the campus to participate in "our last chance to protest the exploitation of our most valuable physical and spiritual asset, East Campus."

On April 25, 1993, a protest demonstration featuring a mock funeral was staged. That week's *Student* provided the following account of the event, which it said had been attended by nearly 100 people: "A crowd gathered in front of Babson Library, complete with signs and megaphones, and marched to East Campus, where it was joined by additional supporters. A symbolic black coffin was carried by students to the Reeds Landing gate, where participants stuffed it with notes, sentiments, and last good-byes to East Campus."

Rev. Childs conducted the "service," which included solemn reflections and a symbolic chaining of the gate on Wilbraham Road. Professor Tom Lachiusa wrote a song for the plants and animals at East Campus soon to be destroyed by the bulldozing, and was well received by the crowd as he played his guitar in accompaniment. Demonstrators also added a "G" to the Reeds Landing sign, transforming the words into "Greeds Landing."

In what may have been a bridge too far, the next day, signs mysteriously appeared in trees along Wilbraham Road urging potential residents of Reeds Landing to look elsewhere: "Glenmeadow is ready to build. Call 567-7800." "Why wait for Reeds Landing? Call Glenmeadow." And "For answers not questions call Glenmeadow."

A private contractor was hired to remove the signs, which had been placed in trees thirty feet off the ground.

Scenes from the April 1993 protest demonstration over the development of a portion of East Campus.

In September 1993, the Springfield City Council voted to reject a petition to return East Campus to its original zoning, which would have killed the Reeds Landing project. The vote was 9-0, and marked the end of organized demonstrations, if not sad feelings, on the part of many on the campus.

Another East Campus issue arose around the same time. Rev. Childs once again voiced his strenuous objections to the use of Loveland Chapel on East Campus as the home of what is today called the Child Development Center. The center provides needed childcare services for faculty and staff, as well as local residents. Loveland Chapel was built during the Locklin years through generous gifts from Norman Loveland, a former trustee, and his wife, Ruth. Rev. Childs' disagreement with the administration on Loveland Chapel actually began during the Falcone years. The crux of the matter was whether or not the terms of the gift precluded the building from being used as anything but a chapel. Based on his contacts with the Loveland family, Rev. Childs insisted the terms of the gift did preclude anything but a chapel, but to date no documents have surfaced to substantiate that view.

BROMERY APPOINTED PERMANENT COLLEGE PRESIDENT

The headline on the lead story in the November 5, 1992 issue of the *Student* was definitely a shock to the campus community: "Bromery Appointed Permanent College President." In his public statements, Bromery had consistently referred to his interim status and emphasized the importance of preparing things for the next president. He had publicly stated that he would not accept the job on a permanent basis. The search committee to identify "the president for the 21st Century" had begun its work, with the help of a search consultant. Now, suddenly, the search was off, the search committee was disbanded, and the College had its eleventh president.

Bromery became the College's eleventh president in November 1992.

What had happened? Many people who were on the campus then believe that Bromery "just sort of fell in love with the place." Bromery himself agreed with that point of view, and readily admitted that he had gone to the trustees and asked to be considered for the permanent position. "Shortly after I came here, I knew I would like working at Springfield College," he said. "SC just rubs me the right way."

Meanwhile, there was a great sigh of relief from the Board of Trustees. Following a difficult time for the College, they had cast their lot, temporarily at least, with Bromery. Things had worked out reasonably well. Now, they could go through a comprehensive, year-long search and hope that lightning would strike twice, or they could re-up with the man who had already proven himself, the man who had "fallen in love" with Springfield College. They chose the latter.

Bromery's formal inauguration was not to occur for nearly a full year. It was a two-day celebration. On Friday, October 29, 1993, some 1,600 enthusiastic students, alumni, faculty, staff, trustees, neighborhood guests, family, and friends of Springfield College gathered in Blake Arena for an evening of presentations, singing, dance, and gymnastics (including the traditional Tableaux). And on Saturday, October 30, the formal inauguration ceremony was conducted in Springfield's Symphony Hall, featuring remarks by former president Glenn Olds.

Bromery with Molly Rau, Joan Patota, and Bob Palmer.

PERSONNEL CHANGES: THE USUAL COMINGS AND GOINGS

In the first three years of the Bromery presidency, the usual comings and goings of senior administration figures was observed:

- Adelaide Van Titus, who had come to the College from Temple University as vice president of academic affairs and dean of the faculty, left the College for a similar position at Cazenovia College. Falcone had given Titus the additional title of provost, but soon after Bromery arrived, a restructuring eliminated that title. Titus left and was succeeded by Molly Rau.

- Dallas Darland, with more than twenty-six years of experience in higher education, mostly in development and public affairs, was appointed vice president of institutional advancement. Darland had been a friend and professional colleague of Bromery's for more than two decades, and was selected to lead the College's fundraising efforts. He succeded Joan Patota.

- Bob Palmer '65 left the College just before classes started in 1994, following disagreements with Bromery. After twenty years in various positions in admissions, financial aid, and development, Palmer had been tapped by Frank Falcone to be vice president of administration. When Falcone left, Palmer was designated as the chief operating officer during the transition to Bromery, who then appointed him vice president for finance and administration in 1992. Palmer was widely loved and respected, and his "resignation" came as a shock to many.

- Bill McGarry joined the College as vice president of finance and administration that fall, in October, but claimed he was not replacing Palmer. "I think I can fill the position, but nobody can possibly replace Bob Palmer," he said. McGarry, with twenty-five years of experience in business and financial management in higher education, dealt confidently and efficiently with a $1-million budget shortfall and quickly became a key member of Bromery's senior team. He left the College in 1999 to become president of Anna Maria College near Worcester, Massachusetts.

- From the faculty, Frank Wolcott '52, the legendary men's gymnastics coach, retired after four decades of service to his alma mater.

THE MIDDLE YEARS

The middle years of the Bromery presidency (1994-96) were quiet and reasonably productive. Bromery was absent from the campus more than he had been in the early years. He continued to live in his family home in Amherst, he still held membership on a number of corporate boards, he took a medical leave in 1995 to undergo radiation treatment for prostate cancer, and he traveled frequently on College business. Still, campus life went on, though some who were there reported feeling "a loss of energy" and "a decline in enthusiasm."

Some highlights from the period:

- In the summer of 1994, prominent Hong Kong industrialist and philanthropist Henry Y.T. Fok made a $1-million endowment gift. The gift established the Fok Ying Tung chair in physical education and would be used to promote sports and athletic relationships between China and the United States. Accepting Fok's gift, Bromery said,

"This gift builds upon past relationships and creates important new opportunities for the exchange of faculty, coaches, and students between the College and China."

- Also in the summer of 1994, Tom Bernard, chair of the education department, was the official Springfield College representative at the 150th anniversary of the founding of the YMCA in Coventry, England. An alumni reception attracted Springfield College alums from Canada, Hong Kong, Japan, and Korea, in addition to the United States. Former President Limbert and Board of Trustees Chair Peter Post G'59 delivered remarks. Also present was Norman Judd, son of legendary gymnastics coach Leslie Judd.

- The following summer brought the 110th anniversary of the partnership between the YMCA and Springfield College. Olympic gold medalist Jeff Blatnick '79 served as master of ceremonies, and famed television celebrity Art Linkletter was a special guest. During the Bromery years, the College's long-standing relationship with the YMCA was strengthened.

- Tuition costs to attend Springfield College increased by 8.5 percent for the 1995-96 academic year. In making the announcement, Bill McGarry, the new vice president, noted that a further increase would be needed for the following year. That increase, as it turned out, was close to 8 percent.

- Helped by a rising stock market, the College's endowment more than doubled over a four-year period, to $26 million in 1996 from $11.5 million in 1992.

- Continuing a tradition of Olympic involvement by people associated with Springfield College, Michael Boulden '96 served on the advance team for the thousands of torchbearers who participated in the Olympic torch's eighty-four-day journey across the U.S. in advance of the 1996 Olympics in Atlanta, Georgia. Boulden took a turn himself, carrying the torch sixth-tenths of a kilometer in Kingsman, Arizona.

Michael Boulden '96 carries the Olympic torch in Kingsman, Arizona, on its journey across the U.S.

SEPTEMBER 1997: CAMPUS IMPROVEMENTS GREET STUDENTS

Students and faculty returned to the campus in September 1997 and were pleasantly surprised at the improvements that had been made in the living and learning environment for students—computer access and networking, food service options, and the overall appearance of the campus.

The number of work stations in the Chatterbox—the café-style computer room in the Beveridge Center where students could go to check e-mail or use the Internet—was doubled, to a grand total of sixteen. Recognizing the trend that was sweeping all of American higher education, this was to be the first year in which all residence-hall rooms were wired for direct access to the College's computer network. The cost of in-room access was reduced to $100 from $180.

The cost of food at Cheney Dining Hall was cut by twenty percent, and the Convenience Store had been well received by students and was open until 11 p.m., providing a new late-night-snack option after the café closed at 10 p.m.

Sprucing-up was evident all over the campus: new synthetic turf for Benedum Field; new gutters and ice-retention roof plates for the Townhouses; handicapped accessibility for Alumni Hall; landscaping outside many campus buildings; and renovations on Blake Track.

Students looking for on-campus jobs now had three places to look: the Career Center, the Financial Aid Office, and the new Career Center home page on the Web.

Welcoming students to the campus, Bromery promised to continue efforts to improve campus communications, which he said were "vital to the health of the College community." He proposed meetings with students in residence halls, "brown bag" lunches, and a "President's Q&A" column in the *Student*.

Bromery also noted that the coming year marked the "mid-point" in the College's strategic planning process, "VISION 2003: Framework for the Future." He said he looked forward to working with the College community on "further developing our strategic initiatives and preparing for a major fundraising effort." The plan itself was completed before Bromery left in 1998, but it was put on a shelf pending the selection of his successor.

In October 1997, at the YMCA Blue Ridge Conference Center in North Carolina, six new members were inducted into the YMCA Hall of Fame, housed in Marsh Memorial Chapel. There was nothing unusual about that, except that one of the inductees in particular stood out for his enduring contributions to Springfield College. He was Laurence Locke Doggett, the legendary president of Springfield College from 1896 to 1936, whose involvement with the YMCA had begun in 1886, when he joined the Oberlin College Student YMCA, and who now, posthumously, was being elected to the YMCA Hall of Fame.

RETIREMENT BECKONS—AGAIN

Near the end of October 1997, "after long and careful consideration about the future of Springfield College, myself, and my family," the College's eleventh president asked board Chair Tom Wheeler to inform the Board of Trustees of his plans to "retire on a basis most appropriate for the College."

Thus, the man who had already retired not once but twice and had been lured back, first to the presidency of Westfield State College, then to the presidency of Springfield College, was going to attempt to retire yet again. Bromery reported that the trustees had accepted his decision and pledged their full support to his continuing leadership of the College "and the many programs to which I have dedicated my presidency."

Trustees also authorized Wheeler to develop a transition plan and a presidential search process, appoint a presidential search committee, and retain a search consultant. For his part, Bromery pledged to "provide continuity of leadership and allow for an appropriate transition."

In a letter to faculty, students, and staff, Bromery said, "I am satisfied that this is an appropriate time for the College to begin transitioning leadership. The mandates for which I was hired are fulfilled. The strong fiscal policy that the College needed is in place and our financial situation is improved."

Bromery added: "I am also satisfied with the progress of initiatives begun under my leadership including advancing our readiness to launch a comprehensive fundraising campaign."

Closing on a personal note, Bromery said, "Serving as president has been, and will continue to be, a most satisfying chapter in my professional and personal life which I shall always cherish."

SOME MEASURE OF DISCONTENT LURKING BENEATH THE SURFACE

In the columns adjacent to Bromery's letter on the front page of the October 31, 1997 *Student* was an account of a rally on Administration Green (today Naismith Green), attended by students and faculty and addressed by the president of the Student Government Association and the presidents of the classes of 1998 and 2000. Among the issues on the agenda were tuition increases, academic restructuring, and College traditions.

To many observers, this rally was a sign that some measure of discontent lurked just beneath the surface of what seemed to be a calm campus. Another sign that all was not copacetic was the emergence in 1996 of *Faculty Voice*, "a journal of opinion by and for the Springfield College faculty."

Faculty Voice was a witty and irreverent newsletter—some senior administrators might have used stronger words—published sporadically to promote a contrarian viewpoint on campus issues. The editorial board for *Faculty Voice* included a number of highly respected faculty members, all plainly identified on the masthead. Also on the editorial board was Rev. Ken Childs, who was *not* a member of the faculty, though he regularly taught classes as an adjunct. He was to become a prolific contributor to *Faculty Voice*.

Rev. Childs had been a key figure on the campus for more than twenty-five years, and was widely loved and respected as the "conscience of the College." Even those who

The *Student* covered Bromery's retirement announcement in the same issue it covered a student rally on Administration Green.

Rev. Ken Childs.

did not agree with his politics, which were decidedly left of center, admired him for his intelligence, passion, humor, and willingness to counsel and help anyone at any time.

Over many years, Rev. Childs had also become the primary collection point (and sometimes the origination point, too) for criticisms and complaints about the president and the administration. According to people who were there, Rev. Childs's views were shared and supported by a number of activists on the faculty, who, from time to time, encouraged him to assume a leadership role on these issues.

That is not to say Rev. Childs was not very much his own man. According to people who were close to him, he needed no encouragement from anyone to take up one cause or another. A Yale graduate with an insatiable intellectual curiosity, he was entirely capable of making up his own mind on issues, staking out a point of view, and pursuing it with great tenacity.

This extra-curricular activity had begun during the Falcone years, and was continuing unabated—some would say more aggressively than ever—during the Bromery administration. One issue of *Faculty Voice*, fairly representative, listed nineteen separate points of difference between the writers and the administration.

The writings in *Faculty Voice* regularly reflected these deep divisions. Indeed, this became the distinguishing feature of the publication. There were those on the campus who believed that *Faculty Voice* was performing a necessary service, forcing the College to face issues that were vital to a successful future. And there were others on the campus who believed that Rev. Childs and his allies on the faculty, although they were clearly fighting for what they believed in, also had been waging an incessant war on two successive presidential administrations—Falcone's, and now Bromery's.

ONE MORE TIME: THE PLAN TO CLOSE ALDEN STREET

Around year-end 1997, the city of Springfield announced it was closing down Alden Street for ninety days, beginning in February 1998, for periodic sewer maintenance. This decision by the city afforded the College the opportunity to study the effects of closing the street permanently.

Sound familiar? It's not known if the legendary Doggett ever tried to close Alden Street, but every president for the past forty-five years had attempted the feat. This is not surprising, since Alden Street, the main connection from Roosevelt Avenue to Six Corners and State Street, is traversed by more than 10,000 motorists every day—a good number of them exceeding the thirty-mile-per-hour speed limit.

Considering the way Alden Street divides the campus in two, and the dangerous speeds of vehicles traveling on the street, closing it made (and still makes) perfect sense in the context of improving the overall safety of the campus. But ask the neighbors, or commuters on their way to downtown offices, how they feel about rerouting Alden Street traffic to, say, King Street, in back of the athletic fields, and you'll hear a much different opinion.

Aware of the potential problems, Bromery emphasized that attempts to close the street permanently would be halted if the effects to the neighborhood were detrimental and if the relationship between the College and its neighbors deteriorated as a result. He promised to work with community leaders in that regard.

On January 15, the College announced its decision to withdraw its application. Some said Bromery's efforts to persuade the community were less than enthusiastic. Commenting on the decision, Bromery said, "I listened to the neighborhood. I heard what they said to me."

CHUN-KWUN WUN, FRANK TORRE, AND *ESCHERICHIA COLI*

In the spring of 1998, two Springfield College professors, working in the College's biology lab in Schoo Hall, made a discovery with life-saving and health-saving potential. Chun-Kwun Wun, a biology professor, and Frank Torre, head of the biology and chemistry department, developed a methodology to detect lethal strains of *E. coli* bacteria quickly enough to enable food-processing plants to prevent the distribution of contaminated food. The two scientists' revolutionary Motility Channel Pathogen Detector, unlike other detection methods in use, was inexpensive, could be used by a technician with three or four hours of instruction, did not require sophisticated lab conditions, and produced reliable results.

Frank Torre: Co-discoverer of a methodology with life-saving and health-saving potential.

ATHLETIC NOTES FROM 1998

The spring of 1998 brought honors to two coaching legends—baseball coach Archie Allen '37 and softball coach Diane Potter '57, who between them won 673 games, pacing the coaching sidelines over a combined span of fifty-two seasons.

With several of his former players in the stands, Allen threw out the ceremonial first pitch at a doubleheader with Clark University on April 4, while Potter threw out the first pitch at a doubleheader with Ithaca College on April 5.

Allen was baseball coach from 1948-78, compiling a 446-250 record for a .637 winning percentage. His teams competed in twelve NCAA tournaments, including the 1951 and 1955 Division I College World Series and the 1970 College Division II World Series. Allen was national coach of the year in 1969.

Archie Allen '37 and Diane Potter '57: Between them, 673 victories for Springfield College.

Potter was a pioneer in women's athletics at Springfield College, serving as the College's first gymnastics coach and first softball coach. She coached the softball team for twenty-one years (1965-75 and 1977-85), compiling a 227-123 record for a 65 percent winning percentage. She had four undefeated seasons and a College record twenty-five victories in her final season. Potter was twice the Northeast-8 Conference coach of the year.

The summer of 1998 was also noteworthy for the death on June 16, at age eighty-seven, of Charles E. "Red" Silvia '34, who attained legendary status during his thirty-eight years as men's swimming coach. Silvia compiled a 210-168-2 record and coached more than 200 All-Americans. Ten of his teams captured New England championships and ten of his swimmers won National Collegiate Athletic Association Division II championship titles. One of Silvia's greatest swimmers was Dr. William Yorzyk '54, the first American swimmer ever to win the gold in the 200-meter butterfly competition. Yorzyk won the gold medal in the 1956 Summer Olympics in Melbourne, Australia.

When Art Linkletter donated the funds for the College's new natatorium in 1967, he said of Silvia, "I gave the money for the natatorium, but Red gave his life to it."

Charles E. "Red" Silvia: Attaining legendary status during thirty-eight years as men's swimming coach.

MEANWHILE...

The formal Presidential Search Committee, formed two months after Bromery had announced his pending resignation in October 1997, continued its work, aided by its search consultant, Ward Howell International. The committee's charge from the trustees had been to solicit nominations, screen applications, interview and assess semi-final candidates, and ensure confidentiality—ultimately recommending a candidate or candidates to the board.

Bill Marsh, vice chair of the Board of Trustees and chair of the search committee, kept the campus regularly informed of the progress of the search through interviews with the *Student* and written communications.

RUPTURE

Like Falcone before him, Bromery had struggled to deal with the continuing opposition to his policies and programs from Rev. Childs. Looking back on it today, Bromery recalls asking Rev. Childs "many times" to come to his office and talk out their differences, seek a compromise that would heal the adversarial relationship. "I never found out where he wanted to go and how he proposed to get there, but it always seemed that where *I* wanted to go, he *didn't* want to go," Bromery says today.

For his part, Rev. Childs said he felt a "moral obligation" to raise issues that affected the future of the College. He viewed his disagreements with the administration as matters of "academic freedom" and, more broadly, "freedom of speech."

Bromery says today that he had contemplated asking for Rev. Childs' resignation for several years. Matters came to a head in early July 1998, when Bromery invited Rev. Childs to his office for a conversation. Two subjects were on the agenda: a leave of absence the minister had requested, and a financial arrangement that would require him to leave the College.

Previously, in June, Rev. Childs had met with human resources personnel, but no agreement had been reached. While Rev. Childs was interested primarily in the leave of absence, in Bromery's mind the two issues were inextricably linked. No separation agreement, no leave.

Bromery recalls the end of their conversation this way:

> *Rev. Childs*: "Are you firing me?"

> *President Bromery*: "I'm not going to renew your contract when it comes due."

Rev. Childs left the office.

Contrary to popular opinion, Rev. Childs' continued employment at the College was not a new subject. Nor was his termination, when it came, "sudden." College records verify that there had been on-and-off negotiations at least since January 1998, when Rev. Childs had requested a paid professional leave of absence for the fall semester of the 1998-99 academic year. In April 1998, Rev. Childs made the request again, and this time added, "I would also like to explore the possibility of an early retirement or buyout package if the College is open to that possibility."

The three-paragraph termination letter was acquired by the *Student*, printed in full in its September 17, 1998 issue, and summarized in subsequent issues of the local newspapers. It was dated July 22, was signed by Bromery, and was delivered to Rev. Childs by Corinne Kowpak, the dean of students and his immediate supervisor. The letter referred to Rev. Childs' "outspoken and caustic criticism and lack of support of administration" and his "fostering of dissention among College constituencies."

Tuesday, July 28, 1998, was another hot and humid day in the Pioneer Valley. Rev. Childs spent the day cleaning out his campus office in the summer-quiet Beveridge Center. Then he drove home to 52 Perkins Street in Springfield's East Forest Park section. After lugging the heavy boxes of books, papers, and memorabilia down to the basement, Rev. Childs came upstairs, collapsed, and fell to the floor, dead of a heart attack at the age of fifty-six.

When Bromery got the news of Rev. Childs' death from Fr. Leo Hoar of Campus Ministries, he was at his home in Amherst. He expressed sorrow, and asked to be kept advised. He then called Bill Marsh, chair of the Board of Trustees, to request a meeting of the trustees' executive committee, to tell them he wanted to move up his already announced retirement to August 21 or sooner. (As noted earlier, Bromery had announced his retirement in October 1997, but had set no specific date.) And he sat at his desk to write a letter to students—"probably the last 'official' communication I will have with you."

In the letter, Bromery outlined "positive changes you will experience when you begin your semester." Among the changes he mentioned were: cable TV hookups in all residence halls; the renovation of what is now Naismith Green, including the elimination of the roadway; other physical improvements; new programs; a new anatomy lab and a new computer lab; several new grants; a new logo and mascot; and new membership in the New England Women's and Men's Athletic Conference (NEWMAC).

In closing, Bromery thanked students, and wished them "all the best for this academic year and for your lives after Springfield College."

Bromery would never return to the campus as president. Not long after, Corinne Kowpak, to whom Rev. Childs had reported, left the College, followed by Jim Robertson, Bromery's executive assistant. Shortly after that, Dallas Darland, Bromery's friend of many years, also left.

Volume 113, No 1.   *Serving the Springfield College Community Since 1910*   **September 17, 1998**

Viva Ken Childs

By Alanna Blinn

Viva Ken Childs, Ken Childs presente! These are the words of Fr. Bruce Teague of St. Brigidt's Church in Amherst who stifled the sniffles and sobs of mourners on a sunny Friday afternoon in an overcrowded Trinity Church on Sumner Avenue in Springfield. This service on August 7, 1998, became the first of many services, tributes, and memorials for campus minister and college chaplain Reverend Kenneth Childs.

Literally translated from Spanish, the words of Teague mean, "Long live Ken Childs; Ken Childs is present." The Spanish version came from the funeral service of migrant worker activist Caesar Chavez, whom Childs met after he completed his graduate studies at Yale University.

Childs died suddenly on Tuesday, July 28, 1998 after cleaning out the contents of his office in Campus Ministry in the Beveridge Center. Having served Springfield for 26 years, Childs was known to students and colleagues on campus simply as "Ken." No title. No Mr. Childs- or Reverend Childs. His humility was his trademark.

Four days before Ken had died, his employment was terminated rather spontaneously by former college president Randolph Bromery. Bromery cited Ken for having a lack of support for the college's administration, senior staff, and their policies, Bromery also dubbed Ken's conscientious and humility as "outspoken and caustic criticism."

Bromery also claimed Ken had been counseled repeatedly about the issue, which none of Ken's closest friends can attest to. Although Ken was fired by Bromery, his immediate supervisor was Dean of Students Corinne Kowpak, with whom Ken had a controversial relationship. Ken claimed he had never been "counseled" by Kowpak, or any other person.

In typical "Ken" fashion, he photocopied his termination letter which bore a confidential stamp at the top. Ken distributed the letter

and discussed his termination of employment openly with those who expressed their concerns and/or support.

Ken also hired prominent Springfield attorney Ephram Gordon to explore his options of being reinstated as chaplain, or seeking an appropriate retirement settlement, since Bromery had offered him none. At age 56, Ken was most concerned about his wife, Donna, and for her welfare.

Prior to Ken's firing, he sought sabbatical leave for the fall semester of 1998, but instead was offered an 18-thousand dollar severance pay by Kowpak in late April. He confided in several friends that he suspected the severance offer was coming, and that others would follow.

Immediately following Ken's

firing by Bromery, anger and confusion prompted the most veteran of faculty, as well as alumni and friends of the college, to meet to try to get Ken reinstated as Chaplain and Director of Campus Ministry. Professor of Physical Education Mimi Murray still believes Ken should be reinstated to his rightful position as the "moral conscience" of Springfield College.

After Ken's untimely death, his picture, which accompanied his

weekly column in the Student, was posted in Marsh Memorial at the altar so that mourners would remember Ken's comforting smile. The picture had been photocopied so many times that hundreds appeared around campus in the student center, outside on light posts, in campus offices and on doors of buildings, and on Ken's office door, on which various people wrote "farewells" and "thank yous"

Campus Minister Fr. Leo Hoar and Murray reported receiving up to a couple hundred phone calls and messages from Springfield alumni all over the world.

Several days later, Bromery announced he would retire officially on August 18, 1998, even before another president had been selected. And Kowpak took a 30-day leave, after rumors of her immediate res-

ignation spread across campus offices.

Four days prior to his death, Ken said to a friend, "I told them [those who began working to have Ken reinstated as Chaplain] that this is not about me. It's not a Ken Childs issue. I want them to keep the focus on academic freedom and free speech, and other issues of that nature."

Yet even more selfless was Ken's professing his passion for the

college to Health Center nurse Nancy Wilson on the afternoon he died. He told Wilson that he still believed in Springfield and its unique philosophy as much as he ever had, and that he still held the institution close to his heart even after his termination of employment.

In the May 8, 1997 edition of the Student, Ken expressed his concerns regarding academic freedom and the future of free speech at Springfield College. He wrote, "Here at SC we are coming dangerously close to that ['official'] truth by mandating a politically correct agenda to which everyone is required to subscribe. We are tip-toeing on the edge of Institutional coercion, and in so doing risk losing the very essence of what an academic community is about."

In light of Ken's passing, his friends, his wife Donna, and his children Becky and Jeff, have memorialized Ken for his simple virtues and random acts of kindness, and of course, his first rate sense of humor.

In the February 28, 1998 issue of the Student, Ken wrote, "Too often, I have had to conduct funerals and memorial services. Invariably, whether the deceased was a well known Individual or an ordinary soul, the memories of loved ones and friends have focused not on great deeds, but on simple virtues: kindness, friendship, humor, concern for others. It is ironic that so much of our lives are focused in becoming and so little focused on being, ...Ouch! I just got spooned by Phil [Dilbert character] for being self-righteous."

Ken's insightful wisdom, sense of humor, and unparalleled compassion not only made him an institution at Springfield College, but also a humble and giving friend to all living things and to whom Ken called our collective mother, "Mother Earth." The next service for Ken will be held during Homecoming Weekend on Sunday, October 18, 1998, at 4 p.m. in Marsh Memorial Chapel.

The Faculty Voice: Another View on Campus

By Michael L. Liuzza

"The Springfield Student" isn't the only source of information of current events on this campus.

"The Faculty Voice" is an often controversial newsletter that is written and financed by faculty members at Springfield College. It was started in May of '97 and has been described as an "underground newspaper."

The Faculty Voice deals with all issues pertaining to Springfield College. This includes political correctness, faculty government, and all those involved in the administration.

"We feel we have a responsibility to speak about these issues," said editorial board member Fernando Gonzalez.

Right now, there are at least ten members on the editorial board.

Much time and effort are put into this newsletter, as issues only come out every four or five weeks.

The journal is aimed at other faculty members as well as members of the administration board. But students are more than welcome to read the issues as well.

"All articles are both welcomed and printed, and that is very

Continued on Page 3

Note

In conjunction with the concept of an In Memoriam issue dedicated to Ken Childs, commercial advertisements have been excluded from this edition.

Front page of the *Student* commemmorating the life and death of Rev. Ken Childs.

After Bromery

When organizations are in crisis, sometimes individuals step up to new challenges in a timely manner and distinguish themselves in an unanticipated way. Such was the case with Springfield College following Rev. Childs' death and Bromery's retirement.

Bill Marsh, who had been elected the new chair of the Board of Trustees just six weeks earlier, following three years as vice chair, returned from a European trip in early August to find himself faced with three daunting priorities:

Bill Marsh, as the new chair of the Board of Trustees, played a key leadership role in the presidential transition from Bromery.

- Starting immediately, he needed to take a personal, hands-on role in running the College, with the help of two key individuals—Gretchen Brockmeyer, the provost and acting vice president for Academic Affairs, whom Marsh had named chief operating officer until the appointment of an interim president; and Mary Lou Dyjak, assistant to the president and secretary to the Board of Trustees.

- Almost as urgent, Marsh needed to identify and hire a suitable interim president who could keep things running smoothly for a period of months, not years, and prepare for the arrival of the College's twelfth president.

- And he needed to continue and accelerate the work of the presidential search committee to identify and hire the "president for the 21st century" to succeed Bromery.

The next several months, Marsh recalls today, brought "the most intensive involvement in any nonprofit institution that I've ever experienced—a difficult and demanding process." Normally, of course, a board member would not be so deeply involved in the day-to-day functioning of an institution.

Bob Aebersold was well respected and well liked during his term as interim president. It was seen by many as "an era of good feeling."

One of the first steps Marsh took was to schedule an open forum meeting for August 25, 1998, in Appleton Auditorium of the Fuller Arts Center. He drove to Springfield from his home near Boston, and patiently took comments and questions for nearly an hour, talking about what had transpired, the ongoing presidential search, the process of hiring an interim president, and related matters.

"There were a lot of concerned people at that meeting," Marsh recalls today. "But through all of this, there were people on the board, in the administration, and on the faculty who really had the best interests of the College at heart. That made a huge difference in how things turned out."

Following that open forum, there were other meetings on the campus, as well as regular printed communications. Marsh functioned in the presidential role for the traditional Fall Faculty Institute, and, when the new students arrived in September, for the New Student Assembly. He made regular drives from Boston to visit the campus, and was in constant contact by telephone, officially to Gretchen Brockmeyer and Mary Lou Dyjak, and unofficially to a number of others who kept him up to speed on the mood of the campus.

The search process for an interim president was nothing if not efficient. A number of candidates were interviewed, and the searchers quickly coalesced around what most believed was the *obvious choice*—Bob Aebersold, who had served fifteen years as president of Slippery Rock University. During his nearly thirty years at Slippery Rock, Aebersold also had served as vice president for academic affairs and chair of the physical education department. Following his recent retirement from Slippery Rock, he'd served as special advisor to the chancellor of the Pennsylvania higher education system. Among many other accomplishments, as a physical education teacher with expertise in exercise physiology, Aebersold had published papers on muscle fatigue.

Aebersold arrived at Springfield College in early September 1998, and left in February 1999. His wife, Nancy, visited frequently, commuting from the family home in Pennsylvania. By all accounts, they were greatly respected and well liked during their brief stay. In announcing Aebersold's appointment, Marsh had taken pains to specify that the interim president would serve "until a new, permanent president takes office." Thus, Aebersold was relieved of some of the burdens carried by permanent presidents, and his time at Springfield College was characterized by some who were there as "an era of good feeling."

One individual who was closely involved in the work done by Marsh and Aebersold during these trying times summed it up this way: "You know, sometimes God gives you what you need. And what this College needed that summer was Bill Marsh, and what it needed for the months after that was Bob Aebersold. And the good Lord took very good care of this little College then."

Interim President Robert Aebersold, Alumni Relations Director Tamie Kidess Lucey '81 G'82, and Alumni Council President Charisse Duroure '80 performed the ribbon-cutting ceremony at the Alumni Park groundbreaking festivities during Homecoming '98.

The twelfth president of Springfield College drove for twenty-six hours to get here, then ran the last thirty yards at full speed in a relentless downpour to get to his new office in this building.

Chapter 12

Flynn: Leading from Integrity

Richard B. Flynn started work as the twelfth president of Springfield College on March 1, 1999, with the new millennium a mere ten months away.

It wasn't just raining. It was the kind of relentless, cats-and-dogs, bone-drenching, cloud-bursting downpour that occurs with depressing regularity in New England in late February. The kind of rain that causes the natives to rationalize: *Well, at least it isn't snow.*

If Dick Flynn had that thought, it was probably small consolation to him at that particular moment.

It was late afternoon on Sunday, February 28, 1999. Flynn and his wife, Jani, had just completed a twenty-six-hour journey of some 1,352 miles from Omaha, Nebraska, in the new maroon Jeep purchased specially for the occasion. His tenure as the twelfth president of Springfield College would begin officially the next day. But right now, parked outside Marsh Memorial, the immediate concern for the new president was more mundane: *How do I get to my new office without getting completely soaked?*

Seeing no other way, Flynn opened the Jeep door and made a run for it, using an accelerated version of the classic loping strides of the athlete he'd been in college. But by the time he reached his office and sat down at his desk for the first time, the man was a soggy mess.

Minutes later, there was a timid knock at the door. Two students appeared, sent by Father Leo Hoar to invite the new president to the Catholic Mass then in progress in the Chapel. Flynn, a lifelong Methodist, demurred, pointing to his completely soaked yellow sweater. Not dressed for the occasion.

The students left, but a moment later, two more students appeared at the door, and one said, more or less: We don't care how you're dressed. Just come in and sit in the back. We promise you won't have to speak or anything.

Persuaded, Dick and Jani Flynn walked into Marsh Chapel, dripping water on the carpet as they went, their shoes making little squishing sounds. Prompted by Father Leo, those in attendance at the Mass stood and applauded the new president and his wife. Welcome to Springfield College!

Promises notwithstanding, Father Leo did ask the new president to speak that day, and Flynn did so. Ten years later, Flynn says he has only the foggiest memory of what he said. But no one is very surprised that, even on this occasion, he was not at a loss for words.

181

Trustee Bill Marsh guided the presidential search process firmly but unobtrusively.

Trustee John Odierna '64 to Mary Lou Dyjak: "I think we just met the next president of Springfield College."

THE PRESIDENTIAL SEARCH

The search for a new permanent president, guided firmly but unobtrusively by Bill Marsh, the trustee chair, had been efficient, inclusive, and relatively transparent to the College community. Given the circumstances, that was essential.

"The process was extremely important," Marsh recalls. "People on the campus needed to understand that they had an opportunity to express their opinions on the things that were important to the future of the College, and also the sort of person we should be looking for. I just felt that this would help us find the right person, and also help the buy-in on the final decision."

As the chair of the search committee, Marsh had carefully put together a strong group in which trustee members were in the minority and other key constituencies—faculty, staff, and students—were represented.

The members of what would prove to be a historic presidential search committee were: Trustees Marsh, Denise Alleyne '73, Sue Lundin '70, John Odierna '64, Thane Pressman '67, George Silcott '52, and Harold Smith; faculty members Mary Ann Coughlin G'84, Joel Dearing '79, Dan Nussbaum, Peter Polito, and Ann Roy; students Matthew Geaughan '99 and Stephen Lovejoy '95; and staff Mary Lou Dyjak, Catherine Banks G'80, and Michele David.

More than eighty candidates had applied for the position. On August 10, 11, and 24, the search committee had interviewed seven individuals in a nondescript function room at the Springfield Marriott Hotel downtown.

Flynn was the first candidate to be interviewed, on August 10. He made a lengthy presentation on his own education, background, and experience, and offered some comments on the history, present condition, and future prospects of Springfield College. Then, standing at the open end of a U-shaped arrangement of eight-foot tables, he proceeded to field dozens of questions from committee members.

As he responded to search committee members' questions, it rapidly became clear that Flynn had taken the time and trouble to do his homework prior to the Marriott meeting. And his answers to the questions were informed by those efforts.

When Flynn left the room during a break, search committee members had a chance to compare notes. Odierna leaned over to Dyjak, sitting in the chair to his right, and whispered, "I think we just met the next president of Springfield College."

Other committee members had similar positive reactions to the man from Nebraska, but Marsh reminded all that there was a process to follow.

Four finalists were invited back to the campus during September for two days of meetings with faculty, students, staff, and others—including an open meeting for anyone who wanted to participate. Flynn visited the campus again on October 5-6—the third of the four to make his return visit.

"YOU'VE REALLY GOT TO GET THIS RIGHT!"

Flynn easily satisfied the primary criteria the committee had established. As dean of the College of Education at the University of Nebraska at Omaha, he'd managed a large educational enterprise, and he'd successfully raised money for his school. He'd taken a professional leave, at the request of the executive director of the Nebraska State College System and with the full blessing of the university's chancellor, for a one-year assignment as interim president of Peru State College in southeastern Nebraska. And he was known nationally and internationally for his expertise in facilities planning and design—an important consideration for a College with obvious needs in that area. Over the years, he'd published many books, monographs, journal and magazine articles on that subject and others.

A native of Bluffs, Illinois, Flynn had earned bachelor's and master's degrees in the areas of health and physical education at MacMurray College and Ohio University, respectively. He also held a doctoral degree from Columbia University's Teachers College. As a student, Flynn had competed in intercollegiate athletics as a shortstop in baseball, a point guard in basketball, and a center halfback in soccer.

Moreover, Flynn impressed his interviewers as intelligent, mature, thoughtful, and responsive. "He was somewhat low key, but still seemed to have some real backbone," Marsh recalls. "He was leading from integrity, and he just made a very, very positive impression on everyone on the committee."

Looking back on the presidential search today, Marsh recalls the faculty member who came up to him after a meeting and warned: "You've really got to get this right!"

"I knew we had done everything we could think of to try to do it the right way, and I couldn't think of a single thing I'd have done differently," Marsh recalls. "But you know, not all searches work out well; you've got to be both smart and lucky at the same time. And I think this search turned out extraordinarily well."

When those visits were over, the committee had some discussion, but little difficulty in voting unanimously to recommend Dick Flynn to the trustees as the College's twelfth president. And as Marsh points out, it was a "legitimate unanimous vote," not requiring any motion to make it unanimous.

GAP ANALYSIS THEORY

Thus began the Flynn presidency. Having come through the rough patch of recent years, many faculty and staff could be forgiven for some early skepticism. But before very long, it became clear that this president was different, in many significant respects.

Over the ensuing ten years, Flynn would have a powerful positive impact on Springfield College in many ways, at a time when the institution was sorely in need of just that. Indeed, in the words of one prominent alumnus, the Flynn years represent "the Renaissance of Springfield College." Among the major achievements:

- Financial capacity, controls, and understanding were greatly strengthened and enhanced.

- A six-year, $40-million fundraising campaign was concluded successfully in 2008, raising $44.5-million.

- The physical appearance of the campus was transformed.

- Collaboration with strategic partners like the YMCA and the Naismith Memorial Basketball Hall of Fame was rejuvenated and expanded.

- Serious attention was paid to the College's infrastructure.

- The international dimension of Springfield College, which had been an integral part of its history since its founding, was energized and broadened.

- Academic programs were formally reviewed and improved, and new ones were added.

- Institutional policies, procedures, and practices were centered around the needs and success of students.

- The image and reputation of the College—in the city, in the country, and in the world —were improved dramatically.

- Strategic goals relating to leadership development, mutual respect, diversity, and sense of community were all addressed aggressively, and progress was made.

Among the management tools Flynn had brought with him from Nebraska was the Gap Analysis theory. Reduced to its essentials, this theory was pretty simple: An institution needed to a) assess precisely its current status, b) determine where it aspired to be, and then c) develop a strategic plan to close the gap to reach its goals.

Flynn recognized that actually following the theory was more easily stated than accomplished. But he was thoroughly convinced that the process involved, first of all, asking questions and listening. As far as the faculty, staff, and students were concerned, that was clearly a step in the right direction.

THE INFORMATION-GATHERING PHASE

Flynn spent a lot of time during the first six months of his presidency in conversations with faculty, staff, students, alums, community leaders, and others. He talked about his views of Springfield College, of course, but mostly he asked questions, probed, challenged, and listened carefully.

As far as the rough patch the College had endured in recent years was concerned, Flynn's approach in conversations was simple: First, remain studiously neutral on questions of who was right and who was wrong about East Campus, the Rev. Ken Childs situation, and similar contentious and divisive issues. Second, as objectively as possible, pose questions to elicit additional facts and opinions about those issues.

In this manner, Flynn was able to avoid taking sides. Nonetheless, he could demonstrate his interest in hearing about the issues, and then seek to relegate them to the past so he, and the College community, might move on to focus on the future.

In his first two weeks on the job, following a full day of meetings, Flynn visited a different residence hall every week night. Using pizza as a lure, he listened to students talk about the things that were on their minds. He learned a lot, and those visits served as a gentle reminder to faculty and staff of the reasons they were at Springfield College— to educate students.

Shortly after Flynn's arrival, a brief printed questionnaire was sent to all faculty and staff, asking three questions: What three things do you like and/or value most about

Jill Russell, a long-time Flynn colleague from Nebraska, rejoined him at Springfield College in 2000. Flynn credits her with playing a key role in the development and oversight of *The Plan for Springfield College.*

Springfield College? What do you consider the two or three major challenges facing Springfield College? What one suggestion do you have for strengthening and encouraging a greater sense of community at Springfield College?

Responding to the questionnaire allowed people to engage in a focus on the future, and served to help bring the campus together.

During this time, Flynn accumulated a wealth of data from hundreds of people. The data served the College well during the subsequent drafting of the strategic plan, later called *The Plan for Springfield College*, and helped in the development, and success, of the largest fund-raising campaign in the College's history.

Flynn valued this input highly, saying it was a big factor in his ability to hit the ground running. And, in fact, many of the improvements to the campus, and to its academic and athletic programs, can be traced directly to a suggestion or comment made during this information-gathering phase of the Flynn presidency.

THE PLAN FOR SPRINGFIELD COLLEGE

James Walsh '64, who served as trustees' chair from 2005-07, recalls that Flynn's byword while developing a strategic plan for the College was "inclusive." "The way Dick brought that strategic plan together brought the entire campus community together," Walsh says. "Everyone had opportunity in terms of providing input, developing the goals, and then figuring out how to meet the goals. It was *everybody's plan*, and it was in everybody's interest to see that it was carried out."

Walsh adds, "As an engineer, that kind of thinking appeals to me. You get everybody involved, you develop a plan that everybody buys into, you have goals and objectives, and you have steps you need to take to meet those goals and objectives. It was just a very inclusive approach, and it worked very well."

In fact, *The Plan for Springfield College* benefited from months of research, listening, and thinking. This included a careful review of the following: the 1998 *Institutional Priorities Report* and the *Vision 2003* Report (both produced under Bromery); the campus master plan existing at that time; the survey of faculty and staff conducted shortly after Flynn's arrival; hundreds of conversations with many constituents and colleagues; a review of recent trends in post-secondary education; and an examination of the effects of dramatic societal and technological change.

Trustee James Walsh '64: "The way Dick brought that strategic plan together brought the entire campus community together. It was everybody's plan, and it was in everybody's interest to see that it was carried out."

There is little mystery attached to determining the elements of a good strategic plan for an institution of higher learning. The list has a certain motherhood-and-apple-pie quality: Academic excellence, leadership development, student support, financial integrity, collaboration with educational partners, diversity, a sense of community, technology, facilities and grounds, image and reputation, and fund-raising.

To improve in these areas over time, however, requires vision, knowledge, wisdom, insight, tenacity, and perhaps a certain degree of luck. More to the point, it requires strategic thinking and a strategic plan.

It is not surprising that these elements, more or less, became the foundation for *The Plan for Springfield College* as it was developed early in the Flynn years—by Flynn himself, and by Jill Russell, a long-time colleague of the new president's, after she arrived at

The College's strategic plan benefited from months of research, listening, and thinking.

Springfield College in June 2000. The vice presidents played an important role in implementing the plan.

Specific goals and objectives—based on voluminous input from faculty, staff, students, and trustees—were identified for each of the ten primary elements of the plan. Serious attention was paid to each of the ten goals, and major accomplishments came to be recorded for each one.

However, there was a special urgency to, and a conceptual linkage among, three of the goals—financial integrity, fund-raising, and facilities and grounds. By the time of the College's 125th anniversary, the accomplishments related to these three strategic goals were being seen as the true hallmarks of the Flynn years. By then it was clear that the College had fixed the finances, raised the money, and transformed the campus.

In developing a strategic plan, an institution always benefits from a clearly stated, long-standing mission statement—one that all concerned know and accept. In this regard, Springfield College was particularly fortunate. Since the College's founding in 1885, its mission had always involved two essential elements—the concept of educating students in spirit, mind, and body; and the concept of leadership in service to humanity. It was (and is today) very likely that, if students, faculty, or staff were stopped on the campus and asked to recite the mission of the school, they would immediately respond with some version of the above.

BUILDING A SENIOR LEADERSHIP TEAM

Practicing a little leadership development of his own, Flynn set about building a senior staff he could count on to help achieve the goals of *The Plan for Springfield College.* Among the four senior administrative positions reporting directly to the president, Flynn could count three interims and one vacancy. But by July 2001, a mostly new senior leadership team was in place, along with the strategic plan, and the President's Cabinet was functioning relatively smoothly:

- John Mailhot, who started at the College in October 1988, was named interim vice president for administration and finance in June 1999. The "interim" in Mailhot's title was dropped in July 2000. Flynn felt blessed to have an insider who provided great insight in all aspects of the College's finances.

- Jill Russell, with whom Flynn had worked at the University of Nebraska at Omaha, joined the Office of the President as executive assistant in June 2000. Russell was named vice president for strategic planning in June 2006, and executive vice president in August 2008.

- M. "Ben" Hogan came to Springfield College as vice president for student affairs in August 2000. He left for health reasons and was succeeded by David Braverman in July 2005.

- Jean Wyld joined the College as vice president for academic affairs in February 2001, benefiting from the experience and ability of Gretchen Brockmeyer, a longtime administrator who had served as interim vice president and would continue to serve the College, as associate vice president, until her retirement in 2009.

- Dave Fraboni '84 returned to the campus as vice president for institutional advancement in July 2001. He succeeded John Kindzerske, who served in the position briefly in 1999 and 2000. Fraboni himself left at the conclusion of the fundraising campaign in 2008. He was succeeded in 2009 by John White, who previously had served as director of development, major gifts officer, and director of sports information.

Along with the senior leadership team, there were other matters, Flynn recognized, that had to be dealt with early on. These matters might have been labeled "housekeeping" if they weren't so absolutely critical to the smooth operation of the College:

Faculty governance: Recognizing the pressing need to heal the faculty/administration relationship, Flynn focused on faculty governance. Working with the Faculty Senate, he championed steps to empower the faculty and provide it with a single, strong voice to speak out on campus issues.

Once implemented, these steps benefited all concerned: Faculty began to feel that the newly empowered Faculty Senate gave them a real place at the table. And the establishment of the single, strong voice for the faculty had the ancillary effect of minimizing the power and influence of a number of unofficial "camps" that had sprung up within the faculty over the years. Almost immediately, the administration's relationship with the faculty began to improve, and an atmosphere of trust began to develop.

One symbol of that atmosphere of trust remains on Flynn's office bookshelf to this day: A ceramic coffee mug with "Trust and Open Communication" printed on it. The mug was a token of appreciation from Matt Pantera, the Faculty Senate president at the time, and Ann Moriarty, the vice president, both of whom worked closely with Flynn during the early years of his presidency.

Infrastructure: Beyond building a senior leadership team, Flynn recognized there were many other aspects of the College's infrastructure that needed improvement. Things like establishing and updating policies, protocols, and procedures; improving campus information technology; tweaking the organizational structure; enhancing facilities; tightening the budgeting process and accountability; and upgrading record-keeping and data storage. In short, addressing the people, facilities, technologies, and other resources needed to do the job effectively.

For example, when it came to decision making, Flynn was a data-driven manager. He believed it was always better to make decisions based on the data available. Upon his arrival at Springfield College, however, he quickly discovered that much of the data he

Ann Moriarty and Matt Pantera, Faculty Senate vice president and president, respectively, during the early years of the Flynn presidency.

Token of appreciation to Flynn from Pantera and Moriarty in 2001.

needed to make informed decisions—on enrollment, or housing, or food service, or anything else—either was not available or was exceedingly difficult to extract.

Flynn began to prod vice presidents and others for data-driven decision making. The first year, his demands may have caused more work. But beginning the second year, with data available, decisions were made more quickly and rationally. A new College Fact Book, collecting a more significant portion of data, was established in 2000 and is now published annually.

Board of Trustees Policies and Procedures: Like any good chief executive officer, Flynn knew very well who his *bosses* were—the men and women on the Board of Trustees. And he knew, too, that any good CEO sought to manage the relationship with the trustees, to maximize efficiency and effectiveness.

Flynn had heard a number of comments from trustees that their policies and procedures badly needed overhauling. He learned that Bob Aebersold, during his term as interim president after Bromery left, had engaged the trustees in a weekend-long self-assessment the previous fall. The retreat had uncovered a number of things that needed fixing. Flynn set to work with trustee chairs Marsh and later Odierna as they streamlined policies and procedures that, in some cases, had not been changed in years.

Mimi Murray '61, a faculty member since 1968, has the honor of leading the academic procession at commencements.

Among many other changes: The size of the board was reduced, board oversight of financial planning and budgeting were beefed up, board committees were made more interactive, regular reports were scheduled from the president of the Faculty Senate and the student trustee, recruitment and cultivation of new trustee candidates was stressed, the relationship between the president and the trustees was defined more precisely, and the prestigious but rather unwieldy Board of Corporators was eliminated as a formal body, though corporators were urged to continue their involvement with the College, and many of them did so. The result was more productive meetings that ran more smoothly than before.

At the same time, Flynn started a practice he would continue throughout his presidency, to great benefit: Using telephone calls, emails, letters, reports, copies of College publications, early-morning breakfasts on campus, lunches and dinners downtown, social gatherings, athletic events on campus—in short, anything and everything he could employ—to remain in close contact with trustees on a regular basis, particularly with members of the board's executive committee, and, above all, with the trustee chairs.

This constant contact between president and trustees enabled Flynn to hear what was on trustees' minds, and trustees to hear what Flynn was thinking about. Both worked to the advantage of the College.

Ed Bilik '57 retired in 1999 following a forty-six-year association with Springfield College—as student, teacher-coach, and athletic director.

Ted Dunn and his players at a football reunion. According to a local newspaper reporter: "Dunn's football career . . . was more about teaching, helping, and caring for the students who were fortunate enough to be associated with him."

PRE-MILLENNIUM HONORS

During 1999, the College honored three of its own for longtime service:

- **Ed Bilik** '57 retired following a forty-six-year association with Springfield College that began as a student in 1953. Bilik was the archetype of the teacher-coach, the winningest basketball coach in the history of the Birthplace of Basketball (322 wins over twenty years), and athletic director during a ten-year period that included a nickname change and new logo for athletic teams, and the move from NCAA Division II to Division III. Later in 1999, Cathie Schweitzer, who had been assistant director of athletics, was named as Bilik's successor, the first woman to serve in the post.

- **Ted Dunn** and his wife, Ann, were saluted at halftime of a football game and were guests of honor at a postgame reception to celebrate Dunn's fifty-year association with Springfield College. As Garry Brown of the *Union-News* wrote on the occasion, "Dunn's football coaching career . . . was more about teaching, helping, and caring for the students who were fortunate enough to be associated with him." Dunn's tenure spanned thirty seasons coaching football, including the College's first unbeaten-and-untied team (1965, 9-0-0)—unless one counts the 1893 team that beat the Massachusetts Aggies in both of the games they played that season.

- **Mimi Murray** '61, professor of physical education and a faculty member since 1968, was honored with her very own "day," Saturday, January 30, 1999. As women's gymnastics coach from 1968-74, Murray's teams compiled a perfect 37-0 record in dual meets and won five Eastern titles and three AIAW Division I national championships. Murray was also involved in the passage of Title IX legislation for women's sports, and was recognized by the Women's Sports Foundation as one of five pioneers in women's athletics. She's a former president of the American Alliance for Health, Physical Education, Recreation, and Dance (AAHPERD) and the National Association for Girls and Women in Sport. Weeks after her "day," Murray was feted again, as AAHPERD bestowed on her its highest honor, the Luther Halsey Gulick Award.

When Ed Bilik retired as athletic director, Cathie Schweitzer, who had been associate director of athletics, was named as his successor, the first woman to serve in the post.

Flynn accepts the presidential medal from Tom Wheeler, immediate past chair of the Board of Trustees and MassMutual CEO.

The inauguration of the College's twelfth president took place October 24, 1999.

PRESIDENTIAL INAUGURATION

By the time the formal Presidential Inauguration rolled around on October 24, 1999, the new president and his elegant and gracious wife, Jani, already were familiar sights on the campus—in Cheney Dining Hall and the residence halls, and at plays, concerts, and athletic events. Faculty, staff, students, and alums commented that Flynn seemed to have brought a new energy and enthusiasm to the College. Rev. Bob Price, president of the Faculty Senate (back then, and again as this is written) and professor of religion and philosophy, put it this way: "He always knows the right things to do and say. He conveys his warmth and caring."

The inauguration itself took place in Blake Arena, as usual, with an audience of 750, including representatives of colleges and universities, elected officials, business and community leaders, members of the College community, and the public.

Del Weber, former chancellor of the University of Nebraska at Omaha, where Flynn had been a longtime administrator, called the new president "an extraordinarily gifted leader," adding that Flynn was "moral, super-organized, and thrives on five hours of sleep a night."

To which Jani Flynn commented to the person sitting next to her, "I only *wish* he would sleep five hours. It's more like four hours."

The new president's remarks centered on the importance of change. "Our future success," he pointed out, "in large part will depend on our willingness and ability to adjust to a rapidly changing society."

Flynn was not under any illusion about the scope of the challenge confronting him and Springfield College. "Rising costs, diversity, a changing student population, advances

Del Weber, former chancellor at the University of Nebraska ay Omaha, spoke at the inaguration, calling Flynn "an extraordinarily gifted leader."

190

in technology, competition by alternative providers, a growing emphasis on outcomes assessment, and the list goes on," he noted, as reported by the *Student* newspaper.

The new president paid homage to former presidents, with special references to two presidents who together had served for more than half of the College's 115-year history —Laurence L. Doggett for forty years, 1896-1936, and Wilbert E. Locklin for twenty years, 1965-85.

One wonders if Flynn was thinking ahead: Today, in the midst of the College's 125th anniversary celebration, he is in the twelfth year of his presidency, and is able to include himself among the three Springfield College presidents with the greatest longevity.

In his remarks as well as his actions, the new president showed that, in his few months on campus, he'd already become a true son of Springfield:

> Since being introduced more than a hundred years ago, the term "Humanics" has been a driving force in defining the College, and the campus community has sustained its commitment to the Humanics philosophy of developing the whole person in spirit, mind, and body for leadership in service to humanity. And, most importantly, our students have been successful and have excelled as graduates, assuming positions in a multitude of professions in all of the United States and throughout the world, and building a reputation for themselves and for the College that has endured over time. The faculty and staff, past and present, can take great satisfaction in the accomplishments of Springfield College graduates. . . . I am very proud to be a part of the Springfield College family."

In attendance at the presidential inauguration, from the right: Daughter Tracy Flynn (now Leonard), wife Jani, and mother Myrtle Flynn.

And just in case someone had missed the point, the new president returned to it a moment later:

> The mission of Springfield College is timeless and enduring. Our goal of educating the whole person in spirit, mind, and body will never diminish in relevance or go out of style. As long as there is a desire for a caring and just society, bringing out the best in others, as long as there is a respect for the multifaceted essence of life, there will be a need for Springfield College and a demand for what it has to offer.

There was little doubt that this president was on the same page as the College's founders, who, in the words of Seth Arsenian, the first Distinguished Springfield College Professor of Humanics, "were not interested in adding just another college of liberal arts to those studding the picturesque Pioneer Valley."

EARLY IMPRESSIONS OF THE NEW PRESIDENT

During the presidential search process, and in the early months of the Flynn presidency, members of the Board of Trustees had opportunities to form first impressions of the new president. Virtually all were positive, and a body of opinion began to form that this president was for real, and would be here a long time.

For one thing, the man's energy and enthusiasm and plain old get-up-and-go were simply breathtaking.

Here are the opinions of four trustees with long-standing ties to the College, as they recalled them from that time:

Bill Marsh: "Dick got everybody in the campus community pulling in the same direction, and that enabled the College to move forward in a lot of different ways."

"I'd get a call from Dick at nine or ten o'clock at night, and he'd be at some athletic event. I'd hear it in the background, and I knew he'd just been so busy he hadn't gotten around to calling during the day. And it became clear to me that he was giving an enormous time commitment to the College."

"Dick really prepared for meetings. He'd sit down and think about what we were trying to accomplish, what we needed to discuss. And if he didn't know the person he was meeting with, he'd get some information on the person from someplace. He just worked very hard at his job, and that really impressed me."

"He had a willingness to take on the tough issues. He was determined to make sure that things were being run the right way; I think he was courageous in that respect."

"The word spread quickly through the YMCA movement that there was a really outstanding president at Springfield College. The work Dick did with the YMCA leadership in building and expanding the relationship with the College has been an enormous plus for both."

Jim Walsh: "Dick was extremely hard-working and very well organized. He knew where we should be going as a college, and really knew how to get us there."

"He was very inclusive. When he started working on the strategic plan for the College, he made the entire College family part of the process. He held everybody's feet to the fire."

"He and Jani stayed with us in Florida when they were attending some alumni events, and we'd get to bed around midnight. Then when you got up in the morning, Dick would already be up and working at his laptop."

"As everyone knows, Dick is a very hands-on guy. He also has a great deal of experience in building educational facilities, so he was able to take a very active role in even the smallest details of some of our major projects."

Harold Smith: "Dick presented us with a vision for the school and a record of professional accomplishments that made us feel this was someone who could take us forward."

"He had the right set of skills and the right sense of direction, and that was terribly important for us at that time. He was someone who understood academia, and could bring order to a rather chaotic personnel situation. And he turned around the finances of the school in a way that I think was almost miraculous. He has financed capital improvements out of cash flow; that's not easy to do."

"Dick built a team. It moves with precision, and with a common sense of purpose and goals. And that's the ultimate accolade in my book."

"The mission of the College was something that was already in him, something he already believed in fervently. His whole value system coincided with what Springfield College has always stood for. The alignment was perfect."

"The campus looks good, and the food is edible. Not just edible, it's actually good!"

192

Peter Andruszkiewicz: "Dick understands the value proposition of the mission of this institution. He knows that our mission is just as relevant today as it was when the institution started. And there are very few institutions of higher education or businesses, or any other endeavor, where that's true. That's what makes this place special."

THE NEW CENTURY DAWNS

Despite all the predictions of technological disaster as "Y2K" approached, the first year of the new century dawned uneventfully.

At reunion weekend in June 2000, the new president, now a veteran with fifteen months at the helm, wasted no time dropping a clear hint with returning alums of what was to come.

Speaking at the David Allen Reed Society reception, Flynn noted the intense competition for students, and said, "Private colleges throughout the U.S. are turning more and more to their alumni, not only as ambassadors to the larger world, but also as recruiters of potential students and important sources of financial support."

Over the summer, Schoo Hall and Woods Hall lost their 1970s yellow brick, as they were given a paint job to match the red brick décor of the rest of the campus. The *Student* newspaper commented: "No longer will our eyes suffer the damage caused by looking at the horrible color scheme designed by the College's forefathers."

Strangely, the change in color for the Schoo and Woods brickwork went mostly unnoticed by alums returning for homecoming and reunion. Even when they were pressed to comment on the "new color" for the bricks on the two buildings, alums generally agreed the bricks had always been red.

Once it was explained that the buildings had been repainted using a special process to color the brick red, alums changed their tune: Yes, it looks much better now.

The yellow brick of Woods Hall (shown here) and Schoo Hall was painted over in 2000 to match the red-brick décor of the rest of the campus. Some returning alums claimed the buildings had always been red. Woods Hall would be razed in 2008 to make way for the new campus union.

The bold line traces the path of Hickory Street from Alden Street through the center of the campus. Bromery eliminated the street to create green space, and Flynn continued the improvements by closing the narrow and dangerous access road between Woods Hall and the Beveridge Center to vehicle traffic.

Before: Over the summer of 1999, this parking lot was transformed into a beautiful (not to mention safer) green space.

After: The parking lot becomes green space. Flynn received "hundreds" of thank-you notes from appreciative students.

Another campus improvement in 2000 followed on the heels of Bromery's elimination in 1998 of the section of Hickory Street that once snaked through campus from Fuller Arts Center to Alden Street. Now, the narrow and dangerous access road from Alden Street that led between Woods Hall and the Beveridge Center and continued at the rear of the Administration Building was closed to vehicle traffic and made safer for pedestrians.

Still another campus improvement, this one also championed by Flynn, had occurred earlier, over the summer of 1999. When students left for the summer, there was a large parking lot in front of Reed residence hall. When they returned, the lot had been transformed into a beautiful (not to mention safer) green space, suitable for sun-bathing, reading, tossing Frisbees, and other pursuits. Flynn recalls today that he received "hundreds" of thank-you notes from appreciative students, and many favorable comments on the change from returning alums.

In September of the millennial year, a committee of educators representing the New England Association of Schools and Colleges, Inc. (NEASC) arrived on the campus to carry out its once-every-decade re-accreditation process. For three years previously, Gretchen Brockmeyer, acting provost and vice president of Academic Affairs, had chaired a twenty-three-member steering committee to be certain the College was fully prepared for this rigorous evaluation.

Upon its departure, the NEASC committee said it was generally pleased with the state of the College. In its verbal feedback, the committee mentioned a number of strengths: the College's distinctive mission and relevance; the commitment of faculty, staff, and students; the progress on infrastructure; the physical appearance of the campus; the active student involvement in governance and decision making; and the positive contributions of the School of Human Services. The committee promised a full written report in the coming months.

Also in September 2000, a new dance major became available for the first time, as part of the visual and performing arts department. Even though dance had been taught at the College for years, the new major revived a significant dance history that had begun in 1933, when modern dance pioneer Ted Shawn joined the faculty as an adjunct.

Ted Shawn's legacy lives: A new dance major became available for the first time in 2000.

Shawn created Jacob's Pillow in the Berkshires with an all-male troupe of College dancers. In the process, he established dance as a legitimate field for men, even for football players and other athletes who needed additional pedal dexterity. Dancers studied with Shawn at the College during the school year, then the top dancers trained extensively at Jacob's Pillow during the summer.

STRENGTHENING IMPORTANT RELATIONSHIPS

Another important initiative that was started in 2000, also part of *The Plan for Springfield College*, was to explore ways to strengthen the College's collaboration with its key partners. Included here was the long-standing bond between the YMCA and the College, which Flynn was to nurture carefully throughout his time as president. The scope of YMCA-related programs at the College expanded greatly. Flynn spoke regularly to YMCA groups, and built strong working relationships with senior-level executives of the YMCA of the USA.

In April 2004, the YMCA of the USA and the College signed an important articulation agreement that "revitalizes the historical relationship between Springfield College and the YMCA of the USA," and "designates Springfield College as a YMCA Leadership Development Center." In June 2009, a successor agreement was signed.

Largely as a result of the negotiations leading to the signing of the 2004 articulation agreement, a close personal bond developed between Flynn and three top YMCA leaders—Ken Gladish, then the national executive director of the YMCA of the USA; John Coduri, national executive director of the Association of YMCA Professionals (AYP); and John Preis, president and CEO of the YMCA Retirement Fund. The four, who started in their new positions around the same time, met periodically, communicated via email and telephone, and came to be known, in some circles at least, as "the Y-Four."

Also important was the relationship between the Naismith Memorial Basketball Hall of Fame (now moved downtown) and the Birthplace of Basketball. The College and the Hall of Fame collaborated on a number of projects that benefited the Hall of Fame, Springfield College students, and the citizens of Springfield.

Students were routinely drafted to help at all sorts of Hall of Fame events, thus gaining important experience in the real world. Flynn was named to the Hall of Fame board of trustees, and Hall of Fame President John Doleva joined the Springfield College Board of Trustees. When the College's first comprehensive fund-raising campaign in thirty-five years went public in May 2005, it occurred at a formal dinner held at Center Court at the Hall of Fame.

THE SCHOOL OF HUMAN SERVICES

In retrospect, it is easy to view the 1988 acquisition of the School of Human Services (SHS) from New Hampshire College as one of the most important achievements of the past twenty-five years at Springfield College.

At the time of the acquisition, there were doubts in some quarters that SHS "fit" with the traditional College. The latter, of course, was self-contained on its main campus and served "traditional" undergraduate and graduate students with a wide-ranging curriculum. SHS, on the other hand, held classes on weekends, year-round, at sites in New Hampshire, serving "non-traditional" students with a human-services curriculum that gave academic credits for life learning, or experience gained on the job. The typical SHS student at the time was a thirty-seven-year-old single mother who worked at a human services job during the week and went to school on weekends.

Left to right: Bob Willey, dean of the School of Human Services; Jean Wyld, vice president for academic affairs; and Dick Flynn.

It was only when one examined the academic focus of SHS, and compared it with the long-standing Springfield College mission, that the absolute brilliance of the acquisition became evident. It was, and is today, a natural way to extend the Springfield College mission (not to mention the Springfield College "brand" and reputation) to serve a totally new segment of the population, in cities throughout the United States.

Better still, three presidents—Falcone, Bromery, and Flynn—clearly saw SHS as a way to help further strengthen the relationship between the College and the YMCA. How? By locating regional SHS campuses mostly in YMCA facilities in major cities throughout the country, and then offering programs that would help YMCA leaders advance in their chosen careers.

Under Bromery, SHS had been expanded, with new regional SHS campuses located in Wilmington, Delaware (1995); San Diego, California (1997); Boston, Massachusetts (1997); and Tampa Bay, Florida (1998). During the first five years of the Flynn presidency, three more regional campuses were established: Milwaukee, Wisconsin (2000); Los Angeles, California (2001); and Charleston, South Carolina (2003). And in September 2008, a major SHS regional campus was established in Houston, Texas, in partnership with the Houston YMCA. The Houston campus is intended to be a model for future SHS campuses.

196

In addition, SHS presented significant international opportunities. Over the years, SHS programs were started on the continent of Africa, in the Caribbean, and in Brazil and Sweden.

When Flynn arrived, the tuition revenues from SHS regional campuses were being used in part to compensate for operating deficits at the campus in Springfield. Flynn thought this was clearly wrong, and vowed to run the Springfield campus so that it was on solid financial footing by itself, independent of funds from SHS. This he accomplished in short order.

Today, the Springfield College School of Human Services is an integral part of the Springfield College educational offering. And the Springfield campus is completely self-sufficient—another example of improved financial condition.

The success and acceptance of the School of Human Services did not happen overnight. Nor did it happen without the unwavering commitment and support of Falcone, Bromery, and Flynn, as well as a number of other individuals:

- Molly Rau, academic vice president under Bromery, who championed SHS from its earliest days;

- Dan Nussbaum, who was dean of SHS until he left the College to join the YMCA in 2002;

- Rick Davila, who served SHS as a "campus starter" in Wilmington, San Diego, Tampa Bay, and Milwaukee, and later was selected to serve a term as the Distinguished Springfield College Professor of Humanics—the first SHS representative to be so honored;

- Jean Wyld, vice president for academic affairs, who, along with Flynn, always referred to SHS as an integral part of the College and was a strong advocate for the school; and

- Robert Willey, an experienced higher-education administrator who was appointed dean of SHS in 2002 and has provided enthusiastic and dedicated leadership to the school.

FINANCIAL INTEGRITY — THE *SINE QUA NON*

There is general agreement among trustees interviewed on the subject that one of Flynn's greatest achievements in his years as president of Springfield College has been restoring and maintaining the College's financial integrity. Trustee Peter Andruszkiewicz '80, for one, says this was a three-part process—stopping the financial bleeding, restoring financial discipline, and raising funds through an ambitious capital campaign "that took a lot of chutzpah."

Andruszkiewicz adds that it was Flynn's dogged work on finances, with the able assistance of John Mailhot, vice president for administration and finance, that "made possible the physical transformation of the campus.

"When Dick first arrived," Andruszkiewicz recalls, "he understood very clearly that he had to stop the financial bleeding, which was caused by the empty beds we had on the campus. He came in and assessed, and understood what needed to be done, and put together a plan, and executed the plan to get those beds filled."

Trustee Peter Andruszkiewicz '80 said Flynn's dogged work on the College's finances "made possible the physical transformation of the campus."

197

The stellar recruiting work by members of the admissions staff was led by John Wilcox '67 and Mary DeAngelo.

A small private college such as Springfield College doesn't have the luxury of a huge endowment to help pay annual operating expenses. Harvard, Yale, and others measure their endowments in billions; Springfield College does not.

Moreover, during the first three years of the Flynn presidency, common stocks suffered through the so-called "dot-com crash," which lowered the Dow Jones Industrial Average by nearly 40 percent and affected college endowments accordingly. (A similar decline in stock prices occurred in 2008.)

Historically, Springfield College has relied almost exclusively on student tuition and room and board payments to cover its annual operating expenses. So if the number of students in attendance were to decline, either budgets would have to be cut or the endowment would have to make up the difference. Neither alternative is attractive.

That appeared to be the case when Flynn arrived in March 1999. The enrollment forecast for the 1999-2000 academic year was not encouraging—190 empty beds.

Student Affairs personnel had begun to suggest alternate uses for the rooms with the empty beds. Flynn had a better idea: Why not, he suggested gently, fill the empty beds with new students? Then, he noted pointedly, the College wouldn't have to worry about what to do with the empty rooms. And the move would also help the College's financial situation.

The empty beds were filled through a combination of more aggressive enrollment management tactics, new recruitment materials, increased faculty involvement, and some stellar recruiting work by members of the admissions staff. And not too long afterwards, the College was breaking ground for its first new residence hall since the construction of the Townhouses in 1989. There have been very few empty beds since then.

What used to be called "freshman beanies" are still worn today, by what are now called "first-year students."

Securing the financial integrity of the College was a coin with two sides. One side was increasing revenues, primarily through more intense focus on scholarships, planned giving, and other development efforts, in addition to filling those empty beds. The coin's other side was getting a firm handle on budgets and costs, and continually looking for ways to increase efficiency without sacrificing effectiveness. With typical enthusiasm, multitasking as usual, Flynn attacked both sides of the financial integrity coin simultaneously.

Andruszkiewicz puts it this way: "Dick is an academic, but he's also a terrific businessman. He brought discipline to the budgeting process. People had to justify the numbers they used, and had to live within their budget numbers, and had to achieve an appropriate return on that investment."

The financial discipline led directly to budget surpluses where there had been break-even results, or even, in some years, deficits. The surpluses allowed the College to begin to work on the long list of deferred maintenance projects around the campus. And that allowed people to begin to dream a bit about what was needed going forward, in terms of facilities.

Former trustee chair Jim Walsh '64 comments on the importance of deferred maintenance to a college: "It may not seem like the most glamorous work, but if you're redoing the bathrooms in a residence hall, that's very important in terms of the quality of student life."

Speaking at the Faculty Institute at the start of the 2000-2001 academic year, Flynn proudly announced the College was now operating on a balanced budget. Moreover, that balanced budget had been achieved notwithstanding a tuition increase of only 2.4 percent—significantly lower than prior years, and also lower than comparable institutions. Clearly, Flynn was not about to balance the budget on the backs of the students —or their parents.

The College was still heavily tuition dependent, Flynn said, and "a significant portion of the operating budget on the expense side would be classified as fixed in nature." He also noted that scholarships and financial aid had increased significantly over the years. "Future budgets will continue to focus strongly on price sensitivity in the marketplace," he added.

2001: GOOD NEWS AND BAD

As calendar 2001 began, the appearance of the campus began to change in relatively small ways, thanks largely to funds freed up for deferred maintenance by more effective financial management. But the changes were a sign of the bigger changes to come later.

In addition to minor renovation projects in the residence halls and classroom buildings, several planting projects took place, enhancing the natural beauty of the campus.

In one of the first significant interior improvements to the campus, the first floor of Marsh Memorial got a long overdue makeover, to give the historic building the appearance it deserved, Flynn said. Funding for the project was courtesy of the Class of 1968, which made a generous gift for the purpose in late 2000.

A new granite tile floor was installed in the foyer in a mere nine days, with a brass rendition of the College seal in the center. In addition, the first-floor foyer and conference room received some badly needed wood stain and polish.

Erected in part with student labor and dedicated in 1913, Marsh Memorial had functioned as the College's library for nearly sixty years, until the 1971 opening of Babson Library.

All in all, inspecting the newly refurbished lobby of Marsh Memorial, one could not resist thinking of President William Howard Taft, who had been the featured speaker at the building's dedication in 1913. During a reception at the Doggetts' home before the ceremony, President Taft, all 300 pounds of him, sat on a chair and unceremoniously broke it.

The lobby of Marsh Memorial received a long-overdue makeover in 2001, thanks to a gift from the Class of 1968.

Meanwhile, the bidding process began for the first of several upgrades of the food service in Cheney Hall. One immediate change was the reopening of the grill in Woods Hall for lunch, after a lengthy absence.

The winning bidder for Cheney turned out to be Aramark Corporation, which immediately brought in a number of innovative food stations. Students who were there at the time surely recall Java City, Pan Geos, Tortilla Fresca, Cranberry Farms, GrilleWorks, and, most popular of all, a Subway franchise. Also available under the new regime were

Massachusetts Senator John Kerry spoke at the 2001 commencement.

smoothies, pretzels, and brick-oven-fired pizza. The new additions were an immediate hit, and Aramark ultimately partnered with the College for a highly successful total renovation of the food service operation in 2005.

In April 2001, the Springfield College family had a scare, when President Flynn checked into Boston's Massachusetts General Hospital to undergo surgery for prostate cancer. The surgery was successful, and Flynn, uncharacteristically, stayed away from the office for a few days, recuperating at his home in East Longmeadow until he regained his strength.

Once he recovered from the surgery, Flynn rarely discussed the topic with anyone except family members. He didn't dwell on it, for the simple reason that he wanted nothing to distract him or anyone else from the task at hand.

Each day, the high-energy president made dozens of telephone calls, sent and received dozens of emails, read everything that was sent out to him, and made every decision that needed to be made during his recuperation. Not missing a beat, he even worked in the passenger seat while he was being driven to Boston for his post-operative treatments.

In May, Massachusetts junior senator and 2004 presidential candidate John F. Kerry spoke at the undergraduate commencement and was awarded an honorary Doctor of Humanics degree.

And then, quite suddenly, it was September 11, 2001 . . . .

THE WORLD WILL NEVER BE THE SAME

The room over the garage had served as Art Linkletter's bedroom whenever he visited the campus. But once President Bromery elected to continue to reside in his longtime family home in Amherst, the president's house on Alden Street was transformed into the Admissions Center.

Seated now at his desk in the middle of that room was John Wilcox '67, executive director of enrollment management. An early riser and early arriver, Wilcox had been at work since about six a.m. He was deep into New Student Orientation matters—wrapping up the 2001 NSO and beginning the planning for 2002 NSO.

The sound of footsteps on the stairs outside his door brought Wilcox back to the present. Mary DeAngelo, then director of undergraduate admissions, peeked around the door jamb with astonishing news: "A plane crashed into the World Trade Center."

News services were reporting that American Airlines Flight 11, out of Boston and headed for Los Angeles, had crashed into Tower One of the World Trade Center. As the two talked, United Flight 175, also out of Boston and also headed for Los Angeles, struck Tower Two. Then, thirty-five minutes later, American Flight 77, Dulles to Los Angeles, crashed into the Pentagon. And twenty-five minutes after that, United Flight 93, Newark to San Francisco, went down in a field in Pennsylvania.

It was, people said later, like the assassination of JFK in 1963: You never forget where you were and what you were doing when you heard the news.

Students at a candlelight service outside Marsh Memorial, on the one-year anniversary of the 9/11 attacks.

A flag draped outside Gulick hall after the attacks.

Wilcox and DeAngelo listened to the news on the radio at the receptionist's desk for a while, then went out into the magnificent early fall morning and walked up to Cheney Hall. Inside, small groups of students clustered silently around the television sets located throughout the room. The mood was somber.

As the full dimensions of the terrorist attack became evident, Springfield College responded. Flynn led the College in an interfaith service in Marsh Memorial Chapel commemorating the victims in New York, Washington, and the field in Pennsylvania. Solace was provided to a shocked campus community.

Reporting later on the events of September 11, *Triangle* magazine stated,

> Though acknowledging the grief felt by all Americans, the College maintained its regular schedule of classes as a way to encourage sharing and support among fellow students, faculty, and administrators and staff. Services provided by several offices, such as the United Campus Ministry and Spiritual Life Center, the Counseling Center, Student Affairs, and Residence Life, remained readily available for individuals in need.

A number of Springfield College people were galvanized into action by the worst act of terrorism ever seen on United States soil. A few examples among many:

• Emergency medical services management majors, all of them certified EMTs or paramedics, ran volunteer ambulances in Massachusetts and Connecticut, allowing regular ambulance staffs to help the rescue efforts in lower Manhattan.

• Bob Hopkins, assistant professor of EMSM, participated in search and rescue operations at the site as a member of the Worcester Disaster Medical Assistance Team.

• Janice Price of the financial aid office spent four days in New York supporting her son (and Springfield College graduate) Jason Gaboury '95. Gaboury was doing chaplaincy work and counseling students day and night at the City Universities of New York.

• And longtime trustee Harold Smith H'98, looking out the south-facing window of his 26th story apartment on Duane Street in the nearby Tribeca neighborhood, saw the first plane hit. Then he heard the sirens of the fire trucks rolling out of the firehouse across the street. Later that day, Smith helped with medical triage in the firehouse, and used his counseling skills with people who were in deep shock. He returned to his apartment, totally exhausted, only to find that the collapse of Seven World Trade Center had caused the generators in his building to stop functioning—no electricity, and no elevators. Hobbled by recent knee surgery, Smith was unable to use the stairs, and was marooned in his apartment for two days with only water and a granola bar for sustenance. On the third day after the attack, his building was evacuated.

Harold Smith H'98, a longtime trustee, lent a helping hand with medical triage and counseling in lower Manhattan following the terrorist attacks.

The football game with Kings Point, scheduled for September 15, was postponed to October 27. Located on the north shore of Long Island, the U.S. Merchant Marine Academy at Kings Point is twenty miles east of New York City. The September 11 attacks put the academy in the thick of search-and-rescue services.

When October 27 arrived, there was a brief but powerful halftime ceremony on the field to honor police, firefighters, and rescue workers—those who lost their lives in the line of duty on September 11, and those who protect the safety and security of the Pioneer Valley. In his remarks for the occasion, Flynn said, "These are difficult times for all Americans, and these public servants play vital roles throughout the Pioneer Valley in preserving our safety and security. They deserve our respect and our thanks."

Two weeks later, on Veterans Day, there was a campus tribute to victims of the terrorist attacks, with patriotic music, a twenty-one-gun salute by a Marine Corps rifle squad, and an address by retired Marine Lieutenant Colonel Hank Detering '72.

The terrorist attacks remained in the memories of everyone. When the one-year anniversary came around, a full program of campus events was scheduled in remembrance of the victims, focusing on themes of healing and new beginning. Alums who had lost family members reflected on September 11 in different ways. Members of the campus ministry staff conducted an interfaith service commemorating those who died in New York City, Washington, and rural Pennsylvania. Students and graduates from the College's emergency medical services management program recited the new Springfield College EMT oath "to rededicate themselves in spirit, mind, and body to serving humankind." And the Class of 2004 staged a candlelight vigil on Administration (now Naismith) Green, in which student leaders lighted candles from the commemorative candle in Marsh Memorial Chapel and watched as candles of other participants were lighted in turn.

In many other ways, the business of the College went on, day after day, with a normalcy that belied the horror of the terrorist attacks.

A huge American flag is traditionally draped over the front entrance to Marsh Memorial for Veteran's Day observances.

202

PUTTING THE PIECES IN PLACE

As Springfield College, like campuses all over the country, was recovering from the September 11 terrorist attacks, Flynn continued methodically putting the pieces in place for what was to become a renaissance at Springfield College.

The College's financial condition was greatly improved, and getting better. The strategic plan had been approved by the Board of Trustees. A totally new senior leadership team was in place. The disruptions of the late 1980s and 1990s were mostly in the past. Groundwork was being laid and preliminary preparations were being made for a comprehensive fundraising campaign that would become the largest in the College's history and its first such campaign since the 1960s. In the words of Flynn himself, "the train was about to leave the station."

Flynn believed that "a college president's primary role is to provide leadership. That includes developing a shared vision for the institution, and then providing encouragement and support for those pursuing that vision." The "shared vision" had been created with input from all concerned. Now it was time for Flynn to provide the encouragement and support.

A NEW PRESIDENT'S HOUSE

The Board of Trustees believed that Springfield College was the kind of institution that ought to have its president living on the campus. At their November 2001 meeting, trustees had voted unanimously to request that Flynn move to the campus, and require all future presidents of Springfield College to live on campus.

In the College's history, several presidents had lived on the campus—either in the big Victorian house built by Gulick that stood about where Babson Library is today, or in the Doggett Memorial President's House a little further down Alden Street. While Bromery had chosen to remain in his family home in Amherst, the trustees now wanted to return to the tradition.

At their November 2001 meeting, trustees voted unanimously to request that Dick and Jani Flynn move to the campus, and to require all future presidents of Springfield College to live on campus. The Flynns moved into this house in April 2003.

203

After the School of Social Work moved to the newly renovated Brennan Center on Island Pond Road, Admissions moved to the space vacated by Social Work on Middlesex Avenue, to make room for the new president's house.

The newly renovated Brennan Center, new home of the School of Social Work.

But where? Doggett Memorial was not a possibility. It had been used as an admissions house since the 1990s, and would require a total renovation to be habitable as a residence once again. More to the point, the building was definitely showing its age, having served as the starting point for many thousands of prospective students and their parents. An architectural analysis of the building concluded that the projected cost of renovations was prohibitive. So trustees concluded that a new president's house ought to be constructed, to provide living space for the Flynns and future presidents, and additional space for presidential meetings and entertainment.

In a game of organizational musical chairs, the School of Social Work moved to the newly renovated and expanded Brennan Center on Island Pond Road, and Admissions happily moved to the space vacated by Social Work on Middlesex Avenue. In March 2002, Doggett Memorial was demolished to make way for new construction, and on April 1, 2003 Dick and Jani Flynn moved from their home in East Longmeadow into the new President's House.

Student residence advisors and residence directors enjoy barbecue in the back yard of the president's house. Inside, a large portion of the house was given over to public space—a dining room for entertaining, two reception rooms for larger gatherings, and a bedroom suite for special visitors to the College.

In an interview with the *Student*, Flynn admitted that "moving is perhaps my least favorite activity." He added, "It would have been much easier for us to have moved to campus when we first arrived, but that was not an option, since the house had already been converted to an admissions center." He might also have observed that the move was not quite as arduous as it might have been; in the basement in the East Longmeadow home were dozens of boxes of stuff that had never been unpacked after the move from Nebraska nearly four years before.

The house itself was a beauty—an enhancement to Alden Street and to the campus as a whole. Looking at it from the street, it seemed quite large at first glance. But visitors inside quickly realized that a large portion of the house was given over to public space—a dining room for entertaining, two reception rooms for larger gatherings, and a bedroom suite for special guests of the

College. With a fundraising campaign in the works, this made perfect sense, and this public space was to get plenty of use in the years to follow.

The Flynns both worked closely with Ray Laplante, a well known area builder selected for the project. This team of three planned the house and decided on all the interior finishing touches. They focused on functionality and the "public" aspects of any president's house, with constant attention paid to costs. Future presidents of Springfield College will be glad to learn they also avoided any overly splashy interior decorating touches.

All things considered, the Flynns were both totally delighted to be living on the campus, and took full advantage of that in the years ahead.

Among the first events hosted in the new house were receptions for seniors and student leaders, at which the Flynns personally greeted every guest. Dick Flynn ponders the benefits of those soirees: "They've proven to be a constructive learning experience for me—asking why students decided to come here in the first place, whether their expectations and dreams had been fulfilled, and what their plans are for the future. When you can get students to reflect on their college experiences and their future plans, it tells you a lot about how well we have done our job in preparing them for life in general, and for the types of positions they are interested in pursuing."

Those receptions for graduating students, as well as ice cream socials for new students, were to become annual events at the new president's house. Along with Faculty Senate dinners, Board of Trustee events, a variety of alumni activities, student leader receptions, and many other events, it became a very busy place.

When the couple finally moved in, Flynn credited Jani with masterminding the logistics of the move, and summarized his own feelings about the new residence this way: "Well, my commute is a lot shorter now, and I don't have to travel far for dinner, then come back for evening events. And I don't have too much trouble finding a parking space."

BILL COSBY AT COMMENCEMENT

Entertainer, author, and education advocate Bill Cosby was the keynote speaker at the 2002 commencement exercises on Blake Field. Bill Marsh, who had served the College so competently and unselfishly following Bromery's retirement, was awarded an honorary degree.

Cosby, who had known Flynn since meeting him at the University of Nebraska at Omaha in the 1980s, focused his no-nonsense remarks on the theme of service, noting the careers many of the graduates planned to undertake. He said academics are sometimes guilty of "writing with a drive-by attitude—that is, without talking to the very people who are the subjects of their reports. They're not in the trenches," he said, adding, "Springfield College puts people in the trenches!" Cheering erupted.

The beguiling Cosby humor was on display, too: "When I received my Ed.D. . . . . my mother was in the audience. At the time I graduated, I was making four million dollars a year. My mother ran over, knocked down the security guard, jumped in my lap and kissed me so hard, and she said, 'Now you have something to fall back on.'"

World-famous entertainer, author, and education advocate Bill Cosby H'02 spoke at the 2002 commencement exercises on Blake Track and Field.

The George I. Alden Center for Interactive Learning was established in 2002 through a grant of $150,000 from the George I. Alden Trust.

Just a couple of old point guards: *Triangle* magazine cover photo of Flynn with Earvin "Magic" Johnson at the Naismith Memorial Basketball Hall of Fame.

A month earlier, Springfield College had scored a real coup with a clean sweep of major awards at the 2002 annual convention of the American Alliance for Health, Physical Education, Recreation, and Dance (AAHPERD) in San Diego: National Athletic Director of the Year: Walter Sargent '65; National High School Teacher of the Year, Carol Swindler Martini '75; National Elementary School Teacher of the Year, Nancy Egner Markos '71; and National Adapted Physical Education Teacher of the Year, Candice Dias McLeod '79.

Try to imagine the shock—and the delight of alums in the audience—as one winner after another was announced, took the podium, and toasted Springfield College. No one there could recall another such clean sweep. Springfield College had always been prominent in AAHPERD, and Mimi Murray '61 had served as the organization's national president. But this was totally astonishing.

In July 2002, the George I. Alden Trust awarded Springfield College a $150,000 grant to establish a state-of-the-art technology learning center. There, students and faculty at the College's main campus could participate in live, interactive learning programs with faculty and students at School of Human Services campuses throughout the country.

When it opened, the George I. Alden Center for Interactive Learning included a "smart" classroom with interactive computer work stations, a board-style meeting room equipped for live video conferencing, and a central control room.

In September 2002, the dazzling new Naismith Memorial Basketball Hall of Fame opened for business on the riverfront in downtown Springfield. And the cover of the next issue of *Triangle* magazine featured Flynn and Earvin "Magic" Johnson shaking hands outside the new Hall.

In October, the 93rd not-quite-annual Springfield College Gymnastics Exhibition Show recreated twenty years of the Home Show's highlight performances, including the show's traditional finale—several tableaux featuring gymnasts in silver body paint forming statuaries. As usual, the Home Show played to sellout homecoming crowds at both performances.

In November, in the spirit of the first Thanksgiving, the College and its Wilbraham Avenue neighbor, the Massachusetts Career Development Institute (MCDI) served traditional turkey dinner free of charge to about 600 individuals and families from the adjacent neighborhoods—Upper Hill, Old Hill, Maple High/Six Corners, and Mason Square. Working in collaboration, seventy-five volunteers from the College joined fifty MCDI volunteers and staff members to decorate the dining room, welcome guests, serve dinner, and clean up afterwards. The dinner has become an annual event.

In December, the Davis Educational Foundation made a three-year, $240,000 grant to the College to create the Davis Center for Information Literacy in Babson Library. The center, featuring twenty-five computer stations, would help students with research assignments to find out what they needed to know, where to go for the information, and how to analyze the information they've found.

Around year-end 2002, two more legendary figures from the College's past died:

- **Charles F. "Chic" Weckwerth** '31, passed away in November, ending a relationship with the College that spanned more than seven decades. Weckwerth served for many years as director of the department of community and outdoor recreation, a program he founded. The Weckwerth Lecture, a scholarly event held in the spring, was established in his honor in 1992.

- **Gilbert Vickers**, who served as music director at the College from 1950 to 1982, died in December. Known as "Coach Vickers" to his choral students, he'd been heard to remark that he was the only undefeated coach at Springfield College. Through the years, he brought his musical talents to the Glee Club, the Scotchmen, the Heathertones, and the Springfield College Singers. He also wrote new arrangements of the alma mater and other College songs.

Charles F. "Chic" Weckwerth died in November 2002, ending a relationship with the College that spanned more than seven decades.

TOWN-AND-GOWN RELATIONSHIPS

The town-and-gown relationship between the College and its adjacent neighborhoods had been periodically rocky over the years, due mostly to the College's repeated (and well-meaning) efforts to close Alden Street.

Most of these plans had suggested rerouting traffic to King Street or other neighborhood roads—a significant disruption to the peace of the neighborhood, in the opinion of many neighbors. As a result, despite the many good things accomplished by Springfield College and its students, faculty, and staff, relations had been a bit tense.

From his first days as president, Flynn sought to change that state of affairs. His philosophy on the subject was summed up in a single sentence: Springfield College wants to be a part of its community, not apart from its community.

"Coach" Gil Vickers, said to be the only undefeated coach at Springfield College, conducts at Springfield's Symphony Hall.

In his first week on the job, he met with a delegation of neighborhood clergy and other leaders. A few weeks later, he took a street-by-street tour of the neighborhood with residents of Old Hill which he found interesting and educational.

With the assistance of Director of Community Affairs Dale Allen '92, existing programs were strengthened, a number of new programs were started, and the College and the community became engaged in significant regular dialogue.

A broad-based neighborhood coalition encouraged and led by Springfield College came together in February 2003 to announce a joint venture to develop a master plan for the Old Hill neighborhood and adjacent portions of Upper Hill. Flynn said the plan would draw on and enhance the area's educational resources, and promised that the College would further expand its current community involvement by increasing its mentoring, student teaching, and recreational programs in the neighborhood. This master planning effort was to serve as a foundation for a number of community initiatives.

Around this time, the College's community relations efforts were featured in a U.S. Department of Housing and Urban Development (HUD) book, part of a series titled *Lasting Engagement*. The series examined four institutions of higher education that had successfully made community engagement central to their missions. Springfield College was the only private college in the series.

The Partnership for the Renewal of Old Hill is a joint venture to develop a master plan for the Old Hill neighborhood and adjacent portions of Upper Hill.

The U.S. Department of Housing and Urban Development book in which Springfield College was featured for its community relations initiatives.

The 104-page book described how the College had shifted over ten years from a "missionary style" model of carrying out its public services, to working in partnership with a broad array of stakeholders in community improvement. The book also included descriptions of the College's current community outreach, and a chapter on ten lessons learned that other institutions could apply to their own efforts to institutionalize community engagement.

In April 2003, the Partners Program, one of the College's most successful community programs, celebrated its tenth anniversary with a big bash at the Naismith Memorial Basketball Hall of Fame. Under the program, more than 600 Springfield College students had been paired as tutors and mentors with children from nearby DeBerry School. The children were transported to the campus after school for an hour of academic help; then the students took the children to dinner in Cheney Hall, followed by a sports event, crafts project, or social time. It was, and is, a practical, hands-on program that has been highly successful and continues today.

UNBEATEN, UNTIED, UNPRECEDENTED

"Who's Number One? It's the greatest question in sports. Bobby Jones or Jack Nicklaus? Barry Bonds or Babe Ruth? We'll never know, but that doesn't mean the debates don't rage on."

That's how John White, then the College's sports information director, and today vice president for development and alumni relations, led off a *Triangle* magazine article on the four greatest football teams in post-war Springfield College history. The success of the unbeaten and untied 2003 football team, coached by Mike DeLong '74, revived a long-standing argument on Alden Street. After all, the 1956 team under Ossie Solem and the 1965 edition under Ted Dunn also had gone undefeated during the regular season. And the 2000 squad, also coached by DeLong, had rung up a record eleven victories against two losses, and went deep into the NCAA Division III post-season competition.

White left his readers tantalizingly short of an answer to the question, and you won't find it in these pages, either—merely a bow in the direction of all four teams, who did the College proud with their outstanding performances.

Football was not the only team to become the toast of the campus in 2003. In April, in Huntington, Pennsylvania, the Springfield College men's volleyball team, coached by Charlie Sullivan '91, topped Juniata College, the home-town team, to win the Molten Division III Invitational National Championships for the third consecutive year. In a remarkable illustration of guts and determination, the team lost the first game 27-30, then came back to win three games in succession, 31-29, 30-24, and 30-27.

Many students, faculty, and staff have seen Flynn hit one of his long sweeping hook shots from the corner. And all are quite astonished, even disbelieving. This photograph was printed on the front page of an NCAA publication.

In May 2003, the College broke ground for a new four-story, suite-style residence hall—the first new residence hall since the construction of the Townhouses fourteen years previously. Here, Flynn gets help from Board Chair John Odierna '64 and 14 other trustees.

EMPTY BEDS? WHAT EMPTY BEDS?

Remember those empty beds Flynn was concerned about when he first arrived on campus in 1999? Not only were they filled quickly, mostly through more ambitious recruitment tactics, but in May 2003, the College confidently broke ground for the construction of a new four-story, suite-style residence hall—the first new residence hall since the construction of the Townhouses fourteen years previously.

The new residence hall, located directly across from the Townhouses, with open green space in between, was designed to accommodate the increasing enrollment, and to make it possible for more seniors to live on the campus. Combined with the Townhouses, the new building created what some called a "senior village."

The amenities in the new residence hall were, indeed, tempting to seniors who had been considering going off-campus to live: Four-person or six-person suites, each with bedrooms for each resident, and a living room, kitchen, dining area, and one or two baths. Every bedroom featured telephone, cable television, and Internet connections. And, it was all air-conditioned.

Equally important, revenues from room and board charges were projected to cover comfortably the costs of building and operating the new facility.

The first year of occupancy was 2004, and that year an amazing 90 percent of seniors chose to live on the campus, up from about 20 percent when Flynn had arrived in 1999. That said something about the accommodations, of course, but it also said something about the many other benefits of living on the campus.

As part of the construction of the new residence hall, a large, tree-dotted parking lot was established between the new hall and the new Admissions Center, and a new walkway was created to lead prospective students from the Admissions Center to the rest of campus in a stylish, elegant manner.

Ribbon-cutting for the Suites, in time for occupancy in the fall of 2004: Left to right, SGA President Aaron Dombroski '05; President Flynn; and trustees John Odierna '64 and Lyman Wood H'06.

Dottie Potter Zenaty '65, who lettered in four sports during her college career, retired as teacher and field hockey coach in December 2003.

LEGEND OF THE FALL

An article in the Summer 2004 issue of *Triangle* magazine described the scene at the field hockey team's year-end banquet the previous December, quoting the coach:

> Dottie Potter Zenaty stepped to the podium to announce the team captains for the 2004 field hockey season. This is an annual rite-of-passage at the end-of-the-year banquet, the passing of the torch from one set of proud captains to the next group of leaders.

> "I told the team that I teach in my Principles and Problems of Coaching class that a coach shouldn't elect or select captains for the next season if the coach is not going to be returning," recalls Zenaty. And with that, one of the greatest college field hockey coaches in history announced that she had coached her last game at Springfield College, leaving a group of players, parents, and friends of the program in disbelief.

Thus did Dottie Potter Zenaty '65, who lettered in four sports during her college career, retire as a teacher and coach in December 2003, after coaching 653 matches in thirty-four seasons at Springfield College—more matches than any other coach in college field hockey history. Her 377 victories rank her tops in New England and fifth nationwide on college field hockey's all-time win listing.

A month later, Zenaty was inducted into the National Field Hockey Coaches Association Hall of Fame.

In her term as the 2003-04 Distinguished Springfield Professor of Humanics, Zenaty created a year-long program that educated students about Alzheimer's disease, in honor of her late husband and constant companion, Bert Zenaty. Until his death, Bert was a fixture at the end of the bench during field hockey games coached by his wife.

Signing the agreement with the YMCA in April 2004 are President Flynn and YMCA president and CEO Ken Gladish. College trustees, College leaders, and YMCA leaders look on.

HISTORIC AGREEMENT WITH THE YMCA OF THE USA

In a historic agreement signed April 7, 2004, the YMCA of the USA designated Springfield College as a premier institution of higher education for YMCA leaders, and Springfield College agreed to annually recruit students interested in YMCA careers from around the country, as well as to expand its range of educational programs for current and future YMCA staff.

Signing the agreement in the Townhouses Conference Room were President Flynn and YMCA of the USA National Executive Director Kenneth L. Gladish. That same afternoon, Springfield College and YMCA representatives in San Diego, California; Tampa Bay, Florida; and Wilmington, Delaware, witnessed a ceremonial signing at the College's George I. Alden Center in Wilbraham Hall.

The agreement expanded more than a century of collaboration between Springfield College and the YMCA of the USA. And it symbolized the growing rapport between the two institutions. The agreement was renewed five years later, in June 2009, by Flynn and Neil Nicoll G'73, Gladish's successor as the YUSA national executive director and a trustee of the College.

As a further indication of the blossoming partnership, at the 118th Commencement in May, the two speakers both carried heavy YMCA credentials: YMCA of the USA CEO Ken Gladish at the undergraduate ceremony, and Rizek Abusharr, retired director general of the Jerusalem International YMCA, at the graduate exercises.

AND SPEAKING OF COMMENCEMENTS . . .

Gladish and Abusharr, in their commencement addresses, both echoed the universal themes of peace and service that had been enunciated forty years earlier by Rev. Dr. Martin Luther King, Jr. In his visit to the campus in 1964, Rev. King had stirred the souls of the audience and left an indelible impression on the minds of many.

Both 2004 commencement speakers had strong YMCA ties: Left to right: Trustee John Odierna '64, Rizek Abusharr, Ken Gladish, and President Flynn.

In his remarks at the 2004 Baccalaureate, Flynn referenced King's remarks: "Nearly forty years ago, in June of 1964, a man came to this campus to speak at commencement. He spoke about change. And his words on that day—as well as other words he said at other times and in other places—were instrumental in bringing about fundamental change in this great nation."

Flynn commented that King had spoken glowingly of Springfield College in his preliminary remarks: "He noted, and I quote, 'a deep sense of appreciation for all that this College has meant to the cultural and humanitarian life of our nation and the world.' And he added, 'I am deeply aware of this rich and great tradition.'"

Rev. King's visit, and the sometimes bizarre circumstances surrounding it, were the subject of a lengthy but fascinating cover story in the Summer 2004 issue of *Triangle* magazine by Marty Dobrow, a member of the Humanities Department. Roughly twice the length of the typical *Triangle* article, it is the best account of the events surrounding King's visit that anyone is likely to read.

One other commencement note from 2004: Flynn returned to his alma mater, MacMurray College in Jacksonville, Illinois, in May to receive an honorary doctor of education degree and to deliver the address at the school's 153rd commencement services. The honorary degree was a nice complement to Flynn's election to MacMurray's Athletic Hall of Fame in 1994. He would receive the school's Distinguished Alumnus Award in October 2004.

NEW SCHOOL YEAR, NEW DINING HALL

As the new school year began, the pace of change in the campus quickened.

One of Flynn's many positive contributions to the betterment of Springfield College was a new definition of "renovation." This was not just a matter of some new carpeting and a coat of paint, with the color determined by what was on sale. It was gutting a building down to its main supporting posts and beams; removing the wiring, plumbing, heating, and air-conditioning; rebuilding from scratch; and replacing worn-out furnishings.

Returning to the campus for the 2004-05 school year, students, faculty, and staff were immediately stunned by the incredibly rapid physical transformation in Cheney Hall. Those who had departed the campus after commencement in May left behind the Old Cheney—an interesting but aging structure badly in need of refurbishment. Returning in September, those same folks were astounded and pleased at the speed and grace with which the building had become the New Cheney. All around the campus, the buzz was the same: Have you seen the New Cheney?

The new Cheney Hall, with the Cheney walkway enclosed to provide additional seating, appeared as if by magic over the summer of 2004.

The Cheney walkway, overlooking the newly renamed Naismith Green, had been enclosed to provide additional seating. But the enclosed walkway was only the beginning. The building's interior had been stripped down to the brick walls, and was now totally new, incorporating Aramark's "Fresh Food Company" concept, a restaurant-style dining experience featuring several different food stations with names like Northern Kitchen, Café Roma, American Bakery, and the Cheney Grille. The big-screen televisions and the pool tables were gone, to promote actual conversation over dinner. Customers were strongly discouraged from taking food out of the dining hall. And the faculty dining room, for many years a perfect way to isolate faculty from students, was closed.

The new dining experience was an instant hit with students, faculty, and staff. And it proved to be a help in the College's recruitment efforts, too.

On Naismith Green itself, the College sign, a fixture in earlier days at the southeast corner of Alden and Hickory, reappeared from the bowels of Facilities and Campus Services. Flynn had encountered the sign while touring a campus warehouse one day. The sign was painted and remounted in a low brick wall of the exact dimensions of the old one (Flynn personally counted the bricks), and located at the front of Naismith Green, facing Alden Street.

The Flynn touch was apparent in this installation, as well, in the Flynn-designed circle-in-a-triangle conversation area in back of the sign. It quickly became a new campus meeting place for one and all. (So popular was the idea that the reverse configuration, a triangle-in-a-circle conversation area, was installed near the new Suites Residence Hall, which also opened its doors at the start of the school year.)

The Flynn-designed circle-in-a-triangle conversation area behind the new College sign.

Students enjoying the cuisine and the camraderie in the new Cheney.

So the fall of 2004 brought with it two ribbon-cuttings (Cheney and the Suites)—and one ground-breaking. The latter took place November 9, 2004, for two multi-purpose fields to be surfaced with state-of-the-art synthetic turf. The grass-covered men's and women's soccer game field was completely renovated and resurfaced, and a second field with synthetic turf was installed next to it, adjacent to the College's softball field. Lights, bleachers, and a press box were part of the project, which covered over 200,000 square feet.

The fields were dedicated at Reunion 2006 as the Irv Schmid Sports Complex, in honor of the legendary men's soccer coach.

86 YEARS OF FRUSTRATION ENDS

The Boston Red Sox—World Champions??? Yes, it sounded funny to a lot of people, but, if you will recall, it actually happened on the evening of Wednesday, October 27, 2004. A four-game sweep of the St. Louis Cardinals, proud champions of the National League, brought the Red Sox their first World Championship since 1918. The Curse of the Bambino was dead, and the Cards never knew what hit them.

Die-hard Cardinals fan Flynn watched game four in the president's house. He'd done the same for game three, in the company of Ben Meyers, managing editor of the *Student*, and other *Student* staffers.

After the Sox won the series, as he walked up the stairs in the house, Flynn heard crowd noises outside, where perhaps 1,000 delirious students had gathered, chanting his name: "We want Flynn! We want Flynn!" They all assumed the president was a Red Sox fan.

Ignoring the advice of campus police, Flynn opened the gate and waded into the crowd, which by now had spilled over into Alden Street. Much to his surprise, the lifelong Cardinals fan wound up with a Red Sox hat on his head.

214

Suitably conciliatory, Flynn congratulated Red Sox fans, acknowledged it was a great day for Boston, and then used the dry wit that should have signaled his St. Louis loyalty. After reminding the crowd that the Cardinals had won their share of World Series, he indicated some concern that the Red Sox might have a problem handling their new role as winners since so much of their past World Series experience had been as losers.

The crowd, caught up in the excitement of the moment, offered another large cheer.

There were stars galore in that World Series, but to the Springfield College community, some of the biggest were not even on the field. Many alums, students, faculty, and staff were focused not only on the players, but also on the head athletic trainers for both teams —Barry Weinberg '73 of the Cardinals, and Jim Rowe '87 of the Red Sox.

A few weeks later, Rowe and Weinberg, who have remained active in the life of the College, spent the day on the campus to chat with old friends, tell World Series stories, conduct an athletic-training seminar, and visit with students, faculty, and staff. Both praised Springfield College for providing them with the foundations and professional preparation for their careers.

Shortly after that visit, the two alums appeared on the cover of *Triangle* magazine, all decked out in their colorful team jackets.

The 2004 World Series featured two teams with Springfield College graduates as head trainers. Barry Weinberg '73 of the St. Louis Cardinals (seated) and Jim Rowe '87 of the Boston Red Sox both visited the campus shortly after the series ended and posed for *Triangle* magazine in their team jackets.

Chapter 13

Flynn: Renaissance!

As 2005 dawned, Flynn contemplated the results so far. He'd arrived at Springfield College six years earlier, and had been surprised at how quickly he had come to love the College and its students. He had listened to all the major constituencies, and had formulated a strategic plan with their help. The plan had been blessed by the Board of Trustees. Then the hard part had begun.

Overall, Flynn was well satisfied with the progress the College had made in most major areas, and he made sure to say just that when he spoke at various campus events. He believed strongly that the strategy was the right one at the right time for this College. But he also knew that strategies did not become realities through the work of just one person.

That is to say, the progress to date had been accomplished because, as Flynn noted more than once, people had "boarded the train before it pulled out of the station"— they had bought in, they had taken ownership, they believed.

This was something for which Flynn was exceedingly grateful, especially considering the state of affairs prevailing when he had arrived. But, clearly, there was still much work to be done. The final verdict on the Flynn presidency, not to mention the College itself, was yet to be rendered.

The former three-sport athlete might have thought about it this way: The big game of the season was still out there in the future, waiting to be won or lost. That big game, of course, was the most ambitious fundraising campaign in the history of the College —a campaign that came to be known as *Leadership for the 21st Century: The Campaign for Springfield College*.

Looking back, Flynn could still recall being asked about fundraising when he was interviewing for the job of president. In response, he had talked generally about the pressing need for fundraising, and offered the opinion that it was time for a campaign at Springfield College.

"I thought I detected some doubts in the audience that the College would ever be able to launch a successful campaign of any size," Flynn recalls today. "But I was totally convinced that a fundraising campaign was an absolute must on my agenda."

The twelfth president of Springfield College sits for an interview for *Triangle* magazine after completing five years in office.

The new Campus Union, capstone building of the successful campaign.

Obsessed with fundraising because he had to be: President Doggett in his younger days.

HISTORICAL NOTES ON SPRINGFIELD COLLEGE CAMPAIGNS

The plain truth is, every single president of Springfield College, to one extent or another, has been positively obsessed with the search for money. And that is because they have had to be obsessed. There has never been any substantial endowment to fall back on when times get tough.

As detailed earlier in this book and elsewhere, the legendary President Doggett nurtured this obsession throughout the forty years of his presidency, from 1896 to 1936. According to Lawrence Hall, Doggett's biographer:

> The story of Dr. Doggett's life at Springfield could be told in terms of his never-ending, relentless search for money. He made a high calling of it, always asking and sometimes receiving, always seeking and sometimes finding, always having too little and sometimes none at all, but always fighting and holding on until he had what was needed to pay his loyal teachers and give them the tools for their work.

Doggett continually solicited funds to cover current expenses. In addition, he directed five separate fundraising campaigns in the course of his forty-year presidency, some more successful than others.

The most ambitious Springfield College fundraising effort had been the $7.3-million campaign embarked upon by Locklin several years after his arrival in the mid-1960s. That campaign had been entirely for bricks and mortar—including Cheney Hall, Babson Library, Gulick Hall, and a new artificial-turf athletic field.

The chair of that campaign had been television celebrity Art Linkletter, who would also serve as the honorary chair of the *Leadership for the 21st Century* campaign—while he was in his nineties.

PRELIMINARY CAMPAIGN PREPARATIONS

In his first days on the job, several people had spoken to Flynn about the false starts on campaigns in recent years, and the lack of resources available to get the job done. It was clear that Springfield College was not prepared to run a campaign of the scope and magnitude Flynn had in mind. That point of view had been strongly reinforced in a consultant's report prepared for—but not distributed to—the Board of Trustees.

At Flynn's first Board of Trustees meeting, Tom Wheeler, the trustee chair, had pulled the report back from distribution at the last moment so the new president, properly, might have a chance to review it before the trustees weighed in.

Reviewing the consultant's report, with its conclusion that the College was not prepared for a major fundraising campaign, Flynn had not disagreed. But he also knew that a

The official campaign logo, which appeared on all campaign materials through the duration of the campaign.

LEADERSHIP
FOR THE 21ST CENTURY:

THE
CAMPAIGN FOR
SPRINGFIELD COLLEGE

major fundraising campaign was an absolute necessity. So he'd set out immediately to enhance the College's fundraising infrastructure and staffing.

Additions to development department staffing were supplemented by new faces and new ways of doing business in related areas—including the alumni relations, advancement services, and marketing and communications departments. These changes had made it easier to practice friend-raising as well as fundraising—identifying prospects who could be called upon during a campaign.

In thinking about the priorities for the campaign, Flynn had established three benchmarks he would follow faithfully:

• The priorities for the campaign must be oriented to students.

• The campaign priorities must be absolutely consistent with the College's mission of educating students in spirit, mind, and body for leadership in service to humanity.

• The priorities must be guided by and consistent with the College's strategic plan.

The priorities ultimately determined for the campaign were straight-forward:

• New facilities and major renovations,

• Pursuit of academic excellence,

• Student scholarships, and

• Support for current and ongoing initiatives.

Flynn had surprised more than a few people by recommending a financial goal of $40-million for the campaign. After all, that was about five times more than had ever been raised at Springfield College. The doubters among the alumni, faculty, and staff had been vocal and definite in their opinion: This will never happen.

Campus stroll (left to right): Randy Locklin, son of former president Bill Locklin; Dick Flynn; Art Linkletter; and Trustee John Odierna '64.

Co-chairs of the *Leadership for the 21st Century* campaign were Trustees Bill Marsh H'02 and Helen Blake G'67, H'09.

But Flynn was determined. "My feeling was, better to set a higher goal and come up a little shy, than to set a lower goal and make it easily," he recalls. "I thought it was important to raise the bar. And I was absolutely convinced that there was no way we were going to come up a little shy."

Despite some early reservations on the ambitious campaign goal by a small number of trustees, the full board was now united in agreement on the need for, and the benefits of, a $40-million campaign. From that day forward, trustees were highly supportive of the campaign and its lofty goal. Shortly thereafter, Trustees Helen Blake G'67, H'09, and Bill Marsh H'02 were named campaign co-chairs, with Art Linkletter, as noted, honorary chair.

Traditionally, fundraising campaigns start quietly and remain "silent" until roughly half of the campaign goal has been raised. After about three years, this campaign's silent phase was about to come to an end, having raised $20-million of its $40-million goal. A major campaign event was already in the planning stages for May 2005, to thank people for their contributions to date, and to officially announce the campaign publicly.

As far as Flynn was concerned, that first $20-million had not been easy, but compared with the second $20-million, it had been a walk in the park. In particular, the role of trustees had been central to the campaign's early success. Trustees and emeriti trustees had stepped up in a major way, accounting for more than $11-million of the first $20-million raised.

Now Flynn was making plans to become much more personally and directly involved in the day-to-day operation of the campaign, and to travel extensively on campaign business over the next three years.

THE RENAISSANCE ARRIVES

In February, as he usually did, Flynn traveled to a number of Alumni Association events, including the Suncoast Alumni Association meeting in Florida. Speaking at the Rosedale Golf & Country Club in Bradenton, Flynn outlined the progress the College was making, and talked about the ambitious plans for the future. But plugged-in alums had already sensed that something good was happening at Springfield College; in introducing the president, Norm Kosciusko '74 noted the progress being made and the upbeat, positive attitudes one encountered on campus.

It was at a meeting of the Suncoast Alumni Association in the winter of 2005 that Norm Kosciusko '74 (second row, second from left) gave a name to the progress at the College over the prior five years—Renaissance.

As Kosciusko recalls it today, he then said something like the following: "Dr. Flynn is leading the greatest change in Springfield College history. No one has had a greater impact on the fortunes of the College than he has. When he took the reins, we were in a period of darkness; now we've entered an age of enlightenment. That's the very definition of a Renaissance."

Kosciusko adds that he believed that when he said it in 2005, and he believes it even more strongly today. "How can you even argue with that point of view?" he asks, rhetorically.

In February 2005, the College received approval to offer a combined bachelor of science and doctoral degree program in physical therapy.

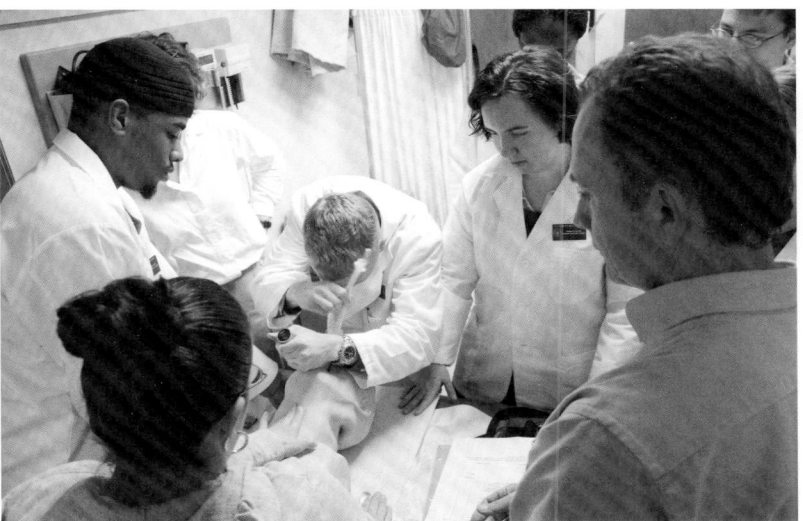

The new School of Health Sciences and Rehabilitation Studies included five undergraduate and graduate programs: physician assistant (shown here), physical therapy, occupational therapy, rehabilitation and disability studies, and emergency medical services management.

IN PURSUIT OF ACADEMIC EXCELLENCE

A number of developments during 2005 exhibited the continuing effort to enhance the academic programs being offered to students. In February 2005, the Massachusetts Board of Higher Education approved the College's plan for a combined bachelor of science and doctoral degree program in physical therapy (DPT). According to David Miller, then the chair of the physical therapy department, the new six-and-one-half-year doctoral program meant the College could "better train our students so that they will enter the field of physical therapy with the level of education needed to meet the demands of today's practice." The new program enrolled its first students that fall.

Students accepted into the new doctoral program would enter as first-year undergraduates and remain at the College until they completed the DPT. Miller added that students in the program would have the opportunity for a traditional undergraduate experience in the first four years, participating fully in athletics, activities, and campus life.

In April 2005, a new School of Health Sciences and Rehabilitation Studies was established, and William Susman, then associate dean for academic programs at the Brooklyn campus of Long Island University, was named the school's founding dean. Susman was successful in his founder's role, but was to leave the College after four years, to be succeeded, on an interim basis, by Miller.

Included in the new school were undergraduate and graduate programs that had been part of the School of Arts, Sciences and Professional Studies: physician assistant, physical therapy, occupational therapy, rehabilitation and disability studies, and emergency medical services management. The change was seen as only logical, and had the added benefit of linking the programs within each school more closely.

A little later in April, a program in Appleton Auditorium celebrated the 100th anniversary of graduate education at Springfield College. Five-time Olympian Willye White H'99 was the featured speaker at the event.

Also speaking that day, Flynn said, "To me, it is nothing less than astonishing that our graduate programs have grown from a handful of students in the early years to more than 1,400 graduate students enrolled today." Flynn also noted that the tuition for a graduate student a hundred years ago was a mere $75 per year, compared with $611 per credit for 2005. Times had, indeed, changed.

Four years later: School of Social Work graduates after the 2009 commencement.

At the June 2005 meeting of the Council of Social Work Education, the accreditation of the Springfield College School of Social Work master's of social work program was reaffirmed for the full eight-year cycle. According to Dean Francine Vecchiolla, the site team had many complimentary things to say about the program: A well-designed and cohesive curriculum; an excellent facility with state-of-the-art technology (thanks to the school's new headquarters in the renovated Brennan Center); highly respected program leadership; a well qualified faculty with a strong commitment to the program; an impressive field education program; an administration that was well aware of the extraordinary professional program within the College; and a committed student body, some of whom regularly traveled some distance to attend classes.

2005 PERSONNEL NOTES

At its annual meeting May 21, 2005, the Board of Trustees elected as its chair a man who was an alumnus and who, earlier in his career, had been a professor at the College. **James E. Walsh** '64 of East Longmeadow succeeded **R. Lyman Wood** of Hampden, who, in turn, had succeeded **John A. Odierna** '64 of Longmeadow.

Father Leo James Hoar, described in a *Student* article as one of the College's "favorite people," went out on leave in the spring of 2005 due to physical ailments. Fr. Leo returned to the campus in 2006 and was the featured speaker at the baccalaureate service that May, but his health limited him to part-time service in the Office of United Campus Ministries and Spiritual Life Center.

In introducing Fr. Leo at the 2006 baccalaureate service, Flynn called him "one of the people who make Springfield College Springfield College. He has been known and loved for his tireless energy, his ready smile, his skillful teaching and mentoring talents, and his unselfish commitment to the College and its mission. He has demonstrated an uncanny ability to touch the lives of students, faculty, staff, and alums in meaningful ways."

A friend and strong supporter of Flynn going back to Flynn's first day on campus, Fr. Leo enjoyed great popularity among students, faculty, staff, alumni, and others. Over the years, he has performed hundreds of weddings for alums who met him when they were students; baptized dozens of children of those alums; and later worked with a number of those children on the campus after they themselves became students at the College.

David A. Hall was named to the new position of director of campus recreation, signaling an intensified focus on developing a comprehensive campus recreation program. Hall was a campus recreation pro, having served in that position at the University of the Pacific in Stockton, California since 2000. While it wasn't widely recognized at the time, Hall's appointment preceded by two years the construction of a wellness center and field house (later named the Wellness and Recreation Complex), which were significant enhancements to campus recreation. Further evidence of the strategic plan at work.

President Flynn was elected to a four-year term on the prestigious Division III Presidents Council of the National Collegiate Athletic Association (NCAA). The NCAA Presidents Council establishes and directs policies of Division III and determines its strategic plan. Flynn was elected by vote of chief executive officers of the 421 Division III institutions.

Fr. Leo Hoar, who went out on leave in the spring of 2005, speaks at the 2006 baccalaureate.

Traditions have always been important at Springfield College. Here, one particularly impressive and beautiful tradition continues—the Baccalaureate ceremony on Naismith Green.

The *Leadership for the 21st Century* campaign goes public: Tables at the Hall of Fame in May 2005.

Speaking at the campaign kickoff event, Flynn said he felt awe and pride to be associated with the people in the room.

THE CAMPAIGN GOES PUBLIC

On the evening of Friday, May 20, 2005, at the Naismith Memorial Basketball Hall of Fame, Springfield College officially went public with its $40-million fundraising campaign, *Leadership for the 21st Century*, to enhance facilities, champion academic excellence, increase scholarship endowment, and support the priorities necessary for the College to fulfill its mission.

The event was a signal that the campaign had already raised half of its $40-million goal —a fact that was confirmed by Flynn later that evening. That was already the most successful fundraising effort in any four-year period in the College's history. "The response to the campaign has been overwhelmingly positive and enthusiastic," he said.

Recalling historical connections, Flynn welcomed the audience in the large Center Court room "as the Board of Trustees of the Birthplace of Basketball gathers here at the Naismith Memorial Basketball Hall of Fame, a world-class museum dedicated to the game that was created in 1891 by Springfield College faculty member James Naismith."

Flynn acknowledged the presence of the heads of two organizations that had worked in collaboration with the College for many years: John Doleva, president and CEO of the Hall of Fame, and Ken Gladish, national executive director and CEO of the YMCA of the USA, who delivered the invocation.

Flynn said he felt awe and pride to be associated with the people in the room. "Every day, in hundreds of different ways, you affirm your belief in the Springfield College mission. Springfield College has always been about people who see possibilities where others see desolation; who see potential where others see only faults; and who know that to serve others brings not only satisfaction, but also deep joy."

Flynn with Hall of Fame CEO
John Doleva at the campaign
kickoff event.

Trustees and former trustees (and corporators) gather for a historic group
photo at the May 2005 campaign kickoff event. Flynn is flanked by Lyman
Wood, then board chair, and Helen Blake, campaign co-chair.

Fourteen-year-old country-
music star Ashley Gearing, a
local resident, produced a stirring rendition of the national
anthem at the kickoff event,
and was presented with a
Springfield College sweatshirt.

In addition to going public with the campaign, the event served as a dinner in connection with the regular meeting of the Board of Trustees. It was the first time that all former trustees (and corporators) had been invited to gather together as a group to be updated on the College's progress—progress they had made possible—and to thank them for their contributions and service. Thirty former board members were in the audience and were introduced, and another twenty had sent notes of appreciation for the invitation.

Flynn said *Leadership for the 21st Century* would "open a new chapter in the proud history of this College. More than that, the success of the campaign is essential to achieving the vision and goals outlined in the strategic plan."

After acknowledging campaign co-chairs Helen Blake G'67 H'09 and Bill Marsh H'02, both of whom spoke following dinner, Flynn introduced fourteen-year-old Ashley Gearing—the youngest female singer ever to make the Billboard country-music charts. Gearing, who had performed with the Boston Pops and the Grand Ol' Opry, and at Fenway Park, produced a stirring rendition of the Star Spangled Banner, following which Flynn presented her with a Springfield College sweatshirt. Gearing is the stepdaughter of Paul Kalill, an adjunct professor at the College.

The evening was thoroughly enjoyed by all present, and proved to be a memorable public kickoff for the College's first comprehensive campaign in thirty-five years. As guests left the Hall of Fame to go out into the warm spring evening, optimism reigned. The bar had been raised.

Over the summer, the level of campaign activity was ratcheted up dramatically, and Flynn continued his intense personal involvement in the campaign—attending planning and strategy sessions, and visiting many of the top-level prospects.

Johnny Coons '50 —"a straight shooter who always told it as he saw it," as Flynn recalled at Coons' memorial service.

Representing the Birthplace of Basketball, Flynn visits with students at the Xian Institute of Physical Education in China in 2006. During his visit, the president actually hit one of his patented long sweeping hook shots from the corner. (See page 208.)

CELEBRATION OF THE LIFE OF JOHN COONS

On June 12, 2005, family members, classmates, teammates, colleagues, players, fellow coaches and others whose lives were touched by John Coons '50 gathered to celebrate the life of a remarkable man, and his intense participation in the life and times of the College he loved over a period of more than fifty years. Coons had died earlier in 2005.

Coons had been hired by Locklin as director of development, following many years at the University of Vermont. He went on to serve every other Springfield College president since then in some development role.

Speaking at the June 12 event, Flynn paid tribute to Coons as a fundraiser: "Now it's true that Johnny's fundraising techniques were not usually by the book, exactly—well, come to think of it, they were not by the book at all. But Johnny had great success as a fundraiser because of a personality and a style to which people just responded favorably, because of his unfailing intuition about people."

Flynn added that Coons was "a straight shooter who always told it as he saw it. Anyone who is head of a college knows how important it is to have people like that around you. I took John's sage advice many times, on many important campus issues. But even when I didn't take his advice, I valued it, and I valued the man who had given it to me—honestly, without any personal agenda."

REPRESENTING SPRINGFIELD COLLEGE ABROAD

Following the celebration of the life of John Coons, Flynn was winging his way, once again, to China in the company of Charlie Smith, longtime men's swimming coach at the College and a kind of freelance ambassador to China.

Flynn delivered a major address on "Liberal Education and Individual Development" at the graduation ceremonies of Lingnan (University) College. He and Smith then traveled to Hong Kong, where they participated in an honorary degree ceremony.

This trip represented just one of many visits to China for Flynn, to connect with long-time alumni and friends of the College, to make major presentations to audiences of thousands, to meet and talk with past and prospective donors, and to visit YMCA leaders in China. Smith was along for a number of those trips, and was very helpful in introducing Flynn to key individuals and sharing the history of the long-time relationships.

The first time Flynn and Smith had traveled together was in 1999. Shortly after the new president's arrival, Smith, who had retired from the College officially ten years earlier, had urged Flynn to accept an invitation he'd received to visit China and Taiwan. Flynn had agreed, with the condition that Smith accompany him, and within three months they were in transit. That trip included a visit to Hong Kong Sports Institute; a meeting with past honorary degree recipients including Bing-lai Wong, Chik-Suen Lam, James Tak Wu, Angela Luk, Philip K. H. Wong, and Henry Y. T. Fok; a reception for alumni hosted by Flynn at the Chinese YMCA in Hong Kong; and a side trip to Taiwan to meet with Henry H. Hsu.

Flynn was hosted repeatedly over the years by Springfield College alumni, including such dignitaries as Ma Qi-Wei G'49, who was past president of Beijing Institute of

Charlie Smith and President Flynn pay a visit to businessman Henry Y. T. Fok at his home in Hong Kong.

In 2007, Flynn was hosted at a luncheon by friends of the College in Hong Kong, all of whom were presented with maroon Springfield College windbreakers to mark the occasion.

Physical Education (now known as Beijing Sports Institute). MaQi-Wei was the son of John Ma '20 G'26, also a Springfield College graduate, who is considered the father of physical education and modern sport in China.

In turn, many delegations from Chinese post-secondary institutions and other organizations came to the College. Some said their primary goal in traveling to the United States was to visit Springfield College.

The faculty and staff at the College who assisted with these extensive international relationships included Ken Wall, International Center director at the time; Deb Alm, the current director; and John (Zhan) Liu, a physical education faculty member who was born and raised in China. Amazingly, Liu had been in the audience as a graduate student in Wuhan, China in 1984 when Flynn had lectured there. Liu came to Springfield College in 1999, the same year as Flynn.

The continuing focus on China was important to the College's international stature and reputation, Flynn believed. In addition, it was not lost on the president that he and Smith usually returned from their visits with significant dollar donations to the College from a growing cadre of international supporters. Two of the most significant gifts were from the Fok Foundation in China and the Hsu Sports and Culture Foundation in Taiwan – both funding exchange programs for faculty, coaches, and students. "I feel very good about what the College has accomplished in China," Flynn says today. "And I know we could not have done it without the very good work of Charlie Smith, John Liu, and our International Center staff."

Smith offers praise for Flynn's skills in international outreach. "Dick came to Springfield College very familiar with the Asian customs, culture, and temperament. He really did his homework with respect to our friends and alumni, and he was able to connect quickly with the very successful educators and businessmen we met in China. At his insistence, our visits were intense and productive. In addition, Jani Flynn was the perfect partner for him on many of these trips," Smith recalls. He goes on to credit Flynn's good listening skills, cultural understanding, and sincere valuing of international relationships for the success in this arena.

DELIVERING ON THE PROMISE

Opening the 2005-06 academic year at the All College Meeting in Dana Gymnasium, Flynn reviewed the list of accomplishments of the year just ended. Over the years, attendees at the All College Meetings had noticed that the lists kept getting longer and longer —not that anyone was really complaining.

"The accomplishments of recent years," Flynn noted, "serve as a confirmation that at least some of our collective dreams and aspirations are being fulfilled. We are, as I have noted, delivering on the promise. We are making a difference, and we can see that difference more clearly, day after day, week after week."

Flynn couldn't resist reminding one and all, once again, of two important correlative facts, in case anyone had missed them: First, that the progress had all been driven by *The Plan for Springfield College*, the strategic road map. Second, the progress was absolutely consistent with the long-standing College mission. "It has been our mission for well over a century, and I'm confident it will still be our mission a century from today," he pronounced.

TWO SIGNIFICANT GRANTS RECEIVED

As calendar year 2005 wound down, the College received two significant grants that would help make possible the total renovation of two facilities on campus that sorely needed it.

In November, the George F. and Sybil H. Fuller Foundation announced that it would award the College a $500,000 grant to renovate Fuller Arts Center, which had been opened in 1984 with major funding from the Fuller Foundation.

Any successful campaign generates a ripple effect—projects that are not technically part of the campaign, but, in some mysterious way, are caused by, or prompted by, or result from, the campaign and the many activities surrounding it. While the campaign was ongoing, discussion were also held with the Fuller Foundation about a total renovation of Fuller Arts Center, which had been built as a centennial project during the Locklin presidency. The foundation was concerned that its named building was out of touch with a transformed campus, and made a generous grant for the renovation—not directly related to the campaign, but happening at least partially because of the campaign.

Work on the renovation and expansion of Fuller Arts Center actually did not begin until the fall of 2008, due to the press of other construction activity on the campus. Work was completed in early 2009.

In December, the George I. Alden Trust awarded a grant of $150,000 to the College towards the renovation and expansion of Schoo Hall into a state-of-the art science teaching facility.

Representatives of the Fuller family and foundation visited the campus in 2009 to celebrate the reopening of the renovated Fuller Arts Center.

TWO FORMER PRESIDENTS PASS AWAY

Calendar 2006 was marked by sadness at the beginning and at the end. Within the space of seven days in March, the College lost two of its former presidents: Wilbert E. Locklin, the ninth president, who served from 1965 to 1985; and Rev. Glenn A. Olds, the eighth president, who served from 1958 to 1965.

The College flag was lowered to half-staff in memory of these two distinguished gentlemen, who will be remembered for their inspired leadership and their lasting contributions to the College.

At the request of the Locklin family, which lived locally, a memorial service was held in Fuller Arts Center, attended by hundreds of people whose lives had been touched by the ninth president. These included Springfield Mayor Charles Ryan, who, coincidentally, had also been the city's mayor during Locklin's early years as president in the 1960s.

Speaking at the memorial service, Flynn said: "As we reminisce about President Locklin we are celebrating a life well lived. His love and inspiration provided the roots that will serve his family forevermore, and his inspired leadership of Springfield College for twenty years provided a strong foundation for this College to reach new heights in the years following."

And in November 2006, another legendary figure passed away—Archie Allen '37, who served as the school's baseball coach for thirty-one years before retiring in 1978 with a winning percentage of .637 (454-257-7). Archie was a part of the College for more than seventy years—as a student, a student-athlete, an alumnus, a coach, a loyal friend, a mentor, a worldwide goodwill ambassador for his College and his sport, and, in his final years, a universally respected and loved elder statesman.

Archie was elected to the Springfield College Athletic Hall of Fame in 1972, as part of the very first group of inductees. Who else was included in the first Hall of Fame class? A basketball guy named Naismith, a football guy named Stagg, and a gymnastics guy named Judd.

Archie's memorial service was held in Marsh Memorial Chapel. A great number of Archie's players were in attendance, most wearing uniform tops as a symbol of their love and respect.

Archie Allen '37, who served as baseball coach for thirty-one years before retiring in 1978, died in November 2006.

"Archie's Boys" were in attendance at his memorial service in Marsh Chapel. Most of them wore their uniform tops as a symbol of their love and respect for the legendary figure.

Speaking at the service, Flynn said Springfield College had "lost part of itself. Coach was one of those rare individuals who just fit into the fabric of this place very naturally. It was as if he'd been here all along, or the College was saving a place for him, waiting for him to arrive. He was comfortable, he made a difference, and he made everyone smile. Unless, of course, you were a player and had just made a bonehead play."

Flynn related an observation made by Barry Weinberg '73, longtime head trainer of the St. Louis Cardinals and one of Archie's players: "Yogi, Shaq, Magic—all in a very exclusive club where one name says it all. For more than seventy years, one name said it all to everyone associated with Springfield College—all knew who you were talking about when you simply mentioned the name 'Archie.' That in itself is quite a marvelous legacy."

TRANSFORMATION OF THE CAMPUS

The transformation of the campus continued at a brisk pace throughout 2006. In March, a ribbon cutting was held for the totally renovated Weiser Hall. On a rainy day in May, there was a groundbreaking for the renovation and expansion of Schoo Hall, which would be renamed the Schoo-Bemis Science Center. And in October, there was the dedication of Herbert P. Blake Hall.

With President Flynn at the March 2006 ribbon cutting for the renovated Weiser Hall are members of the humanities department; Margaret Lloyd, department chair (front row, second from left); and Mary Healey, dean of Arts, Sciences and Professional Studies (front row right).

Weiser Hall, situated between Locklin Hall and Babson Library, is a little jewel of a building that actually started out as an infirmary in the years after World War I. Later, Weiser had housed the department of medical gymnastics, reportedly the forerunner of the athletic training program. According to the 1923 College yearbook, "The building is designed primarily for the reconstruction, re-education, and rehabilitation of post-operative cases, and others who have lost their grip in physical and mental ways, and is fully equipped with the most modern apparatus for this type of work."

The basement of Weiser had housed the laboratory and classrooms of Dr. Peter Karpovich, the Russian immigrant who taught at the College from 1929 to 1969 and was known as the premier exercise physiologist in the country. Karpovich achieved fame as a physiologist, research professor, author, editor, and master teacher. According to a 1974 doctoral paper on Karpovich, students described him as "dogmatic and egotistical, a truly great man, good and kind, warm and cold, and the finest of teachers. He expected hard work and honesty, and his dramatic and vivid style of teaching kept the interest of his students."

When the infirmary was moved down the street to the old electric company building in the late 1960s and began its new life as the Towne Student Health Center, there was some discussion about tearing Weiser down. But Vin Swanberg rode to the rescue. Swanberg, then the director of the facilities department, checked the building out and reported to Locklin: "I am more convinced [than ever] that it should not be razed."

Fortunately, Swanberg prevailed, and Weiser Hall stands to this day. Since its renovation, the building contains teaching spaces to support programs of the humanities department, and new and much needed laboratory spaces for the communications program, including a television studio and a wireless journalism lab. There are also offices for the entire humanities department faculty.

Groundbreaking for the renovated and expanded Schoo-Bemis Science Center in May 2006. Left to right are David Braverman, Steve Lafever, John Mailhot, Jean Wyld, President Flynn, Peter Polito, Frank Torre, and Mary Healey '78.

Helen Blake G'67 H'09 and Prestley Blake H'82, long-time generous supporters of the College, were joined by President Flynn and Jim Walsh '64, trustee chair (right), for the rededication and renaming of Herbert P. Blake Hall in October 2006.

In the continuing game of campus musical chairs, when the humanities department moved out of Schoo Hall and into Weiser, work could begin on the total renovation of Schoo. The groundbreaking ceremony was scheduled for May 19, but that day turned out to be raw and rainy, so the non-groundbreaking part of the ceremony was moved inside the building.

Originally dedicated in October 1963, the full name of the building was The Clarence and Grace Schoo Friendship Hall. The Schoos were local philanthropists who had made an additional gift to the College to match a Kresge Foundation grant. Combined with the gifts of alums, trustees, corporations, other foundations, and friends of the College, the Schoos' gift made the original building possible.

Schoo Hall had served the College extremely well. Many thousands of Springfield College students had trooped up the stairs and into the building over the past forty-plus years. Now, it was undergoing a complete transformation into a state-of-the-art, centralized location for the teaching of, and learning about, science at Springfield College.

In October, the former Standard Electric Time Company building roughly across Wilbraham Avenue from the baseball field was rededicated and renamed Herbert P. Blake Hall, in honor of S. Prestley Blake's late father, who died in 1964. Pres Blake, cofounder of the Friendly Ice Cream Company, and his wife, Helen, have been long-time generous supporters of Springfield College (Blake Arena, Blake Track). The Blakes agreed to make a $2-million gift to support the College through its fundraising campaign, and the College offered to rename the building Herbert P. Blake Hall.

The building's new name had an undeniable logic to it. For many years, Herbert P. Blake had worked in the building, as a vice president for the Standard Electric Time Company. He played a prominent role in the company's expansion and success until his retirement in 1956.

Rip Van Camp '54, a former trustee and one of many devout followers of Peter Karpovich, made a lead gift towards endowing the Karpovich Chair to honor the Russian immigrant who taught at the College from 1929-69 and was known as the premier exercise physiologist in the country. With Van Camp is Tamie Kiddess Lucey '81, director of alumni relations.

THE AMA PRESIDENT-ELECT AND JOHN CENA VISIT

As the transformation of the campus progressed, Dr. William Plested, president-elect of the American Medical Association, came to the campus to talk about health care. Not long after that, John Cena '99, former captain of the football team, and later a major celebrity in World Wrestling Entertainment, stopped by to talk about wrestling, football, and Springfield College.

ATHLETIC NOTES FROM 2006

On the evening of February 7, 2006, Derek Yvon '06 hit a strong lay-up from the left side over Clark University forward Godfrey Duncan with 2:33 remaining in the Pride's 83-67 win over the Cougars in Blake Arena. The shot gave the talented senior his 2,005th point, good enough to eclipse the 2,003-point record set by Hassan Robinson '95.

And in March, also in Blake Arena, Springfield College hosted the NCAA Division III Women's Basketball Final Four Championship. Hope College defeated Southern Maine to win it all, and Springfield College and its athletics department received high praise and recognition for running a great tournament. They performed an encore the following year.

At spring training in Florida, the Birthplace of Basketball demonstrated its skill at Abner Doubleday's game. Flynn tossed the ceremonial first pitch—a perfect strike, naturally—at the Boston Red Sox vs. Minnesota Twins game March 5 at Hammond Stadium in Fort Myers, a contest attended by 150 members of the Suncoast Alumni Association.

Earlier in the same week, Trustee Helen Davis Blake G'67, threw out the ceremonial first pitch at the New York Mets vs. St. Louis Cardinals game at Tradition Field in Port St. Lucie, Florida. Blake, who had no known record as a major league pitcher, didn't allow the diversion to affect her position as co-chair of the College's fund-raising campaign.

John Cena '99, a major celebrity in World Wrestling Entertainment, visited the campus in 2006.

Charlie Brock '76, men's basketball coach, with Derek Yvon '06, who broke the school record for points scored, previously held by Hassan Robinson '95.

Flynn throws a perfect strike in Fort Myers.

Helen Blake G'67, H'09, with no known major league record, serves up a high, hard one in Port St. Lucie.

232

FROM D.P.E. TO PH.D.

A historic moment occurred in March 2006, when the Massachusetts Board of High Education ruled that Springfield College's longstanding Doctor of Physical Education (D.P.E.) program was equivalent to comparable doctor of philosophy programs, and approved the College's request to change the title of its program to Doctor of Philosophy (Ph.D.), effective with the 2006 Commencement.

In granting the change in title, the board considered the program's curriculum quality and faculty credentials, as well as positions earned by its graduates. The college had titled its doctoral program D.P.E. in 1950 to reflect its expertise in the field of physical education.

JANI

There have been very few, if any, presidents of Springfield College about whom one could say: There isn't anyone who doesn't like him. Among past presidential spouses, there are at least a couple of candidates for this kind of extreme like-ability. But most people who have met and come to know Jani Flynn would agree that she is at the top of that list.

Nobody, it seems, doesn't like Jani. And that is not the only reason why she has been such a valued partner to her husband during their years at Springfield College.

A native of Buffalo, New York, Jani grew up in New Jersey, and majored in chemistry and math at MacMurray College in Jacksonville, Illinois, where she met her husband. The decades since then have taken this Flynn team to Ohio, New York City, New Jersey, Nebraska, and now Springfield.

Ask Flynn about Jani and the response is instantaneous: "Jani is a wonderful partner for me to have in this job. Her presence and her contributions have certainly had a positive impact. She truly loves attending student, alumni, and College events, and she's been a valuable ambassador of the College."

Jani: The Flynns seem to fit together well, complementing each other, supporting each other, poking fun when required.

Flynn is quick to point out that Jani "made a huge sacrifice" in moving to Springfield from Omaha. For more than a decade, she had been president and chief executive officer of her own computer software company, Software Solutions for Business. But when the Flynns moved to Springfield, Jani gave up the business to concentrate on the many and varied responsibilities of presidential spouse.

Jani's contributions to the progress of Springfield College go far beyond running the residence and serving as the gracious hostess for countless social events with students, faculty, staff, alums, and others. She's extremely adept at meeting people and putting them at ease. Those maroon banners on Alden Street and Wilbraham Avenue advertising that one is driving through Springfield College were Jani's idea. Many of the interior design schemes of the renovated and new buildings on the campus show the touch of her interior design expertise.

The Flynns demonstrate the value of teamwork, in a marriage and on a college campus.

Jani is an enthusiastic supporter of student activities, and perhaps the only individual to attend more athletic and co-curricular events at Springfield College than her husband.

To anyone who has spent even a little time with them, Dick and Jani Flynn are quite different people in many respects. But observers also note that despite these differences, the Flynns seem to fit together well, complementing each other, supporting each other, poking fun at each other when it's required, and in general demonstrating the value of teamwork, in a marriage and on a college campus.

Jani is predictably modest about her many contributions to the progress of the College. "My role is not defined by any means, by any job description. I feel like I represent the College when I go places or to meetings or in the community—letting people know about the College and what we do here," she says.

A PART OF—NOT APART FROM—THE COMMUNITY

From his first days as president, Flynn was highly motivated to improve the relationship between the College and its adjacent neighborhoods. Over the years, that motivation had been manifested in many community programs and outreach efforts, and the College had received credit for its efforts in many ways. But 2006 was a year when there seemed to be even more activity and more credit than normal in the area of community engagement.

In June 2006, future new housing construction in Old Hill moved from a plan to an impending reality when the College announced that it would secure a $1.5-million acquisition fund for the Neighborhood Collaborative, LLC. The acquisition fund allowed the collaborative to borrow money at below-market rates from TD Banknorth to acquire vacant or abandoned lots to build or rehabilitate housing, strictly for owner-occupants.

Commenting on the new fund, Flynn said, "We're proud to be a partner in this major initiative to make our neighborhood a better place for living, working, and learning. Until today, new housing in Old Hill has been only a dream. I'm especially enthusiastic about the real transformation that we will be celebrating in the next few years."

The AmeriCorps program at Springfield College combines undergraduate and graduate student education with meeting community needs. Pictured here is a small portion of the AmeriCorps neighborhood force.

That September, the College announced the funding of a $3.6-million project to more than quadruple the size of its AmeriCorps neighborhood force. The Corporation for National and Community Service awarded the College two grants to support 125 AmeriCorps students per year for three years. The prior year, the program had operated with just thirty student participants.

The AmeriCorps program at Springfield College combines undergraduate and graduate student education with meeting community needs. Participating students perform services related to their fields of study and directly for persons with needs identified by partnering schools and community organizations.

Announcing the expanded program, Flynn observed, "This is a wonderful example of how a college can serve its community by contributing its expertise and leveraging its resources. Altogether, these students will perform services equivalent to an additional fifty-six full-time employees in area schools and community organizations. We're providing resources for vitally needed services."

The continuing effectiveness of the AmeriCorps program, as well as other programs serving the Greater Springfield community, was one reason why Springfield College was named one of just twenty-five "best neighbor" colleges in the United States. The "Saviors of Our Cities" list, prepared by Evan Dobelle, then president of the New England Board of Higher Education, cited colleges that have dramatically strengthened the economy and quality of life in their neighboring communities through careful strategic planning and thoughtful use of resources.

Before 2006 was over, the College had received two additional awards for its community engagement:

• The Super 60 award from the Affiliated Chambers of Commerce of Greater Springfield, Inc. The Super 60 awards recognize the top businesses in the region that make significant contributions to the strength of the regional economy.

• A proclamation from the Springfield City Council commending the College for its community engagement initiatives and thanking the College for "making the City of Springfield a better place to live." Flynn accepted the proclamation from City Councilor Domenic Sarno, who was later elected the city's mayor.

CHRIS SHARPE AND THE MELBERGER AWARD

The 2006 Springfield College football team had an outstanding year—a 10-2 regular-season record, an Empire 8 Conference co-championship, and an automatic NCAA Division III tournament berth. While there were some remarkable individual stories to tell about this team, it is fair to say the team achieved what it did because its members worked hard together, sometimes literally shoulder to shoulder. Team play, team spirit, team unity, team respect—that's what it was all about.

Having said that, it is still impossible to overlook the astonishing performance of junior captain and quarterback Chris Sharpe in 2006. Sharpe led the Pride in all major offensive categories, breaking six NCAA Division III records and twelve Springfield College records in the process. He finished the year with a College rushing record and NCAA Division III rushing record for quarterbacks—1,941 yards. He also set an NCAA Division III record with thirty-five rushing touchdowns, smashing the old record of twenty. Sharpe provided highlight moments rarely seen at the College. Even though defenses keyed on him on every play, he still led Division III in rushing yardage.

The culmination of Sharpe's year came in January, when he was presented the coveted Melberger Award, emblematic of the top player in NCAA Division III football, and was interviewed by ESPNews co-host, former Heisman Trophy winner, and former Super Bowl Most Valuable Player Desmond Howard.

Chris Sharpe '08, winner of the Melberger Award, with his coach, Mike DeLong '74.

Speaking at the team's year-end banquet, Flynn noted another one of Chris's accomplishments "Chris handled all the commotion and publicity in an exemplary manner."

One other football note: When the Chicago Bears and the Indianapolis Colts met in Super Bowl XLI in Miami in February 2007, Springfield College was there. A total of three strength and conditioning coaches on the two teams were Springfield College graduates—Bears' head strength and conditioning coach Rusty Jones '76, G '86 and his assistant, Jim Arthur '00, G '02, and Colts' head strength and conditioning coach, Jon Torine '95.

GROUNDBREAKINGS AND DEDICATIONS—PART TWO

One key yardstick of the continuing progress in the transformation of the campus was the number of groundbreakings and dedications during 2006. One in April, one in May, one in September, one in October, and one in November. A total of six groundbreakings and dedications, exactly double the number in the previous year. The momentum was not only continuing, but accelerating.

April: Dedication ceremony for the Kakley Graduate Annex, a permanent symbol of Joe Kakley's long-standing commitment to Springfield College and the neighborhood in which it is located. The building now bearing the Kakley name had been constructed in 1989, and marked the real beginning of the College's commitment to housing graduate students on campus.

Joe Kakley had grown up in Old Hill in the 1940s, played sports on the College fields, and rode his bike around the campus. He had walked down Union Street to the South End to court the woman who would become his wife, Joyce.

Today, the Kakleys operate one of the largest home-building supply centers in Western Massachusetts, J.R. Kakley & Sons, Inc.—still in the old neighborhood, over on Allen Street.

May: Groundbreaking ceremony for the new Wellness Center, the new Field House, and the Athletic Training and Exercise Science facility. The three new buildings would be situated between Blake Arena and the Linkletter Natatorium, and would give that area an entirely new look from Alden Street.

Groundbreaking for the Wellness Center, Field House, and Athletic Training/ Exercise Science Facility, May 2006. No less than a dozen trustees attended the event and, with Flynn, wielded shovels.

The precise date of the groundbreaking, May 11, had a previous significance. It was the day, in 1979, that the old Memorial Field House had been ordered closed within twenty-four hours.

Now the College was adding significantly to its athletic, instructional, and recreational facilities. Springfield College already had a School of Health, Physical Education, and Recreation with many programs having long-standing national reputations for quality. It already had one of the premier intercollegiate athletic programs in NCAA Division III. And over the past year, it had begun to establish a top-quality campus recreation program.

So the three new buildings were a perfect example of the principle, often stated by Flynn, that "facilities are to facilitate programs." That seamless integration of facilities and programs would serve the College and its students well in the years to come.

Another athletic facility was to get a major upgrade in 2005 and saw full usage starting in 2006. The Irv Schmid Sports Complex was dedicated in June 2007. The complex includes a synthetic FieldTurf surface that has been called the best two-field complex in the Northeastern United States.

Irv Schmid was one of those remarkable individuals who came to Springfield College as a first-year student and—except for a brief time coaching high school and service in World War II—basically never left. As an undergraduate, he competed not only in soccer, but also gymnastics, lacrosse, and track and field. He served as a coach and teacher at the College for nearly four decades between 1947 and 1985.

Schmid bridged the gap between generations of great Springfield College teacher-coaches. When he arrived, he was welcomed by legendary coaching figures named Judd, Bunn, Allen, Solem, and Silvia. In time, he was joined by such coaching luminaries as Dunn, Bilik, Potter, Smith, Steitz, Wolcott, and Hay. And when he retired in 1985, a new generation of Springfield College coaching-legends-in-the-making was there to say goodbye—DeLong, Bugbee, Dearing, Brock, Posner, Zenaty, Klatka, Graves, Raymond, and others.

In his remarks at the dedication, Flynn told the story of a $500,000 gift from an anonymous donor in honor of Coach Schmid, and the challenge that, if another $500,000 could be raised, the College would name the new sports complex after him.

Aerial view of the Irv Schmid Sports Complex.

237

At the September 2006 dedication of the Schoo-Bemis Science Center are President Flynn, Professors Frank Torre and Peter Polito, and Jean Wyld, vice president for academic affairs.

The renaming of Bemis Hall was part of the September 2006 dedication ceremony for the Schoo-Bemis Science Center. Pictured here are President Flynn and David Braverman, vice president of student affairs, with student leaders.

The success of that initiative was also due in no small part to the hard work of a dedicated group of the coach's former players: Whitey Burnham '48, Page Cotton '69, Chuck Dannenberg '67, Tony DiCicco '70, Bob Nye '58, and current men's soccer coach Peter Haley '77.

September: Dedication ceremony for two buildings totally renovated into state-of-the-art academic facilities—Schoo Hall, renamed the Schoo-Bemis Science Center; and Bemis Hall, renamed, temporarily at least, Hickory Hall.

All of this renaming requires some explanation:

- The Clarence and Grace Schoo Friendship Hall had begun life in 1963 as a general-purpose classroom building. The Schoos were prominent local residents who donated funds toward the construction of the building, and those funds matched gifts from the Kresge Foundation and from alums, trustees, corporations, other foundations, and friends.

- Bemis Hall, which had opened in 1975 and was devoted to the teaching of biology, had been named after William C. Bemis, a noted industrialist and local civic leader. Some twenty years after Bemis's death, his widow, Dorothy, donated the funds needed to complete the building.

- The renovation and expansion of Schoo Hall brought the teaching of science at Springfield College—biology, chemistry, computer science, mathematics, and physics—together under one roof.

- Accordingly, it seemed only logical that the new name of the building recognized, first, the names of Clarence and Grace Schoo, the primary benefactors of Schoo Hall; second, William Bemis, the primary benefactor of the former biology building; and third, the increasingly collaborative nature of the teaching of science today. Hence the new name: the Schoo-Bemis Science Center.

- As for Hickory Hall, formerly Bemis Hall: No longer devoted to the teaching of biology, this building today serves as a popular classroom building and the home of the Academic Success Center. Once the purpose of the building changed, it seemed more appropriate to move the Bemis name to the new science center, and replace it with a place-holder name until a suitable donor could be identified. The building took its new name from the city road that once snaked its way through the campus from Alden Street.

October: Dedication of the newly refurbished football field, formerly Benedum Field, as Amos Alonzo Stagg Field, honoring the memory of the College's first football coach and the only individual ever voted into both the football and basketball halls of fame.

Stagg was a head football coach continuously for fifty-seven years, starting at what is now Springfield College in 1890. He gained his greatest fame at the University of Chicago, where he coached football, baseball, track and field, and basketball before retiring at the age of seventy. He was widely known as the grand old man of football.

Edwin Pope, writing in *The Fireside Book of Football*, summed up Stagg's influence on the game he loved, saying, "He was football's Ben Franklin, Alexander Graham Bell, and Thomas Edison rolled into one."

Stagg truly exemplified Springfield College ideals. Early in his life, he had made a pledge to help the young. He

The new name for Benedum Field is unveiled in October 2006, honoring the College's first football coach, also known as the grand old man of college football—Amos Alonzo Stagg G'91.

achieved that by dedicating his spirit, mind, and body throughout an active lifetime of more than a century. His inspiration as a coach, his many innovations to the game of football, and his contributions to other sports are his legacy, and a proud part of the Springfield College legacy of educating leaders in service to others.

Marking the entrance to the field is a new brick and wrought iron archway emblazoned "Stagg Field." There, the College's teams in football, field hockey, and men's and women's lacrosse play their home games. The surface of the field is composed of a state-of-the-art synthetic grass, similar to that used on the fields of the Irv Schmid Sports Complex.

Later on, attention was also paid to the landscaping surrounding Stagg Field. Rows of evergreens were planted south of the field (to provide a bowl-like effect for players and to shield the parking lot for spectators), and east of the Linkletter Natatorium.

November: Dedication of the totally refurbished basketball court in Blake Arena to James Naismith G'91, who invented the game of basketball at the College in 1891.

James Naismith Court was part of an effort to properly recognize Naismith for his seminal contribution to Springfield College history. That effort came out of an evening meeting Flynn had in the president's office early in his presidency, with three students who were concerned that the Naismith name was not sufficiently prominent on the campus. Flynn listened, and agreed. There would be other

The newly dedicated James Naismith Court in Blake Arena at the Birthplace of Basketball.

President Flynn with members of the Naismith family following the dedication of James Naismith Court in November 2006.

responses to the students' well founded concerns— not just Naismith Court but Naismith Green in 2005 and the James Naismith statue in 2010.

Speaking at the dedication, Flynn said, "In honoring James Naismith, we also honor important values that guided him as an innovator, educator, physician, and minister. He believed strongly that a balanced development of one's spirit, mind, and body is the foundation of a fully realized life and the ability to contribute to the well-being of others. We call that philosophy Humanics, and it has guided all aspects of the Springfield College education for more than a century."

The newly resurfaced James Naismith Court features markings for volleyball and basketball. In fact, the court at the birthplace of basketball was the first in the nation to incorporate the new men's three-point-shot line mandated by the NCAA, a full year before it actually took effect.

The court's central graphic is Springfield College's majestic lion and triangle, symbols of the Pride. The College's wrestling and gymnastics teams also compete on the court.

The dedication of James Naismith Court was a fitting complement to Naismith Green, at the center of the campus, and to Amos Alonzo Stagg Field. Naismith was a friend and colleague of Stagg, and even invited him to participate in the first-ever basketball game, faculty versus students, on March 12, 1892. And turnabout was fair play; playing center on the College's first football team, coached by Stagg, was James Naismith.

THE INTERNATIONAL DIMENSION CONTINUES TO EXPAND

The international dimension of Springfield College had been expanding gradually during the Flynn years. In March 2007, a full-day program on the campus explored the past, present, and future international impact of the Humanics philosophy.

The program was the brainchild of Richard D. Davila, the 2006-07 Distinguished Springfield College Professor of Humanics and director of the Tampa Bay Campus of the School of Human Services. Davila was concluding his one-year appointment as Humanics professor, in which he had focused on the multicultural, multiethnic and international aspects of the Humanics philosophy. Two-hour symposiums had been staged successfully at School of Human Services campuses around the country.

Opening the program were Davila, President Flynn, and vice president for Academic Affairs Jean Wyld, who made presentations related to the international history of the college since its founding in 1885.

Flynn's comments acknowledged that the College's international reputation was perhaps not as widely recognized as its reputation in the United States. However, he noted, "Springfield College alums have also served as university presidents in China, founders of the Olympic movement in Eastern Europe, educational leaders in Central and South America, missionaries in the YMCA movement who started and ran YMCAs in many countries, and countless other leadership positions that make a difference in our world today."

Participants in the March 2007 International Humanics Day program pose with President Flynn. The originator of the event, Rick Davila, the 2006-07 Distinguished Springfield College Professor of Humanics, is in the front row, third from left.

In his remarks, Flynn explored the roles of former presidents of the College in expanding the international dimension. He focused primarily on the two former presidents who, he said, had led the charge most enthusiastically—Doggett and Locklin.

It was in 1965, Flynn said, during the first year of the Locklin presidency, that the Laurence Locke Doggett International Center at Springfield College was dedicated on the top floor of Marsh Memorial. The center, long a dream of Doggett's, was made possible by a $150,000 gift designated by Doggett for that express purpose before his death, Flynn added.

The center's founding director, also designated by Doggett, was Atallah (Ted) Kidess '35, who had been born and raised in Palestine and was the father of the College's current alumni relations director, Tamie Kidess Lucey '81. Flynn said of Ted Kidess: "It seems to me there can be no better example of the way a single graduate of Springfield College devoted his entire life to the international community, the long-standing mission of the College, and the principles of Humanics, which evolved from that mission over time."

Today the Doggett International Center is located in the new campus union complex, and serves as a haven for international students on campus and a resource for Springfield College students studying abroad.

But back to the March 2007 program. Later in the morning, Springfield College graduates serving in leadership positions in other nations presented their views. They were followed, after lunch, by presentations on the College's historical contributions to the Olympic movement; students who had studied in foreign countries; and the College's outreach committee in Mexico.

Closing the day's program was Rizek Abusharr, retired director general of the Jerusalem International YMCA and a recent commencement speaker, who spoke on "International Humanics: Where Do We Go from Here?"

A visit to the Jerusalem YMCA: President Flynn with Rizek Abusharr, retired director general of the Jerusalem International YMCA and a 2004 commencement speaker.

Flynn was a natural choice to be on the program for any exploration of internationalism. His *vita* made it quite clear that someday, when he himself became a former president of Springfield College, he would take his place with Doggett and Locklin in the enthusiastic stewardship of the College's International dimension.

For thirty years prior to coming to Springfield College in 1999, Flynn had consulted and made presentations on management, leadership, and sports-related facilities in Germany, England, Canada, Mexico, China, Japan, Sri Lanka, and other countries.

In the mid-1980s, he had spent a semester in China, lecturing at universities in Beijing, Wuhan, Shanghai, Jinghua, and Guangzhou, and consulting with architects and other government authorities on leadership, management, and facility planning. At that time, two Chinese universities awarded him their Honored Professor designation.

As dean of the College of Education at the University of Nebraska at Omaha, he had been involved in two three-year, $30-million grants to prepare teachers and teaching materials for Afghanistan following the Russian invasion there in 1979.

Since his arrival at Springfield College in 1999, Flynn had represented the College in a wide range of international activities, both in the United States and abroad. He had focused on cultivating longstanding international relationships, enhancing existing international programs, seeking new opportunities for international collaboration, and sometimes serving as a cheerleader to promote internationalism among the faculty and staff.

"I believe the international dimension is an essential element of the uniqueness of Springfield College, and I feel an obligation to encourage others to share that point of view," he says today.

A few months after the program on international aspects of Humanics, Flynn was invited, yet again, to visit China. This time, he delivered the keynote address entitled "The Role of Springfield College in Preparing Chinese Leadership in Sport and Education," at the YMCA and Modern Sports in China Conference in Tianjin, conducted as a run-up to the 2008 Olympic Games.

THE LOCATION OF COMMENCEMENT

Up until 2002, the Springfield College commencement exercises had been held at the Springfield Civic Center for longer than most people can remember. But in that year, the civic center closed for renovation, and the College and other organizations with major events were obliged to go elsewhere.

The Commencement Committee, headed by Jean Wyld, vice president of Academic Affairs, explored a number of possible alternate venues before recommending the closest venue of all—the Springfield College campus. The 2002 commencement, with undergraduate and graduate students combined, took place on the infield of Blake Track. The following year, the undergraduate commencement was again held on Blake Track, but, because of the increased number of graduates, the graduate exercises were shifted to Naismith Green. That procedure had been followed in 2004, 2005, and 2006 as well.

Undergraduate commencement exercises returned to a sleek new MassMutual Center in downtown Springfield in 2007.

Now it was time to return to the tradition of undergraduate commencements in the civic center. Renovations had been completed, and the center had sprung to life again as the MassMutual Center. Graduate exercises remained on Naismith Green.

In addition, construction of new buildings on the campus was about to cause more congestion and a scarcity of parking. In the year ahead, the Wellness Center, Field House, and Athletic Training/Exercise Science facility would be built. The following year would bring the capstone of the fundraising campaign, the new Campus Union complex on the former site of Woods Hall—a site which formed a neat little triangle with Blake Track and Naismith Green, where the commencements were being held.

It had the markings of a traffic and parking disaster—not so much with the smaller graduate commencement, but with the much larger undergraduate exercises.

So the 2007 undergraduate commencement was switched to the sleek new MassMutual Center. The commencement speaker and honorary degree recipient was H. Todd Stitzer, at that time the chief executive officer of Cadbury Schweppes. Stitzer had come from a YMCA family, and had attended Springfield College before transferring to Harvard. He had, in fact, met his wife-to-be, the former Marenda Brown '78, at Springfield College. For this and other reasons, he told the graduates, there was a special place in his heart for Springfield College. Stitzer also was serving on the College's Board of Trustees.

Unbeknownst to most people, Flynn and Stitzer had been having long conversations over several months about Springfield College. Flynn had talked about the great transformation that was in progress on the campus, and Stitzer told Flynn about his and Marenda's days at Springfield College; about his late father, Howard Stitzer, a longtime YMCA leader; and about his brother, Tim Stitzer '77, a lifelong YMCA executive and also a graduate of Springfield College.

The upshot of these discussions was the decision to create the Stitzer YMCA Center at Springfield College. The center would celebrate the rich history of the YMCA movement, its illustrious founders, and its great leaders, past and present; and it would inspire new generations of YMCA leaders to pursue equally ambitious goals for the movement in the future.

From the left: Mark Stitzer, Lucy Stitzer, Marenda Stitzer '78, Todd Stitzer '74. The Stitzer family made a $2-million gift to the College.

Architect's rendering of the planned transformation of East Gymnasium in the campus's first building (1894) into a multipurpose room within the Stitzer YMCA Center at Springfield College.

Three goals had already been established for the new center:

• Celebrate and honor YMCA leaders of the past,

• Recognize and support YMCA leaders of the present, and

• Prepare YMCA leaders of the future.

The collaborative relationship between YMCA and Springfield College had gone back nearly 125 years, to the very origins of the College in 1885. While the College was always clearly a separate entity from the YMCA, a good number of the founders, including David Allen Reed, its first president, had close ties with the YMCA movement.

Given the close collaboration that had been reaffirmed between the College and the YMCA during the Flynn years, the idea of a facility dedicated to that relationship on the Springfield College campus was a natural. Todd and Marenda Stitzer agreed to pledge $1-million to the project, and Todd's brother, Mark, and Mark's wife, Lucy, agreed to pledge another $1-million. With the Stitzer family gift totaling $2-million, the Stitzer YMCA Center was on its way.

Added to the funds for the center was a $500,000 gift already made to the College, with the purpose "to be designated later." The gift was from Harold Smith H'98, long-time trustee of the College and for many years the CEO, president, and chief investment officer of the YMCA Retirement Fund. Also added to the coffers were the net proceeds from the 2008 Harold Smith Dinner, an annual event sponsored by the YMCA Retirement Fund, and gifts from YMCA organizations across the country. (See page 251.)

The Stitzer YMCA Center at Springfield College will be located in a renovated Judd Gymnasia, the oldest building on the campus and a rich historical landmark. The center will house a greatly enhanced, interactive YMCA Hall of Fame (now located in Marsh

Memorial Chapel), which will also be accessible on the Web. And it will be a destination point for students, YMCA professional staff, volunteers, visitors, and others to share in the history of the YMCA and its early leadership, to learn about and embrace the future of the YMCA movement, and to develop the leadership skills and knowledge necessary to its future success.

Flynn's reputation was growing among YMCA leaders. As John Coduri, national executive director of the Association of YMCA Professionals (AYP) put it in the October 2009 issue of the AYP's *Perspective* magazine: "His dedication to the Springfield College/YMCA Movement partnership is unmatched in the past decades."

Fully equipped Springfield College students head off to work on Humanics in Action Day.

HUMANICS IN ACTION DAY'S TENTH ANNIVERSARY

Professor Peter Polito, who started it all in 1998, recalls that the first Humanics in Action Day "was conceived to be a day that really reaffirmed the Humanics philosophy and brought us together as a College community. And, secondly, to bring the initiative into the neighboring communities."

As the 1998-99 Distinguished Springfield College Professor of Humanics, Polito had worked with leaders of the New Student Orientation program to revive and expand an event that had been described in a 1918 Springfield College yearbook—a "work day" in which students worked to improve their still-developing campus.

"I wanted to have the entire College participate in a day to strengthen a true sense of community that would extend into the local neighborhood," Polito recalls. "Students, faculty, staff, trustees, and members of the community worked side by side and shoulder to shoulder to do something good, something that would improve the quality of life.

We reminded ourselves what it means that our institution is focused on a philosophy we call Humanics," he said.

The first Humanics in Action Day in 1998 was intended to be a one-time event, but the idea caught on and quickly became institutionalized. It now serves as the anchor for a broad range of community outreach projects.

The tenth anniversary of Humanics in Action Day, in 2007, like all the previous editions, was a great success. Nearly 2,000 workers gathered on Blake Track, listened to a call to arms by President Flynn, went out into the community, worked hard, and returned to Blake Track in time for burgers and dogs.

Campaign Progress . . . and the Kresge Grant

Momentum was continuing to increase for the fundraising campaign. When Flynn reported to the Board of Trustees in May 2007, the total raised was just over $30-million. But by homecoming in October, the total was up to $33.3-million, well within sight of the $40-million goal.

Peter Polito on the first Humanics in Action Day: "I wanted to have the entire College participate in a day to strengthen a true sense of community that would extend into the local neighborhood."

The number of bequests to the College was growing quickly. Support from corporations and foundations had exceeded $5-million. Online giving, using the College Web site, had been established and was being promoted. As a result of the campaign, there were 116 new President's Council members (annual gifts of $5,000 or more), and the number of David Allen Reed Society members (annual gifts of $1,000 or more) increased by 60 percent, from 329 to 548. Improved gift recognition guidelines, policies, and procedures had been developed and were in use.

The even-better news was that the benefits of the campaign, especially the new Schoo-Bemis Science Center and the anticipation about the new Wellness Center and new Field House, were already having a positive effect on student enrollment and the quality of learning.

According to Jean Wyld, vice president for Academic Affairs, "It was wonderful to see the effect that the new building [Schoo-Bemis] had on the admission of students to our life-sciences programs."

The best news of all about the campaign, however, was the long-awaited word from the Kresge Foundation: YES.

That meant the Kresge Foundation had approved Springfield College's application for a $1-million challenge grant to complete the *Leadership for the 21st Century* campaign. All the College had to do to receive the $1-million "capstone" gift was to raise a total of $39-million for the campaign by July 11, 2008. Thus, meeting the Kresge challenge was going to be key in completing the campaign successfully. The goal having been made clear, the work was cut out for Flynn and his fundraisers.

In granting its approval, Rip Rapson, Kresge Foundation president and chief executive officer, had some complimentary things to say about the College: "We are impressed with your emphasis on revitalization of your neighborhood, your track record of accessibility and persistence rates, and your holistic approach to health, human services, and wellness."

All things considered, the College was in the best condition it had enjoyed in many years. The strategic plan was being followed, and the campaign was on the cusp of a successful completion. Momentum, alignment, strategic partnerships, leverage—it was all coming together.

WRESTLING MAKES HISTORY

The Springfield College wrestling team, coached by Daryl Arroyo '84, made some history in February 2008 with a convincing 31-18 win over Plymouth State in a quad meet that also included Johnson & Wales College and Trinity College. It was the wrestling program's 900th victory, a mark reached by only three other teams in collegiate wrestling. The other three teams to reach 900 wins are Oklahoma State, Iowa State, and Oregon State—all Division I powerhouses.

Reaching the milestone was a familiar occurrence for Coach Arroyo. He had seen the program's 500th win as a team member, and the 700th and 800th wins earlier in his coaching tenure. He credited much of the program's success to his predecessor as coach, Doug Parker, who held the position for thirty-five years, registered 485 victories, and never had a losing season.

This photo showing two representatives from each athletic team ran in the 2008 College calendar.

New YMCA professional studies graduates celebrate at the new College sign following the 2008 commencement.

TRANSFORMATION OF THE CAMPUS—PART THREE

As the transformation of the campus continued, a new sense of urgency was evident. The College was making plans for the groundbreaking ceremony for the new Campus Union at Reunion 2008. And construction workers worked hard day after day to complete the new athletic, instructional, and recreational facilities going up between Blake Arena and the Linkletter Natatorium before the first day of classes at the end of August.

At the same time, faculty offices and classrooms were subject to change as the College worked to find suitable space for everyone while buildings were being built, torn down, and/or renovated. It reminded some of a giant jigsaw puzzle, but in fact there was a well-conceived plan.

Groundbreaking for the new Campus Union was held June 13 before an appreciative Reunion audience of alums, students, faculty, staff, and trustees.

The site selected for the new Campus Union was venerable Woods Hall, which was to be demolished later that summer to make room for the new building. The Beveridge Center, adjacent to Woods Hall, was to be completely renovated and incorporated into the new Campus Union.

Flynn's excitement was plainly visible as he described the new building at the groundbreaking. And who could blame him? Situated at the foot of historic Naismith Green, the new Campus Union would provide a much needed central point for the campus—for students, faculty and staff, alums, and visitors. It would contain space in support of international programs, student organization offices, career services, spacious lounge, activity space to encourage student interaction and collaboration, a food court, the College bookstore, postal services, a convenience store, and a 6,000-square-foot multipurpose room capable of housing large campus events. In Flynn's words, "the new Campus Union will foster a sense of community for the campus."

Appropriately enough, a group of student leaders were special guests at the groundbreaking, even though classes were no longer in session: Matt Fenlon '09, incoming Student Government Association president; Ben Cannon '09, student trustee; Kelsey Bishop '09 and Krystelle Magbanua '09, incoming chairs of the Student Alumni Association; David Clark '11, outgoing president of the Student Society for Cultural Diversity, and Emerging Leaders Program mentor; and two recent graduates, Julie Gniewek '08, outgoing senior class president, and Christine Brayfield '08, outgoing senior class treasurer.

As usual, several trustees were present at the groundbreaking for the Campus Union. One longtime trustee who has been involved with virtually all of the numerous construc-

Campus Union groundbreaking, June 2008, President Flynn with trustees in attendance. Left to right: Sue Lundin '70, Jim Walsh '64, President Flynn, Denise Alleyne '73, Lyman Wood H'06, and John Odierna '64.

Woods Hall, quite an elegant building when it was constructed in 1904, was razed to make room for the new Campus Union.

tion and renovation projects during the Flynn years is prominent Springfield business-man Mike Wallace. In addition to providing key guidance and counsel on projects as needed, the self-described "physical plant guy" has been delighted that Flynn shared his opinions on the importance of deferred maintenance. "The bathrooms, the roofs, the windows, the steam pipes—these are not glamorous projects, but they need to be taken care of before they become emergencies. More than most presidents, Dick Flynn recognized that," Wallace says today. "He's a visionary who came out of the Midwest with knowledge and experience, and with the guts to raise money and spend it productively and wisely," Wallace adds.

Throughout the campaign, Flynn had been circumspect about predicting success. Concluding his remarks at the groundbreaking, Flynn dropped a broad hint, for the first time, that the current fundraising campaign might well exceed its $40-million goal: "Come June 30—the official end of the campaign, a little over two weeks from today —it is very likely that we will be announcing that we have succeeded in reaching and perhaps surpassing the campaign goal of forty million dollars," he said.

Flynn officially broke that good news to faculty and staff at the All-College Meeting opening the 2008-09 academic year, saying: "It's my very great pleasure to announce to all of you officially today, for the very first time, that we succeeded in not only reaching our campaign goal, but also surpassing that goal by a comfortable margin."

Before the public announcement came, however, there was one other piece of business to attend to: Cutting ceremonial maroon and white ribbons with an oversized pair of wooden scissors to officially open three new buildings with over 160,000 square feet of space—the new Wellness Center and the new Field House, together now called the Wellness and Recreation Complex; and the new Athletic Training/Exercise Science facility. That was accomplished at a noontime ceremony on September 25, 2008. The complex had unofficially opened a few days earlier, to rave reviews from students. Flynn summed it up:

President Flynn with student leaders at the September 2008 ribbon-cutting ceremony for the Wellness Center and the Field House, now collectively referred to as the Wellness and Recreation Complex.

> Together, these three new facilities represent a significant improvement to our athletic, recreational, and instructional programs. Take it from a guy who knows: They are among the finest facilities of their kind in the country today, and they have been built in support of some of the finest academic and co-curricular programs in the country.

Flynn's evaluation of the new facilities would be validated in April 2009, when the Springfield College Wellness and Recreation Complex received national recognition, including the 2009 Outstanding Sports Facilities Award at the annual conference of the National Intramural-Recreational Sports Association (NIRSA).

The Springfield facility was one of six winning entries chosen from around the country. "These six facilities represent the very best and the very latest in collegiate recreational centers," said Jeff Huskey, NIRSA's selection committee chair. "They not only provide a location for physical activity, but also create a sense of community on their campus."

FINALLY, THE OFFICIAL ANNOUNCEMENT

After making certain that all the details were in order, the College issued the news release with the first tally on October 22:

SPRINGFIELD, Mass., Oct. 22, 2008—Calling it "historic," Springfield College President Richard B. Flynn announced that the largest fundraising campaign in the College's 123-year history has closed at a record $44.5-million, exceeding its goal by more than eleven percent.

"Our supporters have given a ringing endorsement to our unique mission of educating students in spirit, mind, and body to become tomorrow's leaders by contributing more than five times the amount that has ever been raised in a Springfield College campaign." Flynn added.

"Their generosity helps assure that current and future students will benefit from superior educational programs supported by state-of-the-art facilities and high-quality campus life. We are deeply grateful to all who worked and contributed to put this campaign over the top," Flynn added.

President Flynn pays a visit to Louise Appleton H'05 in Florida. The Appleton family has been involved with the College since its founding, and has been generous in its support.

The College had entered the public phase of the campaign in 2005 with $20-million raised. The Kresge Foundation announced a $1-million challenge grant if the College were to raise $39-million by June 30, 2008. The challenge was met. Altogether, the College received ten gifts of $1-million or more, sixty-seven gifts of $100,000 or more, and 376 contributions of $10,000 or more. There were more than 15,000 donors from all across the United States and fifteen foreign countries.

Supported by campaign funds, the College constructed its new Wellness and Recreation Complex, expanded and renovated Schoo-Bemis Science Center to create an interdisciplinary science teaching facility, and broke ground for the new Campus Union and renovated Beveridge Center. It also established fifty new endowed scholarships and sixteen named funds supporting the College.

The seven-figure gifts had come from Louise Briggs Appleton H'05; Helen Davis Blake G'67, H'09 and S. Prestley Blake H'82; Maurice Schlossburg '51 and Amy Schlossberg '52; Jane Davis-Kusek '78; Earl Hamilton Chamberlain '27; H. Todd Stitzer '74 H'07 and Marenda Brown Stitzer '78; Mark Stitzer and Lucy Stitzer; Aramark Corporation; Jenzabar Corporation; and the Kresge Foundation.

Jane Davis-Kusek '78 (third from left) made a leadership gift to the campaign, and the Davis Foundation has been an ongoing supporter of the College. Paying a visit to the campus and President Flynn with Davis-Kusek are, from the left: Mrs. John Davis (Robyn), Mrs. Mary Davis, John Davis, and Stephen Davis.

It's also important to note that the YMCA movement, including eighty YMCAs throughout the United States, contributed a total of $2.2-million to the campaign, largely due to the efforts of Jack Lund G'82 and Clark Baker, heads of the New York City and Houston YMCAs, and Neil Nicoll G'73, head of the YMCA of the USA. The $2.2-million in contributions was over and above the annual scholarship support the College received from a large number of YMCAs.

Campaign Celebration Day on the campus included campaign success T-shirts for everyone.

President Flynn celebrates the successful campaign with grandson Flynn Leonard.

CAMPAIGN CELEBRATION DAYS ARRIVE

In late October 2008, a variety of activities and events on the campus officially celebrated the campaign's conclusion and success.

On October 23, a large tent was set up outside the front doors of Cheney Hall. Students, faculty, and staff had the opportunity to sign one of three oversized Thank You boards, later displayed at a formal and festive event for key donors, as well as to enjoy celebratory cake and receive campaign T-shirts.

The following evening, in Blake Arena, under a ceiling of twinkling lights and amid numerous standing ovations, President Flynn thanked donors, as well as members of the faculty and staff for their contributions to the future of Springfield College.

Flynn singled out the Board of Trustees for special thanks. He said the College was fortunate to have trustees who were so supportive and "went the extra mile." In particular, he cited Helen Blake and Bill Marsh for their additional responsibilities as co-chairs of the campaign.

During Jim Walsh's term as board chair, he bore the brunt of all the various campaign-related activities that were coming to a peak as the campaign cranked up for the home stretch. Honoring Walsh, Flynn noted wryly that Walsh had "probably participated in more groundbreakings and ribbon cuttings these past three years than any board chair in the College's history."

At the October 2008 Campaign Celebration, four former board chairs—all of whom Flynn noted, "went the extra mile," get together: from the left, Jim Walsh '64, Lyman Wood H'06, John Odierna '64, Bill Marsh H'02.

Flynn also had high compliments for previous chairs Odierna and Wood: Odierna, Flynn said, had "served as a confidant of sorts—listening, discussing, offering opinions on a wide range of matters." And Wood, Flynn noted, "was never the least bit reluctant to express his opinion on any matter before the board. When the matter was related to finance, Lyman was tenacious and relentless in seeking a complete understanding of the issue at hand—a quality any president should value highly."

In closing the festivities for the evening, Flynn had parting thoughts, right from the heart: "All of our campaign priorities, and all of our accomplishments, were student-centered and student-focused. This should not come as a surprise to anyone here

President Flynn with campaign co-chairs Bill Marsh H'02 and Helen Blake G'67 H'09, at the campaign success dinner in Blake Arena in October 2008.

Students, alums, faculty, staff, and friends of the College all celebrated the campaign's success in Blake Arena, under a ceiling of twinkling lights and amid numerous standing ovations.

tonight, since everything that goes on at Springfield College goes on for the ultimate benefit of our students. Our current students, and the prospective students who will enroll here in the future—they are the beneficiaries of our campaign's success."

And Flynn added this closing thought: "All of you in this arena tonight can feel pride for contributing to the transformation of Springfield College while maintaining the legacy of its Humanics mission and its long-standing tradition of academic excellence. In participating in this campaign, you have enhanced the vibrancy of our campus, and helped to secure its future."

In reporting on the campaign celebration, *Triangle* magazine commented on "an academic year that had a different feel than those of previous years. Perhaps it was because of a noticeable increase in move-in day pandemonium; the Class of 2012, at 618 strong, represents the largest first-year class in the College's history. Perhaps it was the newest additions to campus—buildings that had sprouted out of dirt and cement, shed their winter plastic wrap, and transformed into the new Wellness Center, Field House, and Athletic Training/Exercise Science facility. Or maybe it was seeing the feverish work of landscaping crews, who were planting trees, shrubs, and perennials at a fast-forward pace."

Two Days Later, Off to Sorocaba

A mere two days after the campaign soiree at Blake Arena, Flynn was on his was to Sorocaba, Brazil, to sign a new five-year letter of agreement between Springfield College and the YMCA of Sorocaba. With him was Bob Willey, dean of the School of Human Services.

The first letter of agreement between the two institutions had been signed in 1998, while Bromery was president. But for Flynn, the relationship had started in September 1999, when a delegation of Brazilian YMCA leaders had made the long trip to Springfield to represent their country and their YMCAs at his inauguration.

Flynn had reciprocated by traveling to Brazil and Uruguay in 2002 and 2003, deliver-

Ribbon-cutting at the new Houston Campus of the School of Human Services. From the left: Isaac Williams, assistant dean and campus director in Houston; Bob Willey; Clark Baker, president and CEO of the YMCA of Greater Houston; President Flynn; and Jean Wyld.

ing major remarks at historical YMCA ceremonies. A side trip in 2003 had included a stop at Camp Cururu, a YMCA camp in the Amazon jungle, where faculty members from the College, Professors Robert Barkman and Charles Reddington, had preceded him conducting biology and botany research.

The primary vehicle for the Sorocaba partnership, from the college's standpoint, was the School of Human Services. For the YMCA of Sorocaba, it was the highly regarded Technical Institute for Professional Development, an important aspect of the College's international dimension. As Flynn said, "This relationship demonstrates once more the high regard in which Springfield College is held internationally for its leadership development work."

On the way back to the United States, Flynn and Willey made a brief stop in Uruguay to discuss another articulation agreement with the Montevideo YMCA.

A week after his return to Springfield, Flynn was jetting off to Houston in the company of Willey and Jean Wyld, vice president for academic affairs. They were to participate in the official grand opening and ribbon cutting for the Houston Campus of the Springfield College School of Human Services. The new regional campus in Houston became the eleventh SHS campus nationwide, and is expected to serve as the model for future SHS regional campuses.

HONORS FOR COMMUNITY ENGAGEMENT

As calendar 2008 ended, Barack Obama had won out over John McCain to become the nation's president, and Springfield College was honored by a number of organizations for its longstanding commitment to community engagement; the recognition continued into the early months of 2009:

- In December, the College was one of only nine colleges and universities selected to receive the highly coveted Jostens NADIIIAA Community Service "Award of Merit" for projects completed during the 2007-08 academic year. This prestigious awards program, co-sponsored by the National Association of Division III Athletic Administrators and by Jostens, recognizes contributions made by Division III student-athletes to their communities.

- In February 2009, the Carnegie Foundation for the Advancement of Teaching selected Springfield College to receive its Community Engagement Classification. The College was cited for a curriculum that involved students and faculty in addressing community needs, and for outreach and partnerships that benefited both the community and the campus.

- Also in February, the College was named to the President's Higher Education Community Service Honor Roll for its exemplary community service programs by the Corporation for National and Community Service in Washington, D.C. The honor is the highest federal recognition a college can receive for its commitment to service-learning and civic engagement.

The College received another honor around this time that was not related to community engagement: In November, the entire twenty-five-member 2008 graduating class of the physician assistant program passed the national certification exam on the first try, a highly unusual occurrence. Following graduation, all twenty-five class members were employed as physician assistants.

254

NOTES ON PEOPLE FROM 2008

Sally Griggs of Northampton succeeded Jim Walsh as trustee chair, following Walsh's three-year stint. The election of Griggs—a longtime community volunteer at Clark School for the Deaf, the Hampshire Regional YMCA, and Cooley Dickinson Hospital, among other organizations—was historic: She became the first woman to serve as the chair of the Springfield College Board of Trustees.

Brian Rose '07, a former student trustee, used his bachelor's degree in criminal justice and psychology as a launching pad to one of the nation's most competitive internships —judicial intern at the Supreme Court of the United States. In 2007, Rose had been selected to be one of two judicial interns in the office of the administrative assistant to the chief justice. Following his internship, in early 2008, he was hired to work in the office of Justice Stephen Breyer.

Charles Redmond '68, who came to Springfield College as a first-year student in 1964 and never left, was named dean of the School of Health, Physical Education, and Recreation, effective June 1, 2008. Redmond, an internationally known athletic training educator, succeeded William Considine, who retired as dean and continued at the College as professor of physical education.

John Wilcox '67, G'69, retired at year-end following four years as an undergrad, one year as a grad student, and thirty-nine years in a variety of key jobs in admissions, financial aid, facilities, enrollment management, and even, for a little while, student affairs. An additional job Wilcox loved, though it was not part of his job description,

Sally Griggs of Northampton became the first woman to serve as chair of the Board of Trustees in June 2008, succeeding Jim Walsh '64, G'00.

Charlie Redmond '68, who arrived at Springfield College as a first-year student in 1964 and never left, was named dean of the School of Health, Physical Education, and Recreation in June 2008.

Bill Considine, who served as dean of the School of Health, Physical Education and Recreation until his retirement as dean in 2007.

Brian Rose '07, a former student trustee, used his bachelor's degree in criminal justice and psychology as a launching pad to one of the nation's most competitive internships—judicial intern at the Supreme Court of the United States. Following the internship, Rose was hired to work there.

Harry Rock (right) director of YMCA relations, with YMCA legend Fred Hoshiyama (center), and, from the left, Natalie Brown, Brittany Mitchell, and Kayla Mitchell, all YMCA Club members. Rock was named director of YMCA relations in December 2007, succeeding Paul Katz (2001-2007), who had succeeded Kurt Kramer (1994-1999) in this important liaison position.

Roy Burch '08 and Justin Zook '08, varsity swimmers, participated in Olympic and Paralympic competition in Beijing in 2008. Zook took home a gold medal.

Alden H. "Whitey" Burnham '48, the only alum to become a triple Alumni Award recipient, died in December 2008 at the age of 85.

was the eleven years he spent as a supervisor and advisor to New Student Orientation. Ask Wilcox what he liked best about Springfield College, and he will tell you: the students.

Harry F. Rock, executive director of the YMCA of Greater Westfield since 1991, was named director of YMCA relations at Springfield College in December 2007. Rock has senior staff responsibilities for managing and expanding the College's partnership with the YMCA of the USA and its programs and supporting services for students preparing for YMCA careers. Rock also has key responsibilities for overseeing the development of the Stitzer YMCA Center and YMCA Hall of Fame on the campus.

Alden H. "Whitey" Burnham, '48, the only Springfield College alumnus to become a triple Alumni Award recipient (Distinguished Alumni Award, Tarbell Medallion, Athletic Hall of Fame), died in December 2008 at what he would have called the "ripe old age" of eighty-five. Whitey was a true Son of Springfield who led a double life for his last forty-eight years, after being named the new soccer and lacrosse coach at Dartmouth College in 1960. He wore his maroon blazer at Springfield College, and his green blazer at Dartmouth. The ruse worked: When Whitey retired from Dartmouth, he got a soccer field named after him.

Springfield College swimmers **Justin Zook** '08 and **Roy Burch** '08 participated in Olympic competition in Beijing in 2008. Burch represented Bermuda in the Summer Olympics, and Zook won a gold medal for the U.S. in the Paralympics.

The renovated Linkletter Foyer of Fuller Arts Center.

A REMODELED FULLER ARTS CENTER

The remodeled Fuller Arts Center was unveiled in March 2009, thanks to a generous lead gift from the George F. and Sybil H. Fuller Foundation.

Speaking at the unveiling, Flynn said, "The Fuller Arts Center has been a center of activity on our campus and in our community for a quarter of a century. Now, with technology and enhancements that make it more useful, accessible, comfortable, and attractive, it is equipped to present the sophisticated arts events and college programs that are integral to first-quality higher education and the cultural life of our region."

Renovations included a significantly expanded entryway and foyer, with a façade of glass, brick, and limestone. In Appleton Auditorium, the center's performance space, there is a computerized stage lighting system and the floor has been raised to improve views of the stage. The stage itself got a new floor and curtains, and the seating area new carpeting. Enhancing sound were a new ceiling, sound system, and acoustical wall panels.

President Flynn and John Mailhot do the honors at the March 2009 ribbon cutting for the newly remodeled Fuller Arts Center. Also participating are the College's five academic deans: Bob Willey, Francine Vecchiolla, Mary Healey '78, Bill Susman, and Charlie Redmond '68.

MBA Program Announced

Recognizing the growing need for professional management training, particularly in the nonprofit sector, Springfield College announced in April 2009 that it would offer a master's of business administration (MBA) degree program with concentrations in nonprofit organization management, and business management, beginning in the summer of 2010.

Commenting on the program, Jean Wyld, vice president for academic affairs, said, "It's a solidly designed thirty-credit program for students to achieve the MBA competencies identified by the Association to Advance Collegiate Schools of Business."

Flynn noted that the MBA program "is a natural for Springfield College. Since 1885, we have been preparing leaders for the YMCA and other nonprofits. We have a national and international reputation for conducting managerial and leadership training programs across a wide spectrum of disciplines. Our guiding philosophy of service leadership is especially relevant today as businesses and organizations seek ethical managers who structure their success as integral to the well-being of society as a whole."

Wellness Notes

In September 2009, the College opened a new Center for Wellness Education and Research to conduct groundbreaking research, to be a national source of the latest wellness information, and to design and present public wellness-education programs. The program was a natural outgrowth of the construction of one of the nation's premier wellness facilities on the campus.

Along the same lines, the College established a partnership with the spa industry leader, Canyon Ranch, to develop a bachelor's degree specialization in spa and wellness management. The new specialization is offered in the applied exercise science major within the School of Health, Physical Education, and Recreation.

President Richard B. Flynn Day in Springfield

Proclaiming the day as "President Richard B. Flynn Day," Springfield Mayor Domenic Sarno H'09 honored the College's president on June 19, 2009, for Flynn's ten years of leadership that have benefited the city and the region.

Sarno read a proclamation at a City Hall ceremony attended by representatives of the offices of the mayor and the governor of Massachusetts, city officials, community leaders, and representatives of the College and its Board of Trustees.

The proclamation cited Flynn's leadership through major campus construction, national recognition for excellence in academic programs, growth in the student body, and strong community relationships and service.

Flynn, a survivor of the prostate cancer he battled in 2001, also was honored in the spring of 2009 by the American Cancer Society with its Omar T. Pace Award, honoring community leaders who have made a difference in the lives of cancer patients and their families throughout Western Massachusetts.

Springfield Mayor Domenic Sarno H'09 hosts the Flynns in City Hall on "President Richard B. Flynn Day" in the city.

Both Flynn and Springfield College are long-time supporters of the American Cancer Society. The College has hosted the Relay for Life since its inception seventeen years ago, and Flynn was its chair in 2002. The annual twenty-four-hour event features teams of runners and walkers who raise awareness and funds in the fight against cancer.

COLLEGE RENEWS PARTNERSHIP WITH YMCA

The College renewed its historic partnership with the YMCA of the USA (YUSA), as Flynn and Neil Nicoll G'73, the YUSA's president and chief executive officer, signed a new five-year agreement on the campus in June 2009. The agreement recognized Springfield College as a premier institution of higher education for YMCA leaders, and expanded educational programs and services for current and future YMCA professionals and volunteers.

Both institutions agreed to support recruitment of qualified students interested in YMCA careers for the College's undergraduate and graduate degree programs and the subsequent placement of graduates in YMCA positions.

The new agreement extended more than a century of collaboration between the College and the YMCA of the USA. In particular, it recognized "the special and unique relationship between the parties, including the historic bond, mutual goals, and shared programming initiatives."

Later in the summer of 2009, the third annual Springfield Youth Olympics, a fun-filled array of track, field, tennis, and golf competition open to local youths aged 5-22, was held on the campus. The event took place on the campus, and was sponsored by the College and the YMCA of Greater Springfield. James Morton, president and CEO of the YMCA of Greater Springfield, noted, "Our goal is to provide area youth with an enjoyable and rewarding way to stay fit, and to offer families an opportunity to come together. This collaboration with Springfield College enables us to help build strong kids, strong families, and strong communities."

Demonstrating admirable weekend informality, Neil Nicoll and President Flynn sign the documents renewing the historic partnership between the YMCA of the USA and Springfield College in June 2009.

"The Y-Four": John Preis, president and CEO of the YMCA Retirement Fund; John Corduri, national executive director of the Association of YMCA Professionals; Flynn; and Neil Nicoll G'73, president and CEO of the YMCA of the USA. (Nicoll, a trustee of the College, succeeded Ken Gladish in the top job in May 2008.)

259

INTERNATIONALISM AT SPRINGFIELD COLLEGE

Leaders of sports in China, including coaches of 2008 Chinese Olympic gold medalists, converged on the campus in July 2009 for the Summer Sport and Exercise Science Institute, a series of presentations and experiential learning activities on cutting-edge topics in sports science led by faculty members from the School of Health, Physical Education, and Recreation.

The Guangzhou Sports Bureau selected Springfield College to conduct the program, which was funded by the Chinese government. Charles Redmond, dean of the school, negotiated with the sports bureau and arranged the curriculum and faculty.

In addition to Olympic coaches, the group included coaches and representatives from the city's sports bureau, vocational college of sports, badminton center, water sports management team, and shooting and archery center.

Also during the summer, two groups of students and scholars from Japanese universities got a taste of Springfield College.

Two scholars from Mukogawa Women's University in Tokyo came to the College to pursue research on two subjects: the management and administration of fitness clubs and sport gyms in corporate settings, and the lives of female wheelchair basketball athletes.

And students from Nihon University, also in Tokyo, got an introduction to student life at the College, as well as an introduction to lacrosse and practice on the climbing wall in the Wellness and Recreation Complex and on the East Campus high-ropes challenge course.

Later in the year, Flynn and the College hosted Mayor Hiroshi Tamura of Takikawa, Japan and a delegation of nine educators, musicians, and officials of that city for a tour of the College. A separate group of Takikawa high school students also participated in the visit, and were dinner guests in homes of local families.

A BANNER YEAR FOR THE HEADLEYS

Steve Headley '10 concluded his junior year over Memorial Day weekend by winning his second NCAA individual championship. Running at the NCAA Men's Outdoor Track & Field Championships, Headley cruised to a win in the 100-meter dash in 10.51 seconds.

In addition, Headley finished third in the 200 meters, and anchored his 4X100 relay to a sixth-place finish.

In March, at the NCAA Men's Indoor Track and Field Championships, Headley won the 55-meter dash in a blazing 6.24 seconds.

All of which landed him in *Sports Illustrated* magazine and earned him the moniker "the fastest man alive in Division III."

Steve's dad, Sam Headley, is not quite in his son's class when it comes to speed, but Sam had a pretty decent year, too. The Springfield College professor of exercise science was the recipient of a new $228,000 grant from the National Institutes of Health.

Steve Headley running. His dad did pretty well, too.

The Museum of Springfield History

In October 2009, the new Museum of Springfield History opened just down Chestnut Street from the Quadrangle in downtown Springfield.

The museum features a number of exhibits on the city's development as a manufacturing center, focusing on its industries, transportation, inventions, education, and more. Also included: exhibits on the Indian Motorcycle Company, Milton Bradley Company, and Bee Gee planes.

The Springfield College exhibit highlights a number of important contributions made to the city, and to the world, over more than a century. These include the invention of basketball, the partnership with the YMCA, Olympic connections, community engagement, and faculty research.

In addition to large display panels that tell the College's history through photographs and text, a number of College artifacts are also on display, including a copy of "basket ball" rules from 1893, the electrogoniometer created by Peter Karpovich to study motion and athletic performance, and a letter from Rev. Martin Luther King, Jr.

Flynn reviews the Springfield College exhibit at the new Museum of Springfield History, adjacent to the Quadrangle in downtown Springfield.

OKAY, WHAT'S NEXT?

The summer 2009 issue of *Triangle* magazine seemed to capture the situation very well on its cover: Flynn, in shirtsleeves, holding a rolled-up sheaf of construction plans, flanked by vice presidents David Braverman and John Mailhot, also in shirtsleeves, hard hats by their sides, against the backdrop of a partially completed Campus Union. The cover headline: "A Decade of Change."

The expressions on the faces of the three men said something, too: Yes, there was pride and a certain satisfaction. But also there was a restlessness, an urgency, an attitude that seemed to say, After this is complete, what's next?

This is the attitude that seems to have pervaded the Flynn years at Springfield College. We took a parking lot and made it into a lush expanse of green lawn; okay, what's next? We totally renovated the dining commons and made the food service much better; okay, what's next? We built a state-of-the-art Wellness and Recreation Complex; okay, what's next?

May 2009: David Braverman, President Flynn, and John Mailhot review the progress of the Campus Union construction project. The new building opened to the public in January 2010.

There was always a little time for congratulations, of course. But there was always something that was next. The job was never done. Next year and the year after that, there would be more changes, and that was a *good* thing.

And there was something else: A confidence that the choices made would be the right ones, and that the job would get done properly, and on time. Students, alums, faculty, staff, the vice presidents, and Flynn himself *believed*.

You name it, and it has been improved or enhanced over the past decade: Facilities and the physical plant? Check. Faculty governance? Check. Academic excellence? Check. Financial condition and performance? Check. Student activities? Check. Neighborhood engagement? Check. International outreach? Check. Collaboration with the YMCA and Naismith Memorial Basketball Hall of Fame? Check. Fundraising? Check. High morale and optimism about the future? Check.

And through it all, we've remained sensitive to the essential importance of the things about Springfield College that *can't ever change*: The Humanics philosophy, and the mission to educate students in spirit, mind, and body for leadership in service to humanity.

John White, formerly the College's director of sports communications, major gifts officer, and director of development, was named vice president for development and alumni affairs in November 2009.

Okay, what's next? Always looking ahead, Flynn meets with Steve Jablonski (left), architect for the renovation of Judd Gymnasia, the oldest building on the campus, and the planning for the Stitzer YMCA Center. With them are Jill Russell and Harry Rock.

Logo for the celebration of the College's 125th anniversary.

CELEBRATING THE QUASQUICENTENNIAL

With the 2009-10 academic year underway, the 125th Anniversary Steering Committee, established in 2008 as an advisory committee to the president, got busier with the planning and directing of a year-long series of activities, projects, and events designed to engage the Springfield College community in recognizing this milestone in the College's history.

All of the major constituencies of the College were represented on the committee—students, faculty and staff, the Board of Trustees, alumni, parents, emeritus faculty and retired staff, donors and friends of the College, the surrounding neighborhood and the city of Springfield.

The steering committee carried overall responsibility for ensuring that the theme, "Celebrating 125 Years of Great Ideas," reached not only the main campus but also all regional campuses, and touched the following bases:

• The strength of the academic programs across a wide variety of disciplines

• The strength, consistency, value, and stewardship of the College's mission

• A strong sense of community and pride; a local college with a global outreach and impact

• Historical contributions of the College to sport and society

Cabinet (seated) and President's Council, December 2009.

- Success and achievements of alumni in their respective professions, their leadership in professional organizations, and the scholarly accomplishments of students, staff, and faculty

- The diverse student body

- A framework for the future

Throughout the 2009-10 academic year, the 125th anniversary was observed in a wide variety of ways, including special events at Homecoming and Reunion, a series of historical posters, an art exhibition titled "The Founders' Show—A Look Back," the Founders' Day dinner, and, in the Spring of 2010, "Celebrating the Birthplace of Basketball: James Naismith and His Legacy"— featuring the dedication of a bronze statue of James Naismith G'91, the inventor of basketball.

The 125th Anniversary Steering Committee was co-chaired by Betty Mann, recently retired professor and administrator, and Mary Lou Dyjak, special assistant to the president. Committee members included: Deborah Alm, Amanda DiPaolo, Barbara Ernst, Jani Flynn, Tamari Kidess Lucey, Ronald Maggio, Jeffery Monseau, Mimi Murray, Craig Poisson, Laura Maggio, and Harry Rock.

Betty Mann

Mary Lou Dyjak

REGARDING THE PAST, SERVING THE FUTURE
Poem in Honor of the 125th Anniversary of Springfield College
By Dr. Margaret Lloyd

Stirring life on Winchester Square in 1885,
Passion listened to its heart and raised the first building,
Rang the first song, echoing in the first sixteen rooms,
Imagined the move five years later to the lake,
Nourished mission-bound young men and later women,
Gathering in the classroom, on the green playing fields.
Faith and international fame hand in hand.
Imagine it. And turn your head slowly around today.
Examine the evolution. Buildings are not just buildings,
Land is not just land, and the dead are not simply dead—
Doggett, Naismith, Gulick and the other figures providential.

Communicating with us down the years and stirring
Obligation, eyes of passionate students in old photographs
Look at us as we look at them, perhaps asking that we
Locate our potential and longing for justice, that we
Evolve and seize this day, this hour, this minute.
Gathering together in our hearts, the great spirits
Endure with us, though everything changes and moves.

Always there is more: triumphs, failures, new games,
New buildings, sites, landscapes of the spirit, mind, and body.
Nourishing ourselves and others, we teach, learn,
Imagine, coach, play, serve, lead. The strong
Vein of human striving gathers us together.
Empathy and the desire to know what can be known
Raises the old song, but makes new music,
Stirring the air as in the beginning on Winchester Square,
Arriving at this year, 2010, on Lake Massasoit,
Regarding the past, serving the future, new students
Yearn, dream, and still throng our spacious gates.

The Richard B. Flynn Campus Union by night on February 4, 2010—ready for the Founders' Day Dinner.

Flynn family guests at the morning dedication, from left: daughter Tracy Leonard, granddaughter Mollie Magee, daughter Kerry Magee, and Jani and Dick Flynn.

The crowd packed the main lobby of the Campus Union.

Epilogue

$\mathbf{F}$ebruary 4, 2010 dawned as a classic New England winter day—a crisp 21 degrees, with bright sunlight and a cloudless sky. One imagined it was the sort of weather that might have prevailed on January 25, 1885, when the School for Christian Workers received its charter from the Commonwealth of Massachusetts.

And like that day in 1885, February 4, 2010 was to become a true watershed date in Springfield College history:

- The Richard B. Flynn Campus Union, the 58,500-square-foot capstone project of the College's highly successful fundraising campaign, was dedicated in a joyous noontime ceremony attended by hundreds of students, faculty, staff, alums, trustees, and other friends of the College; and

- The Founders' Day Dinner that evening turned out to be no less than an elegant, formal celebration of the College's 125th birthday, which technically had occurred a week earlier.

DEDICATION

11:50 a.m.: A selection of College songs emanating from the prominent bell tower of the new campus union called participants to the main lobby of the new building for the noontime dedication ceremony.

Sally Griggs and Iain Bradbury unveil the "placeholder" plaque.

There was a cheerfulness and camaraderie among the large crowd that gathered by the building's grand staircase. Most of them had seen quite a number of dedications and ribbon cuttings over the past decade, but somehow this one was different.

Speaking from a podium to the left of the staircase, Sally Griggs, chair of the Board of Trustees, presided, graciously. Iain Bradbury '10, the student trustee, represented the student body, eloquently. David Braverman, vice president for student affairs, kept the program running, smoothly. And the man of the hour seemed to take to his triple role as patriarch, president, and honoree quite naturally. The twelfth president was accompanied for the occasion by his wife (and the College's first lady) Jani Flynn, daughters Kerry Magee and Tracy Leonard, and granddaughter Mollie Magee, representing the Flynns' eight grandchildren.

To the left of the podium, some forty special guests sat as witnesses to the historic event. Contractors, subcontractors, suppliers and vendors, including representatives of Symmes, Maini & McKee Associates, the architects, and Erland Associates, the builders. Major donors to the project. Trustees and emeritus trustees. Student leaders. And two

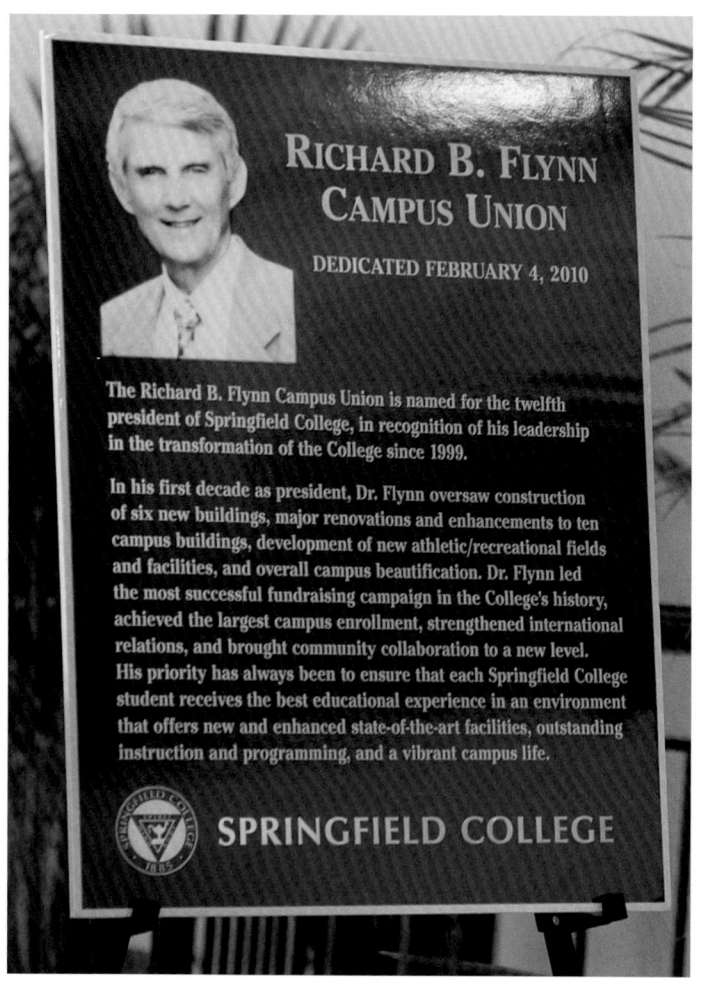

Closeup of the "placeholder" plaque.

alums from the class of 1959, Tom Johnson and Owen Houghton, who had been present more than 50 years ago when the original Beveridge Center was dedicated.

Video cameras rolled, still cameras clicked, local news reporters interviewed people and scribbled notes.

Bradbury noted that the new facility "puts a wide array of resources at the fingertips of the students. We've seen incredible growth and change on this campus, and it's made an already rewarding experience on the campus even more enjoyable." So much so, Bradbury added, that after graduation, he planned to return to campus as a graduate student.

One of Griggs' first official duties as board chair had been to preside at the October 2008 dinner on campus celebrating the success of the College's first comprehensive campaign in more than three decades. Now, she said, she was bearing witness to another "very special and joyous occasion" for the College and its students.

"A decade ago, there were many things that people did not believe possible for Springfield College," Griggs said. "Then, in March 1999, Dick Flynn became our twelfth president . . . . And today, the Springfield College I always valued has become the Springfield College I treasure."

"Look around you," Griggs continued, "and think about the thousands of details in this building that were thought of, discussed, coordinated, and implemented before we could stand here today. The design, the construction, the feel of the interior details and furnishings, the attention to program needs. I think all of us now understand what President Flynn means when he says that facilities do, indeed, facilitate programs. He made sure that a campus union was part of the plan, from the beginning."

Speaking more broadly about the great progress the College has made during the Flynn presidency, Griggs said, "The result of his leadership is a physical plant that has been transformed. Where academic excellence has thrived. Where at least 75 percent of incoming students identify Springfield College as their first-choice college. Where student-athletes can be described as student-scholars. Where leadership development programs guide and inspire. Where faculty know their students. And where students know their president—and, I might add, their first lady."

Griggs said the Board of Trustees had determined months ago to name the new facility after its twelfth president for one basic reason: "Dick Flynn's student-centered leadership. Since day one, his priority has been to ensure that each Springfield College student receives the best educational experience, and to do so in a learning and living environment that offers new and enhanced state-of-the-art facilities, outstanding instruction and programming, and a vibrant campus life." (Griggs added parenthetically that the twelfth president needed to be persuaded to accept the honor, but had come around in the end.)

For his part, Flynn said he was "honored and humbled" to have his name on the new facility. In a personal reflection, he said, "I've been blessed with many satisfying and

268

President Flynn makes the ceremonial ribbon cutting with the help of student leaders.

memorable work-related moments throughout my life. This day may well be the most honored and humbling moment of my professional career. These last eleven years at Springfield College have been truly a labor of love . . . and nothing could be more meaningful to me."

Having his name on the new campus union, Flynn said, was "expressive of my belief in the importance of campus community. I know from my reading of the College's historical documents that this belief was in the minds of the founders, and it is knitted into the very being of the College—its students, alumni, faculty, and staff. It has inevitably been true that the College has succeeded most when it has held the interests of its students in the forefront."

In passing, Flynn noted two nearby ongoing projects: In the months to come, as part of the College's celebration of its 125th anniversary, a life-sized bronze statue of James Naismith, the Springfield College instructor who invented basketball in 1891, would be placed outside the front entrance of the campus union. And right across Naismith Green, renovation work was continuing on the oldest building on the campus, Judd Gymnasia, to transform it into the Stitzer YMCA Center at Springfield College.

After the unveiling of a "placeholder" plaque by Griggs and Bradbury, the first of several ceremonial snippings of maroon and white ribbons was performed by Flynn and eight student leaders. It was an entirely appropriate choice for this most student-centered of campus buildings. More ribbon cuttings followed, with trustees, special guests, and others who expressed a desire to be a part of Springfield College history.

Then the celebration adjourned to the lower level, where a commemorative cake was cut and quickly consumed, and commemorative gifts were distributed to one and all. Those who had not been through the building availed themselves of a tour of the premises, led by students.

CELEBRATION

5:55 p.m.: The crowd gathering in the upstairs lobby of the newly dedicated Richard B. Flynn Campus Union for the formal observance of the College's 125th anniversary was growing in size and sound. Mixing freely and excitedly at the reception were students, faculty, staff, trustees, alums, major donors, and other friends of the College. Dinner was served down the hall, in the Dodge Room, overlooking the lake.

The theme selected for this Founder's Day Dinner was "Celebrating 125 Years of Leadership at Springfield College," and each of the eight speakers contributed to the mosaic of leadership that emerged from the evening's festivities. As with the morning's dedication, David Braverman served as interlocutor. Greetings were proffered by Matthew Ferry '10, Student Government Association president, from students; and by Rev. Bob Price, Faculty Senate president, from the faculty. Rev. Leo James Hoar, associate campus minister, provided a fulsome invocation. Margaret Lloyd, professor of humanities, presented the first public reading of her "Poem in Honor of the 125th Anniversary of Springfield College" (see page 265) and dedicated it to the College's twelfth president.

Board of Trustees Chair Sally Griggs offered a toast to the founders at the conclusion of her remarks: "Let us raise our glasses and toast the founders of Springfield College, those visionaries who collaborated to found the School for Christian Workers, and those who nurtured the mission and philosophy that continue to guide Springfield College 125 years later. Cheers to them!"

U.S. Congressman Richard E. Neal was an honored special guest for the evening. Congressman Neal had been present at the College's centennial celebration twenty-five years previous, in 1985, while serving as mayor of Springfield. He also had served briefly as an adjunct professor at the College, while still a young man. Neal had flown in from Washington, D.C. just for the occasion, returning later in the evening to his Congressional duties.

Massachusetts Congressman Richard E. Neal, shown here sharing stories with trustee Bob Sullivan, was an honored special guest and speaker at the Founders' Day Dinner.

President Flynn conversing with student leaders. He visited each table at the Founders' Day Dinner.

270

In introducing Neal, Flynn characterized the congressman as "a great friend to Springfield College, and a great friend to me."

Neal's perspectives on leadership centered on the founders of the nation, who were also its early leaders. The congressman compared and contrasted the founders with the governmental leaders of today, and found some unexpected similarities. In the process, he was able to provide a fascinating picture of the ways in which government works, and the reasons why it is so critical to the future success of the nation.

In terms of the evening's theme of leadership, the task of historical heavy-lifting fell

Pre-dinner reception on the second floor of the Campus Union.

to Flynn, who rose to the occasion with a concise lesson on the founders. Noting that "the history of Springfield College is a history of leadership and leadership development," Flynn said "the success of our focus on leadership development distinguishes Springfield College students when they embark on their careers.

"Our founders and early leaders had a tremendous impact, not only on this College, but also on the nation and the world," Flynn continued. "All were prominent during their lifetimes, but it is only with hindsight that we begin to understand what remarkable visionaries they were. Their pioneering efforts laid the foundation for our own efforts today, in fields that often didn't even exist during their time. We don't know if they realized the impact they would have, if they knew that what they began in 1885 in Springfield, Massachusetts would continue to influence people around the world 125 years later."

The Founder's Day reception extended into the rotunda of the Campus Union, with its prominent terrazzo College seal.

Flynn mentioned several "recurring themes" he had encountered in his historical reading on the College: "Optimism and innovation, outreach and collaboration, commitment to an ideal, care and respect for one's fellow man, inspired by the spirit of determination and leadership that has blessed our enterprise throughout its 125 years of existence."

The president noted that leadership "is not a new idea at Springfield College. It is who we are. It is what we do. It is not a fad, or a friendly marketing concept. The environment in which we live, work, play, and serve others is very different from the environment of our founders. But true leaders don't get stuck in fads or befuddled by change. Leaders adapt, while remaining true to and focused on core values. Our mission and humanics philosophy have stood the test of time, and are as relevant today as they were more than a century ago."

In closing, Flynn summed up: "Our legacy is deeply rooted in leadership. Handle it with care, and nurture its growth. It's our great privilege to share it, but also our responsibility to preserve it."

Transformation of Campus Facilities
2000-2010

"Enhancing our campus to accommodate growth and progress provides a compelling view of our institution and its future.

Facilities support achievement of the College's mission by creating teaching/ learning and living environments that are both student-friendly and designed to address program goals. After all, facilities are to facilitate programs."

— Dr. Richard B. Flynn, President

New Construction

RICHARD B. FLYNN CAMPUS UNION

This central location for student services and activities, comprising 58,500 square feet, contains space for student organizations and activities, international programs, career services, volunteer programs, residence life, and the administrative staff of the student affairs division. It features a food court with a two-story atrium for casual dining, sports bistro with large flat-screen televisions, and the spiritual life center with a meditation room. Other facilities include a large sub-dividable multi-purpose room with LCD projectors, bookstore, convenience store, post office, several conference rooms and lounges, and activity space.

New Construction

THE WELLNESS CENTER

The 47,840-square-foot Wellness Center, part of the Wellness and Recreation Complex and located closest to Alden Street, offers cardio and weight-training space, a climbing and bouldering wall, four multi-purpose teaching/activity spaces, fitness-testing laboratories, and more.

New Construction

THE FIELD HOUSE

The 93,820-square-foot Field House, located behind the Wellness Center, part of the Wellness and Recreation Complex, incorporates a six-lane running track with a Mondo "FTX" running surface; four multi-purpose courts, each with the ability to be closed off by a netting system; locker rooms; a fully equipped 9,000-square-foot strength and conditioning facility; concessions; and more.

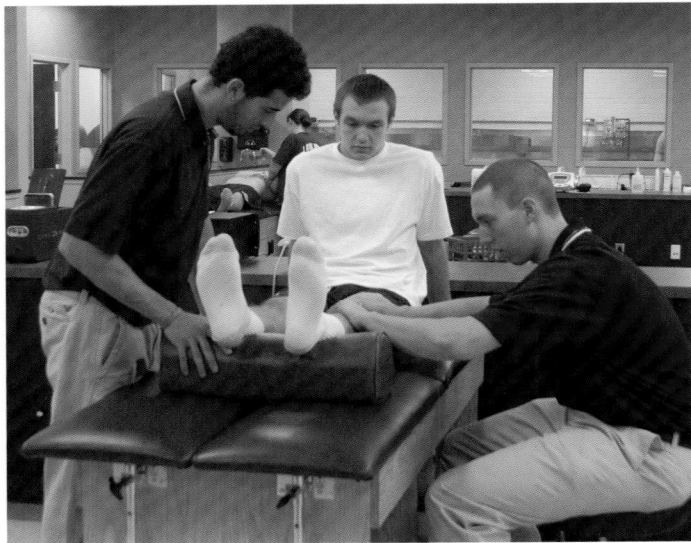

THE ATHLETIC TRAINING/
EXERCISE SCIENCE FACILITY

This two-story, 18,900-square-foot facility provides students and faculty with interactive and experiential learning environments, as well as dedicated research space for the study of all aspects of wellness and human performance. The new athletic training room offers student-athletes access to athletic health care at the highest level.

The Wellness and Recreation Complex and the Athletic Training/Exercise Science Facility officially opened in September 2008. On April 2, 2009, the Wellness and Recreation Complex received the 2009 Outstanding Sports Facilities Award from the National Intramural-Recreational Sports Association.

New Construction

IRV SCHMID
SPORTS COMPLEX

Two synthetic-turf fields—including the College's resurfaced Brock-Affleck game field—lighting, bleachers, parking, ticket booth, concessions, rest rooms, and fencing make up the Irv Schmid Sports Complex, dedicated during Reunion 2007. Completed in 2005, the 210,000-square-foot Complex provides play and practice facilities for the men's and women's soccer teams, as well as for other team practices, physical education classes, and campus recreation. Named for the legendary men's soccer coach and teacher, the Complex has been called "the finest two-field synthetic complex in the Northeast."

New Construction

SENIOR SUITES

Completed in fall 2004, the 60,400-square-foot Senior Suites, which is home to 225 students, created a Senior Village when placed adjacent to the Townhouses. The Suites changed the trend toward off-campus living among upper-class students and has attracted seniors and graduate students back to campus. The residence hall has been filled to capacity since its opening.

New Construction

PRESIDENT'S RESIDENCE

Newly constructed and completed in the spring of 2003, the President's Residence fulfilled the desire of the Board of Trustees to have the current and future presidents reside on campus. It also provided much-needed space for presidential entertaining of students, faculty, staff, and friends of the College.

Improvements or Enhancements

FULLER ARTS CENTER

The newly remodeled Fuller Arts Center, completed in March 2009, is home to the College's performing arts programs. Renovations to the Linkletter Foyer include a new entrance, a new façade of glass, brick, and limestone, new flooring, and a track-lighted ceiling. The floor in Appleton Auditorium, the Center's 300-seat performance and lecture space, has been raised to improve visibility of the stage. Other improvements include new stage flooring and curtains, a new computerized stage lighting system, a new ceiling and sound system, and new acoustical wall panels. All of these improvements are designed to enhance the presentation of sophisticated arts events and programs—dance, theater, lectures, musical performances, and more—in the 11,500-square-foot facility.

Improvements or Enhancements

JAMES NAISMITH COURT

The basketball court within Blake Arena has been formally named James Naismith Court, in honor of Springfield College Professor James Naismith, who invented the game of basketball while teaching at the College in 1891. The newly named and refurbished court includes James Naismith's name proudly displayed. The maple wood flooring, which was also installed in Dana Gymnasium, allows for a variety of athletic contests, classes, lectures, and shows. Rollout bleachers can accomodate more than 2,000 spectators.

HICKORY HALL

This facility, previously named Bemis Hall, provides the College community with general classroom space. An extensive renovation was completed in the fall of 2007. The 17,000-square-foot building contains seven classrooms, each with capacity for 30-50 students and one tiered classroom seating 80, as well as state-of-the-art instructional technology. It also houses the newly expanded Academic Success Center.

Improvements or Enhancements

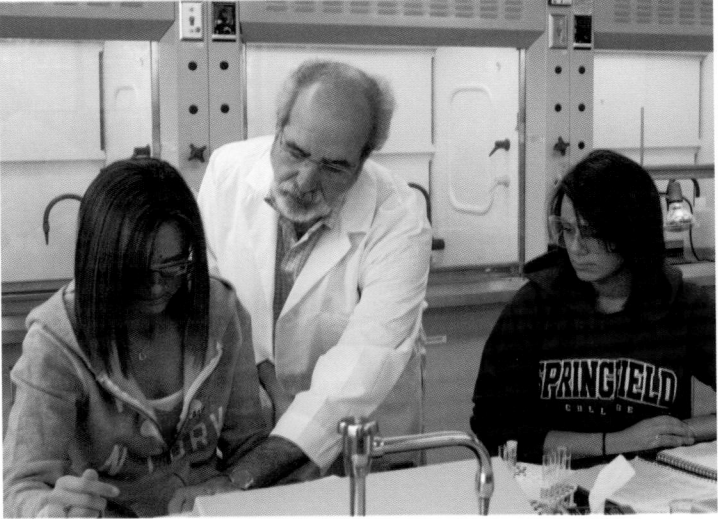

SCHOO-BEMIS SCIENCE CENTER

An expansion and complete renovation of the Schoo-Bemis Science Center (formerly Schoo Hall) was completed in the spring of 2007. The building includes 36,000 square feet and houses the biology/chemistry and physics/math/computer sciences departmental and faculty offices. The space provides an integrated, centralized location for science instruction that allows for interdisciplinary collaboration. Eighteen classrooms, lounges, and event space complete the facility's offerings.

Improvements or Enhancements

STAGG FIELD

Stagg Field (formerly Benedum Field) was resurfaced with a new state-of-the-art synthetic surface and enhanced by extensive landscaping in 2007. With seating capacity for more than 3,800 spectators, Stagg Field is dedicated to Amos Alonzo Stagg, the College's first football coach. The field is utilized for football, field hockey, men's and women's lacrosse, and campus recreation.

WEISER HALL

Weiser Hall is home to the humanities department faculty offices, classrooms, and the television studio and journalism labs. A renovation to the 10,600-square-foot space was completed in spring 2006.

Improvements or Enhancements

CHENEY HALL

The 26,500-square-foot Cheney Dining Hall was expanded and renovated in 2004. Cheney Hall provides a state-of-the-art dining experience for students, faculty, staff, and visitors. The external walkway was incorporated into the interior, and the glassed seating area offers sweeping views of Naismith Green, as well as numerous seating options. Food preparation areas are located in the front of the facility, allowing for quality food choices made to order. Also renovated were meeting rooms and food service offices.

Improvements or Enhancements

ADMISSIONS CENTER

The 5,800-square-foot undergraduate and graduate Admissions Center was expanded, renovated, and completed in spring 2003 to provide improved facilities to serve the College's prospective students.

BRENNAN CENTER

The expansion and renovation of the 19,300-square-foot Brennan Center, completed in fall 2002, houses the School of Social Work, the College's conference center, and the Springfield College Archives (scheduled to be moved to the new Stitzer YMCA Center in the fall of 2012). The renovation was undertaken to provide enhanced space for its inhabitants and to support meeting-space needs.

Improvements or Enhancements

HERBERT P. BLAKE HALL

Blake Hall houses the School of Human Services; the departments of visual and performing arts, emergency medical services management, physician assistant, sport management and recreation, and social sciences; and the Alden Center for Interactive Learning. It was renovated in the fall of 2001 with the goal of returning all traditional undergraduate programs to the main campus, and to consolidate SHS faculty and staff. The 55,000-square-foot building was dedicated in honor of Herbert P. Blake in 2006.

Beautification and Landscaping

CAMPUS BEAUTIFICATION

Beautification efforts are visible throughout the Springfield College campus and include new triangle-shaped conversation spaces on Naismith Green and adjacent to the Senior Suites, expanded green space, extensive landscaping including tree planting, enhanced accessibility, information kiosks, and wrought-iron fencing. Vista pruning efforts have re-established the campus' connection with Lake Massasoit. Beautiful views of the water are once again a prominent landscaping feature from many vantage points on campus.

Honors and Awards

SPRINGFIELD COLLEGE PRESIDENTS

1885-91
David Allen Reed

1891-93
Henry S. Lee

1893-96
Charles S. Barrows

1896-1936
Laurence L. Doggett

1937-46
Ernest M. Best '11

1946-52
Paul M. Limbert

1953-57
Donald C. Stone

1958-65
Glenn A. Olds

1965-85
Wilbert E. Locklin

1985-92
Frank S. Falcone

1992-98
Randolph W. Bromery

1999-PRESENT
Richard B. Flynn

BOARD OF TRUSTEES CHAIRS

For many years, the president of Springfield College also served as the chair of its Board of Trustees. In May 1954, the College's bylaws were amended so that someone other than the president of the College would serve as chair of the Board of Trustees.

Accordingly, this listing begins with 1954, the first year in which the chair of the Board of Trustees was a separate position from that of the president of the College.

1954-61
Edwin E. Bond '26

1961-62
Chester O. Fisher

1962-69
Norman C. Keith '36

1969-72
Charles H. Schaaff

1972-76
Joseph B. Burns

1976-80
Richard C. Garvey

1980-82
Willis H. Hayes

1982-85
William J. Clark

1985-88
John E. Mann

1988-91
John F. Cauley, Jr.

1991-92
Walter C. Wilson

1992-95
Peter B. Post G'59

1995-98
Thomas B. Wheeler

1998-2001
William B. Marsh

2001-04
John A. Odierna '64

2004-05
R. Lyman Wood

2005-08
James E. Walsh '64, G '66

2008-PRESENT
Sally M. Griggs

HONORARY DEGREE RECIPIENTS

1906
Jacob T. Bowne
Luther Gulick

1907
John W. Cook
W. W. Hastings
Edward Hitchcock

1908
Dudley A. Sargent

1909
George J. Fisher
Loring W. Messer

1910
Frank H. Burt
James Naismith
George Poole
David Allen Reed

1911
Hanford M. Burr

1912
George B. Affleck
William Henry Ball
Burt B. Farnsworth
Thomas D. Patton
Lory Prentiss
Frank P. Speare
Amos Alonzo Stagg

1913
William Knowles Cooper
R. Tait McKenzie

1914
Thomas M. Balliet
Max J. Exner
Walter M. Wood

1915
Henry J. Gray
Herbert P. Lansdale
Chester S. McGown

1916
Henry H. Bowman
John Brown
Ralph L. Cheney
John H. Crocker

1917
Laurence L. Doggett
Henry F. Kallenberg
John J. Virgo

1918
Jess T. Hopkins
Herbert L. Pratt
George A. Warburton

1919
Ernest M. Best
William Jessop
George L. Meylan
B. Thomas Pest
Frederick J. Smith

1920
Martin I. Foss
Dirk J. Van Bommel

1921
William G. Ballantine
George D. Chamberlain
Ferdinand Foch
Karl Fries
Raymond P. Kaighn
William D. McRae
Paul C. Phillips
L. R. Welzmiller

1922
Arthur N. Cotton
Robert E. Lewis
Palmer E. Pierce

1923
Frederick D. Fagg
August E. Metzdorf
James H. Post
Edward C. Schneider

1924
William Burdick
Benjamin A. Franklin
Fred B. Messing
James A. Rath
Jefferson C. Smith

1925
William G. Anderson
Blake A. Hoover
Worthy F. Maylott
Horace A. Moses
William Skarstrom

1926
Jessie H. Bancroft
Darius A. Davis
Henry W. Gibson
Mortimer L. Schiff

1927
Clifton A. Crocker
Philip L. Gillett
Guerdon N. Messer
Ernest L. Mogge
Charles W. Savage

1928
Charles B. Powter
Edgar M. Robinson
Carl L. Schrader
James E. West
Samuel W. Wiley

1929
Henry Breckinridge
Charles A. Coburn
Robert C. Cubbon
Ernest T. Seton

1930
Wilbur C. Batchelor
Fletcher S. Brockman
Martin L. Dinsmore
M. W. Ireland

1931
Howard S. Braucher
Hugo Cedergren
Edward S. Elliott
Herbert S. Gott

1932
Philip M. Colbert
Edward K. Hall
Pierson S. Page
Wilbert B. Smith

1933
Gustavus T. Kirby
Jay B. Nash
Herbert S. Smith
J. Max Yergan

1934
Harry B. Burns
Henry D. Dickson
John E. Manley
Joseph E. Raycroft

1935
Frederick Brush
Willard S. Richardson
Roy F. Seymour
Frank L. Smith

1936
Jerome H. Bentley
Edwin M. Shawn
James E. Sproul

1937
Berg Esenwein
Eduard C. Lindeman
C. Lawrence Walsh

1938
Joseph A. First
Robert J. H. Kiphuth

1939
Norman W. Fradd
Charles E. Hendry

1940
Charles S. Botsford
Avery Brundage
Judson P. Freeman
Elisha A. King

1942
Ray E. Johns
John N. Richards

1947
William R. Barry
Frank S. Beveridge
Carroll L. Bryant
William Burger
Ellis H. Champlin

1948
Ruth Evans
Henry A. Field
Francis M. Greene
Edgar Herbert
George Hjelte

1949
Theodore P. Bank
Harold S. DeGroat
Gustav-Adolph Gedat
Charles C. Noble
E. Kent Swift

1950
Mary O. Pottenger
Earl C. Sams
William H. Short
Regino R. Ylanan

1951
Serafin Aquino
George F. Briggs
William F. Briggs
Fred W. Dickens
Cleveland E. Dodge
Alonzo G. Grace

1952
Laurence L. Doggett
James C. Donnell II
John H. Gulick
Francis Oakley
Seward C. Staley
John E. Wallace

1953
Judah Cahn
Frank Carlson
Carlton Harrison
John Heuss
John McCurdy
Gilbert Montague

1954
Ralph J. Bunche
Alvin R. Kaufman
Eugene R. McCarthy
Louise R. McCarthy
Norman L. Munn
Albert J. Nesbitt
George Paik

1955
James V. Bennett
Robert Cutler
Henry A. Field
Charles F. Hall
William E. Hall
Christian Herter
Mildred M. Horton
William L. Hughes
Joseph Prendergast

1956
Olive D. Doggett
Eldon V. Johnson
John F. Kennedy
Clarence E. Pickett
Paul A. Samson

1957
Erwin D. Canham
George K. Funston
Caroline W. Gannett
Lawrence K. Hall
John Merrill Olin
Arthur A. Schuck
Roberts J. Wright

1958
Francis E. Gray
Beatrice H. Hill
Ray F. Jenney
H. Parker Lansdale, Jr.
Bonnie Prudden
Wesley F. Rennie
William E. Speers
Harry G. Stoddard

1959
Paul T. Babson
Luis A. Ferre
Louis L. Little
Shao-Hsien Pang

1960
Leland John Kalmbach
Paul Moyer Limbert
Arthur Gordon Linkletter
O. Ronald Lippitt
Thornton W. Merriam
Thomas E. Rivers

1961
Jennie Rose Cournoyer
Arthur Sherwood Flemming
A. Hugo Grassi
Edward J. Hickox
Gunsun Hoh
Henry R. Luce
Charles D. Sherman

1962
Edwin E. Bond
Marion Bayard Folsom
Alfred M. Gruenther
Leslie James Judd
Lam Po Kwok

1963
R. William Jones
Eugenio Mendoza
Paul A. Schilpp
R. Sargent Shriver, Jr.

1964
P. Matthew Joseph
Martin Luther King, Jr.
Carl D. Smith
Mary E. Switzer
Ellen Winston

1965
Joseph Albert Brunton, Jr.
Julia Bessie Buxton
Glenn A. Olds
Eva B. Olds
Winston Paul
Paul Tillich
Stuart Lee Udall

1966
Julius H. Appleton
Milton S. Eisenhower
Norman C. Keith
Elliot L. Richardson

1967
Reynold E. Carlson
Liselott Diem
Chester O. Fischer
Frederik J. D. Franklin
Edmund T. Manley
Wilbur M. McFeeley
Joseph C. Wilson

1968
Clifford B. Fagan
Robert Staffanson

1969
Richard R. Higgins
Frederic R. Mann
Bernard H. McMahon
Abram L. Sachar

1970
Olga E. Ellis
Chik-Suen Lam
Lij Endalkachew Makonnen
Richard P. Towne

1971
Paul E. Brown
Ruth E. Cameron
Arthur Fiedler
Gordon L. Lippitt

1972
Paul G. Benedum
Orville H. Emmons

1973
Porter McKeever
Frederick A. Purdy
Charles H. Schaaff
Jayne B. Spain
Maurice F. Strong
Roy Wilkins

1974
Enrique C. Aguirre
Seth Arsenian
John W. Bunn

1975
Candido Bartolome
John W. Galbreath
Edward W. Pastore
Richard W. Tapply

1976
R. B. Frost
John M. Turnbull

1977
Joseph B. Burns
Jayne Shover

1978
Walter Byers
Dean W. Jeffers
Timothy J. Nugent
Francis W. Scanlon
Arthur MacDougall Wood

1979
Russell Wilbur Peterson

1980
Leonel J. Castillo
Victor T. Ehre
William M. Savitt

1981
Lucy Wilson Benson
John Brademas
James R. Martin

1982
S. Prestley Blake
Solon B. Cousins
Richard C. Garvey
Lawrence F. O'Brien

1983
Edith Y. Babson
Edward P. Boland

1984
William Aramony
Ma Qi-Wei
Rachel Robinson
J. Paul Sticht

1985
Louise B. Appleton
John W. Kessler
Brian O'Connell
Darryl F. Stingley

1986
Harold Amos
Willis H. Hayes
Richard F. Schubert
William E. Simon

1987
Jeffrey C. Blatnick
Richard F. MacPherson
Lucile C. McCabe
Charles F. Weckwerth

1988
William J. Clark
Edward T. Dunn

1989
Archie P. Allen.
Kenneth B. Clark
Eli A. Finn
Harold Grinspoon
Eugene M. Lang

1990
Tracy Kidder
John E. Mann
Charles E. Silvia
Christine Zajac

1991
Robert J. Cousy
Julius W. Erving

1992
Roscoe C. Brown, Jr.
Wayne A. Budd
John F. Cauley, Jr.
Setsu Kamiyama
Lee Soo-Min

1993
Edward J. Brennan
Randolph W. Bromery
Deborah Prothrow-Stith

1994
Fr. Laurence Bohnen, S.D.B.
Sr. Mary Caritas, S.P.
Henry Y. T. Fok
John E. Jacob
Wilbert E. Locklin
Walter C. Wilson

1995
Tenley Albright
Douglas P. Beal
Henry H. Hsu
David R. Mercer
Bing-lai Wong
James Tak Wu

1996
Madeleine H. Blais
Cleveland E. Dodge, Jr.
Angela Luk Chiu Kwan-Hung
Peter B. Post
LeRoy T. Walker
Philip K. H. Wong

1997
Jean Bertrand Aristide
Leonard Baskin
Sandra Eagleton
I. Ira Goldenberg
William H. Gray III
Yuan Shu
David Starr

1998
Lucinda W. Adams
Richard L. Bruno
John G. Gallup
Harold C. Smith

1999
Robert N. Aebersold
John Casey
Eddie Robinson
Thomas B. Wheeler
Willye White

2000
Donna de Varona
Kin-Yuen Luk
Peter J. Negroni

2001
Michael J. Albano
Ronald E. Burton
Florence P. Kendall
John F. Kerry

2002
William H. Cosby, Jr.
Nancy Hogshead-Makar
Fred Y. Hoshiyama
William B. Marsh

2003
Richard B. Flynn
Richard E. Neal
Robin Roberts
Liz Thompson

2004
Rizek Abusharr
Kenneth L. Gladish

2005
Charles J. Casserly
Sui Lau
Brian P. Lees.
John A. Odierna
Lan Sun Tai

2006
Edward M. Kennedy
Yanbao Li
R. Lyman Wood

2007
Julius Jones
Paul E. Lefebvre
Andrew Wing-Kee Luk
H. Todd Stitzer

2008
Father Leo James Hoar
Stuart H. Reese

2009
Helen Davis Blake
Keith Daly
James Frank
Domenic J. Sarno
James E. Walsh

DISTINGUISHED SPRINGFIELD COLLEGE PROFESSORS OF HUMANICS

NAME	YEARS	DISCIPLINE
Seth Arsenian	1966-1969	Psychology
Harry H. Giles	1970-1972	Human Relations
Charles Weckwerth	1972-1975	Recreation
Holmes VanDerbeck	1975-1976	Religion
Charles Silvia	1976-1978	Health, Physical Education, & Recreation
Walter H. English	1978-1979	Psychology
Josephine L. Cecco	1979-1980	Education
Henry J. Paar	1980-1981	Psychology
Edward J. Sims	1981-1982	English
Edward T. Dunn	1982-1983	Health, Physical Education, & Recreation
Jesse L. Parks	1983-1984	Health, Physical Education, & Recreation
Jean F. Ross	1984-1985	Biology
Herbert Zettl	1985-1987	History
Paul U. Congdon	1987-1988	Education
James Robertson	1988-1989	Physical Education
Diane Potter	1989-1990	Physical Education
Joel R. Cohen	1990-1991	Biology
Janice C. Eldridge	1991-1992	Chemistry
John Cox	1992-1993	Psychology
James Genasci	1993-1994	Physical Education
Martin Dosick	1994-1995	Sociology
Elizabeth Evans	1995-1996	Physical Education
Margaret Lloyd	1996-1997	English
Joel Dearing	1997-1998	Physical Education
Peter Polito	1998-1999	Physics/Computer Science
Barbara Jensen	1999-2000	Physical Education
Delight Champagne	2000-2001	Psychology
Frank Torre	2001-2002	Chemistry
Bernard Graney	2002-2003	Rehabilitation & Disability Studies
Dorothy Potter Zenaty	2003-2004	Health, Physical Education, & Recreation
Charles Redmond	2004-2005	Athletic Training
Ronald Maggio	2005-2006	Art
Richard Davila	2006-2007	Human Services
Mimi Murray	2007-2008	Health, Physical Education, & Recreation
Albert Petitpas	2008-2009	Psychology
Robert Accorsi	2009-2010	Sport Management & Recreation

ATHLETIC HALL OF FAME

The Athletic Hall of Fame was established in 1972 by the Class of 1933 to honor members of the College community for outstanding achievements on the "playing field" and/or for service, dedication, and commitment to athletics and athletic programs.

1972
Amos Alonzo Stagg 1891
James Naismith 1891
Leslie Mann '14
Leslie J. Judd '20
Archie P. Allen '37 G'49

1973
Edward J. Hickox '14
Erastus W. Pennock '14 G'29
Frank J. Civiletto '23
Bernard F. Mooney '23 G'31
Charles E. Silvia '34 G'40

1974
James H. McCurdy 1890 G'07
Elmer Berry '02 G'08
John D. Brock '10 G'24
Raymond F. Oosting '24 G'30
Robert T. Berry '26 G'39

1975
John L. Rothacher '14 G'28
Alvin L. James '28 G'49
Joseph A. Shields '34

1976
Daniel J. Kelly '13
Fred O. Duncan '29
William A. Yorzyk '54

1977
Arthur A. Schabinger '15
Thomas K. Cureton, Jr. '29 G'30
Warren L. Huston '37

1978
William G. Morgan 1894
Leonard A. Watters '22
Lyle Welser '33 G'34
Irvin R. Schmid '43 G'50

1979
Hartley Price '27
William Footrick '32 G'36
Frederick R. Lanoue '32 G'36
L. Stuart Parks '35 G'40

1980
Harold S. DeGroat '14
Richard F. Crawley '26 G'36
Leo Netter '31 G'35
Raymond E. Schmidt '41

1981
Warren B. Woodson '26
Ralph W. Erickson '27 G'35
Fred A. Johnson '27 G'38
Edward S. Steitz G'48 DPE'63

1982
Rudolph H. Lavik '20
Wendell D. Mansfield '25
George A. Cella '36
Douglas E. Parker, Jr. '51 G'58

1983
J. Bruce Munro, Jr. '40
Victor F. J. Obeck '40
Edward J. Shea '41
Vernon W. Cox '44 G'49
Frank A. Wolcott '52 G'60

1984
H. Richard Redding '40
Karl Kurth, Jr. '42
Robert M. D'Agostino '51 G'52
Alan A. Schutts '53

1985
Dale W. Lash '23
Clarence C. Chaffee '34
Edward J. Smyke, Sr. '43

1986
Floyd H. Warner '33 G'37
Robert M. Whitelaw '50 G'50
Charles J. Butt '53 G'56
Samuel J. Coursen '53

1987
Jim F. Lineberger '43
Kathy Corrigan Ekas '66
Jeffrey C. Blatnick '79

1988
Donald J. Grant '41
Richard F. MacPherson '58
Archie F. Moore '63
Neil J. Stam '64 G'73

1989
Mark S. Randall '33
Diane L. Potter '57 G'63
Hugh B. Mendez '58

1990
Ralph A. Piper '28
Bruce Hutchinson '55 DPE'72
Thomas F. Waddell '59
Dottie Potter Zenaty '65

1991
Victor S. Kodis '35 G'37
Richard F. Garber '50
Carlton L. Snitkin '72 G'78
Susan Petersen Lubow '75

1992
Edward T. Dunn G'47
Delene Johnson Darst '62
John F. Curtis '71 G'73
Diane E. Schumacher '75

1993
A. Huntley Parker, Jr. '33
Geoffrey A. Cardinali '61 G'63
Mimi Murray '61 G'68
Denise M. Desautels '77

1994
Gordon D. Gray '41
Matthew J. Sanzone '63 G'64
Nancy M. Darsch '73
Pamela Hixon '73 G'77
Anthony V. Jeffreys '81

1995
Roger K. Leathers '34 G'36
Edward R. Bilik '57 G'62
Carl R. Samuelson '57 G'63
Leslie C. Plumb '58
Anthony D. DiCicco, Jr. '70
Judi Markell '72

1996
George H. Grover '35 G'36
John Y. Squires '35 G'37
L. Curtis Guild '54
Paula Deubel Phillips '57
R. Davis Hart, Jr. '68
Garry St. Jean '73 G'76

1997
Irvin G. Walmer '23
Raymond L. Flint '39
Joseph J. Alissi '56
George E. Benedict '57
Denis B. Clark '71
Patti Corrigan Dunne '72

1998
Russell E. Peterson '32 G'37
John Wesley Patterson '51
Eric Moyer '62 G'63
Charles J. Casserly '71 G'72
Ivan Jose Olivares '86
Martha Grinnell '89

1999
Ossie Solem
Vincent Bradford '36
David J. Martens '57
Richard M. Aronson '58 CAS'71
Robert E. Nye '58 G'59
Francis C. Meyer Jr. '70

2000
Clifford E. Clark '35 G'45
Robert C. Hawkes '44
Raymond Cieplik '67
Katherine Kolemainen Vailliencourt '75
Anita C. Thomas '82 G'84
Hassan S. Robinson '95

2001
William A. Gibney '41 (posthumously)
Alden "Whitey" Burnham '48 G'52
Robert M. Litchard '57 G'61
Charles N. Roys '61 G'67
Robert A. Cobb '64 G'67 DPE'70
Jeffrey D. Coelho '84 G'85

2002
William R. Campbell '49 G'53
Angelo (Angie) Correale Jr. '50 G'51
Gail A. Goodspeed '74 G'75
Charles E. Duggan '76
Kerri L. Camuso-Lavoie '97

2003
Robert "Rabbit" White '32 (posthumously)
Nicholas A. Sabetto '42
Edward W. Reed, Jr. '65, G'66
David B. Bennett '67
Richard E. Munroe '76
Shelley L. Antone-Cormier '89

2004
Frank "Dutch" Holland '36 (posthumously)
William H. Hillman '53, G'56
Miller A. Bugliari '57
Barbara Jacobs Jordan '57
Carson "Missy" Wassell Foote '74
Edward Carey '91

2005
Alan C. "Dinty" Moore '50
Erik Kjeldsen '54, G'62
Theodore Alflen '69
John Martin '71
Michael McCombs '78
Janet Williams '86

2006
Robert Knowles '49
Joseph Marshall '53 G'55
Albert Jackson '60 G'61
Roy Samuelson '77
Branwen Smith-King '78, G'79
Laurence Jordan '86 G'94

2007
Frank Robinson '48 G'49
Charles Redmond '68 G'71
Christina Wielgus '74
Tim Murphy '78 G'79
W.F. Newhall '80
Tom Hay (posthumously)

2008
Theodore A. "Ted" Smith '48 (posthumously)
Lawrence "Larry" Mulvaney '49
William "Fritz" Wiedergott '58
Robert Elsinger '65
Michael "Spider" Brown '80
Brenda Bradley Hogan '91

2009
Paul D. Assaiante '74
Alton B. Doyle '49, G'50 (posthumously)
Nan Duga Campbell '01
George Robert Hamilton '58, G'63
Belinda Perry Beaulier '94, G'95
Robert Piehler '84

DISTINGUISHED ALUMNUS/ALUMNA AWARD

The Distinguished Alumnus/Alumna Award, established by the Class of 1940 in 1966 to annually recognize professional excellence and outstanding service to community, state, and/or nation.

1966
O. Ronald Lippitt '36
Harold Amos '41

1967
H. Harrison Clarke '25
Richard L. Burt '38

1968
George H. Grover '35 G'36
E. Parker Johnson '38

1969
William A. Howes '39
Edward J. Keyes, Jr. '43

1970
Thomas K. Cureton, Jr. '29 G'30
Hugh A. Noble '38

1971
Francis J. Moench '20
Benjamin Hargrave '41

1972
Enrique C. Aguirre '15
Max H. Andrews '44 G'47

1973
Gunsun Hoh '23
Charles F. Weckwerth '31 G'34
Robert H. Atkinson '39
Roscoe C. Brown '43

1974
Norman C. Keith '36
Edward S. Steitz G'48 DPE'63
Jose G. Cervantes '50

1975
Thomas F. Johnson '40
Thomas C. Best '43
Khwaja S. Ahmed '54

1976
Herman N. Neilson '30 G'36
Albert Wollenberger '39 G'41
Dale B. Lake '49 G'50

1977
H. Hubert Wilson '32
Lloyd C. Arnold '49
Ann M. Briley '59

1978
George W. Garniss '14 G'20
Herbert P. Almgren '38
Benjamin Ricci '49 G'50

1979
Guido Graziani '22 G'31
Candido C. Bartolome '29 G'29

1980
Ferenc Hepp '35 G'36
Matthew G. Maetozo, Jr. '51 DPE'65

1981
Carlton B. Greider '38
Robert M. Pate '44

1982
Karl H. Oermann '38
Otis E. Finley, Jr. '50

1983
Howard E. Thompson '38
Walter F. Ersing '54

1984
Ralph A. Piper '28
Daniel F. Riva '40

1985
Donald I. Minnegan '27
David M. Boswell '58 G'59

1986
Seward C. Staley '17
Edward J. Shea '41
Joyce A. Wise '75

1987
Stephen M. Bresett '52
Jean C. Kraemer '54

1988
Mark S. Randall '33
Louis J. Segalla '41

1989
Richard B. Brooks '30
Robert J. Winglass '57

1990
William W. Moore '41
John J. Wydro '41
Alexander Melleby '52

1991
Alden H. Burnham '48 G'52
Donald G. Spencer '50
Thomas R. Bedecki G'54

1992
Sundaram Srivatsan G'56
Charles J. Casserly '71 G'72

1993
Nancy E. Gary '58
Richard L. Bruno '77

1994
Alan C. Moore '50
David M. Auxter '51 G'56

1995
Samuel E. Molind '62
Donald S. Broas '63

1996
Robert C. Hawkes '44
John D. Evangelista '72

1997
Donald J. Grant '41
David P. Beaver '57 G'58

1998
David H. Clarke '52
David S. Liederman G'58

1999
Howard G. Knuttgen '52
Mimi Murray '61

2000
Darlind J. Davis G'72
Barry J. Weinberg '73

2001
Patrick N. Allen '84
Eugene B. Defilippo '72

2002
Margaret C. Locke, Jr. D.P.E.'59
Harold A. Vasvari '66

2003
Jeffrey Cadorette '72, G'73
James Frank G'56, D.P.E.'63

2004
Stanley F. Battle '73
Michael J. Boyle '81, G'82

2005
Norman C. Chambers '71
Craig P. Shirley '78

2006
Walter L. Sargent '65
Kurt Aschermann '71

2007
Lawrence F. Locke '52 G'53
Bridget A. Belgiovine G'87

2008
Russell R. Pate '68
Judith Ford Baumhauer '83

2009
Steven G. Scott '72
Thomas E. Yeager '72, G'75

TARBELL MEDALLION

The Tarbell Medallion, a facsimile of R. Tate McKenzie's "The Joy of Effort," first presented in 1935 as a gift from Edward Norris Tarbell, Class of 1889, and given annually to an alumnus or alumna out of school at least twenty years who has demonstrated outstanding service to his or her alma mater.

1935
James Naismith 1891
Raymond P. Kaighn 1893
Martin I. Foss 1899 G'20
Carl D. Smith '14

1936
Herbert S. Smith '06
Ernest M. Best '11

1937
Ralph L. Cheney '01
Wilbur C. Batchelor '13 G'30

1938
Willard S. Richardson 1891
Stanley L. Metcalf '15

1939
John W. Cook 1889
August E. Metzdorf '05 G'23

1940
Lewis E. Hawkins 1898
Kenneth E. Smullin '14

1941
Amos Alonzo Stagg 1891
James S. Summers '11 G'21

1942
Frank N. Seerley 1890
William H. Ball 1891
George O. Draper '08
Frank L. Smith '11

1943
None Awarded

1944
George B. Affleck '01
Arthur E. Dome '21

1945
None Awarded

1946
Edgar M. Robinson '01
Edward J. Hickox '14
Leslie J. Tompkins '18
Arthur G. Jeffrey '20

1947
Elmer Berry '02 G'08
William H.J. Beckett '06

1948
Paul A. Samson '20
A. Hugo Grassi '25

1949
Archie J. Stearns '10
Arthur T. Noren '21

1950
J. Henry Gray '04 G'15
George G. Deaver '12

1951
Frederick F. Bugbee '03
John D. Brock '10 G'24

1952
Louis C. Schroeder '12
Floyd S. Field '27

1953
Fay S. Mathewson '21
Ernest M. Ford '27

1954
Arthur S. Lamb '12
Charles W. Davis '18

1955
Thomas S. Smith '11
Leslie J. Judd '20

1956
C. Lawrence Walsh '12 G'37
George D. Ritchie '27 G'34

1957
Elmer B. Cottrell '19 G'24
Norman S. Loveland '24

1958
Channing R. Mann G'16
Edmund T. Manley '27

1959
Erastus W. Pennock '14 G'29
Willard P. Ashbrook '24
Richard C. Lancaster '26

1960
Albert M. Chesley '00
John G. Lang, Jr. '24

1961
Edward J. Keyes, Sr. '16
Frank M. Simmons '23

1962
Edwin E. Bond '26
Roberts J. Wright '32

1963
Robert T. Berry '26
Henry G. Ellis '33 G'39

1964
Harold S. DeGroat '14
Warren R. Balentine '25

1965
Wendell D. Mansfield '25
Orville H. Emmons '29

1966
Walter W. Bell '15
R. William Cheney '33
Norman C. Keith '36

1967
Fred W. Dickens '14 G'51
James P. Haughey '22
George R. Taylor '27

1968
Frank J. Civiletto '23
Rene J. Kern '28

1969
Otis Finley, Sr. '24
Kenneth C. Chapin '29 G'42
Harry T. Hall '34

1970
George H. Aylsworth '23
James T. Laidlaw '25
Wilmot S. Babcock '30

1971
William R. Fenstemacher '31
William W. Moore, Jr. '41
Robert W. Emery '43

1972
Earl N. Taraldsen '22
T. Erwin Blesh '30
Joseph A. Shields '34
Alfred C. Werner '40 DPE'60

1973
Harry A. Engleman '23
William H. Pendleton '28
Kenneth L. McEwen '43
Arthur H. Christ '44 G'51

1974
Herbert Evans '24
Paul E. Johnson '27
Dorothea Poulin Woodside '39
Robert R. Thompson '44

1975
Wayne C. Barnes '25
Donald W. Purrington '33
William J. Knowles '40
J. Robert Eddy '41 G'48

1976
Fred S. Coles '16
Oscar L. Elwell '21
Harry C. Thompson '31
Harold J. Jennifer '43 G'48

1977
Edwin C. Johnson '28
Harry L. Lippincott '36
Jack F. George '37

1978
Charles F. Weckwerth '31 G'34
Howard L. Gilson II '44

1979
Samuel E. Pond '12
Britton C. McCabe '27
W. Gordon MacGregor '31 G'41
Robert Van Camp '54

1980
Fred M. Dickerson '32
Henry A. Bonnet '50 G'54
Robert H. Reardon '51

1981
Theodore T. Abel '33
Calvin J. Martin '34 G'35
Jesse Brown '36
Harold Amos '41

1982
R. Berle Thompson '44
Philip J. Brown, Jr. '52

1983
L. Stuart Parks '35 G'40
Archie P. Allen '37 G'49

1984
Edward J. Keyes, Jr. '43
Harold E. Potts '50 G'61
Carol Jeffers Claflin '57

1985
Salvatore Sannella '14
Hubert F. Hill '35
Philip W. Breux '38
Roger H. Fulton '57

1986
Emil F. Faubert '43
Richard J. Brigham '50 G'54
Lynn L. Russell '66 G'00

1987
Harold G. Lynch '41
Judith Witham Moss '56

1988
Michael P. Pagos '39 G'46

1989
John A. Odierna '64

1990
None Awarded

1991
Robert R. Ward '41 G'56

1992
Alden H. Burnham '48 G'52

1993
Edward T. Dunn G'47

1994
Angelo Correale, Jr. '50 G'51

1995
Irvin R. Schmid '43 G'50

1996
Thomas L. Johnson '59

1997
Linda Cruse Moffat '73

1998
J. Rockwell Allen '69 G'70

1999
John R. Savoia '59

2000
Michael A. West '65 G'66

2001
Susan E. Lundin '70

2002
Robert B. Hoffman '57 G'58

2003
T. George Silcott '52 (posthumously)

2004
Barry J. Weinberg '73

2005
Joseph W. Valentine '50

2006
Robert J. Winglass '57

2007
Philip "Buzzy" Ernst '74, G'79

2008
David R. Boyle '83

2009
Helen Davis Blake G'67

YOUNG ALUMNUS/ALUMNI AWARD

The Young Alumnus/Alumna Award, established by the Class of 1966 in 1974 and presented to a graduate in the Tenth Reunion class in recognition of professional excellence and outstanding service to the College, community, state, and/or nation.

1974
Lynda M. Barry '65

1975
Craig J. Kelly '67

1976
Lynn L. Russell '66 G'00

1977
I. David Marder '67

1978
Dennis H. St. Jean '73

1979
Paula Warren Broydrick '71

1980
Deborah Mitchell Stoddard '70

1981
Steven E. Fulford '71

1982
David W. Gilson '72 G'73

1983
Ann G. Rutherford '73 G'75

1984
Eliott G. Baker '74 G'75
Mark E. Chrusz '74 G'75

1985
Daniel C. McBride '77

1986
Patricia Roland LeShane '76

1987
Sue Ann Hedenberg Dubois '77

1988
Pamela Monfort McDonough '78

1989
Jeffrey C. Blatnick '79

1990
Timothy J. Anderson '80
Charisse F. Duroure '80

1991
Phoebe T. Kitson-Davis '81

1992
Mary Anne Gaul Nagy '82

1993
Judith Ford Baumhauer '83

1994
Marc F. Brassard '84 G'89

1995
Maureen Nolan Fitzgerald '85

1996
Karen A. Lachapelle '86 G'88

1997
James W. Rowe, Jr. '87

1998
Tamra M. Stokes '88

1999
Malcolm C. Lester '89

2000
Mark D. Straubel '90 G'92

2001
Stacey Hall '91

2002
Theresa J. Riethle '92

2003
Keith A. Crowley '93, G'95

2004
Dr. Mark A. Kenton '94 G'96

2005
Steven P. Dion '95, G'97

2006
Scott W. Heaney '96

2007
Kelleyrobin Mulvihill '97 G'98

2008
Stacey Franz '98 G'99

2009
Richard J. Wood '99, G'01

ALUMNI COUNCIL PRESIDENTS

Wilbur C. Batchelor '13	1931-33		George H. Grover '35	1965-66
Stanley L. Metcalf '15	1933-34		Thomas Collins III '42	1966-67
Carl D. Smith '14	1934-35		Donald K. Hacker '50	1967-68
Herbert S. Smith '06	1935-37		Joseph A. Shields '34	1968-69
Ralph L. Cheney '01	1937-38		Edgar G. Craver '51	1969-70
Roberts J. Wright '32	1938-40		Vernal P. Davis '57	1970-71
Arthur E. Dome '21	1940-42		Thomas F. Johnson '40	1971-72
Charles C. Wilson '17	1942-43		Stanley G. Van Arsdale '49	1972-73
No Council	1943-45		Craig J. Kelly '67	1973-74
Norman S. Loveland '24	1945-47		Howard L. Gilson '44	1974-75
Henry G. Ellis '33	1947-48		Joseph A. Robitaille '66	1975-77
Philip W. Breux '38	1948-49		John R. Savoia '59	1977-79
Karl Kurth Jr. '42	1949-50		D. Irving Conrad '62	1979-80
Robert T. Berry '26	1950-51		John A. Odierna '64	1980-81
Richard C. Lancaster '26	1951-52		Paul A. Tierney '68	1981-83
Warren L. Huston '37	1952-53		John A. Odierna '64	1983-85
Harry N. Memery '35	1953-54		Alden H. Burnham '48	1985-89
Robert W. Emery '43	1954-55		Sharon Catley Kelly '62	1989-92
Kenneth C. Runquist '43	1955-56		Angelo Correale, Jr. '50	1992-94
Harold Amos '41	1956-57		Barbara Meyers Kenney '83	1994-96
Kenneth L. McEwen '43	1957-58		Robert B. Hoffman '57	1996-98
Jack F. George '37	1958-59		Charisse F. Duroure '80	1998-2000
Robert H. Reardon '51	1959-60		Charles R. Dannenberg '68	2000-02
Wesley G. Woll, Jr. '43	1960-61		Denise Alleyne '73	2002-04
Alfred C. Werner '40	1961-62		J. Mitchell Finnegan '82	2004-06
Benjamin Ricci '49	1962-63		Carl J. Pavano '69	2006-08
John F. Donahue '51	1963-64		Matthew R. Siegel '94	2008-10
J. Robert Eddy '41	1964-65			

CHENEY AWARD RECIPIENTS 1980–2009

The Cheney Award, established in 1980, recognizes a member of the Springfield College family who has worked unselfishly for the best interests of the College. The Springfield College family may be considered to include anyone who wants to be a part of what Springfield College represents.

John Brainerd	1980	Elizabeth Gibney	1995
Jean Ross	1981	Richard Whiting	1996
Gilbert Vickers	1982	Betty Mann	1997
John Odierna	1983	John Wilcox	1998
Scott Taylor	1984	Rita Pellerin	1999
Laura Jo Judd	1985	Peter Polito	2000
Eleanor Fuller	1986	Mary DeAngelo	2001
Amy Kissel	1987	Jean Welles	2002
Susie Baschwitz	1988	Father Leo Hoar	2003
Marcia Mayas	1989	Charles Redmond	2004
Judith Mefen-Sculley	1990	Cynthia Moriarty	2005
Robert Palmer	1991	Ellen Bletsos	2006
None	1992	Angie Haley	2007
Charles Weckworth	1993	Mike Delong	2008
John Wilson	1994	Mary Healey	2009

INDEX

AUTHORS

RICHARD C. GARVEY (1923-2004) was editor of the *Springfield Daily News* and chair of the Springfield College Board of Trustees. He was widely known

throughout Massachusetts as an author and lecturer on the history of Western Massachusetts. He was president of the New England Society of Newspaper Editors and the recipient of several journalistic honors including the Grenville Clark National Award and the Allan

B. Rogers Memorial Award for outstanding editorial writing. In addition to receiving the William Pynchon Award for community service, the Northampton, Massachusetts native was awarded honorary doctorates by Springfield College, the University of Massachusetts, and the College of Our Lady of the Elms.

RONALD S. ZIEMBA (1943-) worked in newspapers and corporate communications before coming to Springfield College in 2000, a year after the arrival of

Richard B. Flynn. After serving seven years as director of Marketing & Communications, he moved to the Office of the President, where he is responsible for various projects of an editorial nature. His newspaper experience includes the *Springfield Union* (sister paper to Garvey's

Springfield Daily News) and *The Wall Street Journal*. His corporate communications experience includes Travelers, New England Life, Chesebrough-Pond's, Eastern Enterprises, and Reliance Group Holdings. Born and raised in Chicopee, Massachusetts, he graduated from Chicopee High School and Amherst College, and lives in Springfield, a mile from the campus.

Photography courtesy of the Springfield College archives, Springfield College Office of Marketing & Communications, President and Mrs. Flynn, Paul Schnaittacher, Dann DeWitt, Andrew Kesin, and Fred LeBlanc.

Designer: John Devanski, Guy With Glasses Design

Project Manager: Kelly Gonya, Springfield College Office of Marketing & Communications

Printed by Universal Millennium, Westwood, Massachusetts

Binding by ACME Bookbinding, Charlestown, Massachusetts

308